This book is an advanced text in applied welfare economics and its application to environmental economics. The author goes far beyond the existing literature on the valuation of environmental benefits, deriving sets of cost-benefit rules which can be used to assess private and public sector projects which affect the environment. He explains how valuation studies can be augmented so as to yield the information necessary for decision-making, showing how externalities, taxes, unemployment, risk, irreversibilities, flow and stock pollutants, discounting, and intergenerational distribution should be treated in social cost-benefit analysis. Drawing on a number of empirical illustrations, this book will be of interest not only to those taking advanced courses in environmental economics, welfare economics and public economics, but also as a reference for those undertaking project evaluations in government and business.

Per-Olov Johansson is Professor of Economics at the Stockholm School of Economics. His previous books include *An introduction to modern welfare economics* (1991) and *The economic theory and measurement of environmental benefits* (1987).

Cost-benefit analysis of environmental change

Cost-benefit analysis of environmental change

Per-Olov Johansson
Stockholm School of Economics

Published by the Press Syndicate of the University of Cambridge
The Pitt Building, Trumpington Street, Cambridge CB2 1RP
40 West 20th Street, New York, NY 10011-4211, USA
10 Stamford Road, Oakleigh, Victoria 3166, Australia

First published 1993

Printed in Great Britain at the University Press, Cambridge

A catalogue record for this book is available from the British Library

Library of Congress cataloguing in publication data

Johansson, Per-Olov, 1949–
Cost-benefit analysis of environmental change / Per-Olov Johansson.
    p. cm.
ISBN 0-521-44318-0 – ISBN 0-521-44792-5 (pbk)
1. Environmental policy – Cost effectiveness. I. Title.
HC79.E5J645 1993
338.4'336373 – dc20   92-38887 CIP

ISBN 0 521 44318 0 hardback
ISBN 0 521 44792 5 paperback

Contents

Figures

Preface

There is now a considerable literature on the economic theory and measurement of environmental benefits. At least in part this is explained by the fact that there is a growing concern in many countries about what we are doing to our environmental resources. This has created a need for economic analysis of environmental problems. When reading the reviews of my own 1987 book on environmental benefits, I was struck by the fact that several reviewers demanded a book on the cost-benefit analysis of environmental damage. As teachers, they had to complement the benefits literature with other books and articles covering the remaining corner-stones of cost-benefit analysis. I had expected somebody immediately to try to fill this gap in the literature on environmental economics. In any case, I finally decided to try to produce a survey of the literature on cost-benefit analysis, and, in so doing, adapt the approach so as to make it suitable for the evaluation of environmental changes. This book is the result of my labour, which I hope has been at least partly successful.

The book is an advanced text in applied welfare economics and its application to environmental economics. It is intended for PhD courses in environmental, welfare, health and public economics. The book also provides simple sets of project evaluation rules ('rules of thumb') on such matters as the treatment of different kinds of taxes, unemployment, risk and externalities. For this reason, the book should also be useful as a reference work for those undertaking project evaluations in government agencies and private firms.

I am grateful to Peter Högfeldt, Bengt Kriström, Karl-Gustaf Löfgren and Rauli Svento for helpful discussions and comments upon parts of earlier drafts. Parts of chapter 7 were written for the European Science Foundation's programme on environment, science and society. My colleagues of the programme's task force group on valuation, risk and uncertainty contributed with many helpful comments on my material. I also owe a lot to the four anonymous referees provided for me by Cambridge

University Press. Their detailed comments helped me to improve the manuscript greatly. Special thanks must go to the fifth referee, Caroline Dinwiddy, whose name was revealed during the refereeing process. She not only commented on the manuscript in the usual way, but also made many valuable comments and suggestions in private correspondence. At Cambridge University Press, my editor Patrick McCartan provided me with support during the long and sometimes painful process that a book project represents. The English was scrutinized by John Haslam at the Press, and by Ann Brown. I am also grateful to Monica Peijne for her excellent work in typing the manuscript.

In spite of all the help that has been provided by outsiders, there are undoubtedly errors, flaws and 'Scandinavianisms' remaining. As a matter of good form, I remind the reader that they are the responsibility of the author.

1 Introduction

1.1 Scope of the study

Most real-world policy changes create conflicts of interest. For example, if a forest which is used as a recreation area is cleared, those owning the forest will gain, while those visiting the area or those concerned about an endangered species living there will lose. Nevertheless, a decision must be taken whether or not to cut down the forest. The decision-maker must implicitly or explicitly transform all values to a single 'dimension' to compare them. Only then can he decide whether or not the value of the timber exceeds the value of the preserved forest. The economist's way of performing this transformation is to try to express all utility changes in monetary terms. This is the essence of *social cost-benefit analysis*. Once all benefits and costs have been expressed in monetary units, the social profitability of the considered project can be assessed.

The beginnings of cost-benefit analysis date back over a century to the work of Jules Dupuit, who was concerned with the benefits and costs of constructing a bridge; Dupuit's famous paper 'On the utility of public works' was published in 1844. In particular, Dupuit introduced the concept of the consumer surplus, i.e. the fact that benefits are measured by an area under a demand curve, not by what is actually paid. The next major contribution to cost-benefit analysis seems to have appeared almost one hundred years later.

In a well-known paper, 'The general welfare in relation to problems of taxation and of railway and utility rates', published in 1938, Harold Hotelling, among other things, formulated the case for marginal cost pricing: 'The efficient way to operate a bridge is to make it free to the public, so long at least as the use of it does not increase to a state of overcrowding' (Hotelling, 1938, p. 158).

The first attempts to apply cost-benefit analysis to empirical decision-making also date back to the thirties. The United States Flood Control Act

1

of 1936 introduced the principle that a project is desirable if 'the benefits, to whomsoever they may accrue, are in excess of the estimated costs'. However, the precise meaning of a 'benefit' remained unclear, and individual agencies often approached similar projects from different standpoints. This stimulated academic interest in the subject. Beginning in the late fifties, an extensive literature on the foundations of cost-benefit analysis emerged: see Eckstein (1958), Krutilla and Eckstein (1958), McKean (1958), Maass (1966), Marglin (1967), Harberger (1969, 1971), Musgrave (1969), Little and Mirrlees (1968), Dasgupta *et al.* (1972), Boadway (1975), Lesourne (1975), Srinivasan and Bhagwati (1978), Diewert (1983), Drèze and Stern (1987), and Starrett (1988), just to mention a few. Tinbergen (1952), Meade (1955), and Arrow and Kurz (1970) are examples of related works which have influenced the development of cost-benefit analysis.

The basic idea of a (social) cost-benefit analysis can be illustrated by means of a simple example. Suppose that the air quality in a particular area can be improved. Since this improvement is associated with a cost, perhaps for filters and other equipment, the question arises whether the investment is worth its cost. In other words, are people really willing to make the sacrifice the investment represents? By examining the total sum people are willing to pay we get a monetary benefits measure that can be compared with the investment cost, so that the profitability of the investment can be assessed. An individual's *willingness to pay* is simply the maximum sum of money he is willing to give up to ensure that the suggested project is undertaken. Alternatively, we may want to find the minimum *monetary compensation* the individual needs in order voluntarily to accept that the proposed project is not undertaken. This amount of money makes him as well off as if the project had actually been undertaken, i.e. compensates him for the 'loss' of the project. Summing over all affected individuals yields the overall or aggregate compensation requirement, just as summing each individual's willingness to pay produces the aggregate or overall willingness to pay. These aggregate sums of money can then be compared to the project's total costs, and the project's social profitability assessed. (This aggregation procedure is a common, though highly questionable one, as is shown in chapter 7.)

For a long time, it was widely believed that it was difficult, if not impossible, to value empirically public goods or 'bads' such as pollution of the air and the water. They were often classified as intangibles. There has, however, been a progressive development during the past two decades, with the result that many goods and services that were earlier classified as intangibles are now classified as measurable. In turn, this means that the possibility of undertaking cost-benefit assessments of activities that affect the environment has increased dramatically.

This study is an attempt to introduce PhD students to the theory of cost-benefit analysis of projects or changes that positively or negatively affect the environment. The focus of interest is therefore on the evaluation of activities that either provide public goods or create external effects. This means that some issues which are highlighted in many earlier contributions, such as the treatment of taxes and market imbalances, although in no way ignored, play a secondary role in this book. Instead, issues that are focused upon include the following: valuing public goods and externalities in a general equilibrium context, the treatment of flows and stocks of both natural resources and pollutants, intragenerational and intergenerational aggregation, evaluation of risky projects, the treatment of irreversibilities and health effects, and assessing projects which affect other countries, e.g. transboundary pollution. Throughout, reference is made to various empirical methods and approaches that can be used in applied project evaluations. For example, a separate chapter is devoted to different methods that can be used to measure the willingness to pay for public goods, and in other chapters the methods used in empirical studies to assess various kinds of benefits and/or costs are reported.

Although there has been a great deal of development in the theory as well as the measurement of environmental benefits and costs, much remains to be done. Cost-benefit analysis can capture and express in a single dimension (monetary units) many, but never all, of the effects of environmental projects. Such analyses enlarge as well as improve the information set available to policy-makers. Nevertheless, given all the unresolved issues in cost-benefit analysis, some of which will be hinted at in this book, such analysis can seldom constitute the one and only factor in decision-making. Usually, the decision-maker also wants to consider a proposed project's private profitability, its impact on the governmental budget, its political consequences, and so on; see, for example, Mueller (1989) for details. Still, if cost-benefit analysis is to be used in decision-making, it is essential that it is based on solid theoretical foundations and the best available practical empirical methods. Hopefully, this book constitutes a step, however small, in this direction.

1.2 Plan of the study

Cost-benefit analysis is applied welfare economics. As a service to the reader, an initial chapter on basic tools in welfare economics has been included. The chapter starts by defining indirect utility functions and profit functions, and presents some of their properties. These tools will play a central role in later chapters. The chapter then turns to a brief presentation of the properties of the perfect market economy. A perfect market economy attains a general equilibrium characterized by equality between supply of and demand for each and every commodity provided, such that it is impossible to improve the situation of some individual(s) without making at least one other household worse off. In the present context, the importance of this Pareto superiority result lies in the fact that it is the point of departure in welfare economics for analysis of real-world economies as opposed to the perfect model economy. The chapter then introduces public goods, and derives conditions for the Pareto-optimal provision of such goods. It is important to stress, however, that if one changes the distribution of endowments across households, a new equilibrium is reached. Unfortunately, the Pareto criterion is unable to rank changes which produce both winners and losers. What is needed is some further ethical criterion for choosing among allocations. Such a concept, namely that of a social welfare function, is introduced. The function is used to characterize the properties of a social welfare optimum. After this digression into general welfare economics, the rest of the book is devoted to applied welfare economics.

The benefit side is extremely important in assessing environmental projects. There is a large and growing literature on both the economic theory and the measurement of such benefits. This is hardly surprising given that many of the services provided by the environment are unpriced. There is therefore a need for money measures of utility change caused by 'commodities' that can be viewed as public goods or externalities, and for methods for the practical evaluation of such money measures. Chapter 3 introduces consumer surplus measures, concentrating on the concepts of compensating and equivalent variation. Measures of a *ceteris paribus* change in the provision of a public good as well as of complex changes involving many prices, wages and public goods are presented.

Several different practical methods of measuring the willingness to pay for public goods and unpriced private goods have been suggested in the literature. Chapter 4 is devoted to a brief review of the most frequently used methods: the contingent valuation method, travel cost methods and hedonic price approaches.

Private firms are often considered as causing a considerable proportion of our environmental problems. However, in many cases firms are also affected by pollution. Therefore, in order to assess projects which affect the environment, producer surplus (change) measures are needed. The first section of chapter 5 is devoted to a presentation of such measures. These are a necessary input in any evaluation of a project's social profitability, since firms are ultimately owned by households. This is true even if a firm is directly owned by a pension fund or the government, for example. These institutions are ultimately owned by households. The different pieces, i.e.

consumer surplus measures and producer surplus measures, are put together in section 5.2 and a general equilibrium type of evaluation of a small environmental project is undertaken. The rest of the chapter considers the evaluation of large projects as well as the treatment of distortionary taxes and unemployment in project assessments.

A typical feature of many environmental projects is that their consequences last for many years. Intertemporal evaluations are the topic of chapter 6. Natural resources, renewable as well as non-renewable, are introduced and the treatment of such resources in a social cost-benefit analysis is explored. An optimal-growth theory model is used to derive cost-benefit rules for flows as well as stock pollutants. This model is also used to discuss the concept of sustainable development and the shortcomings of traditional national income accounts as regards flows of environmental services and changes in stocks of natural resources and pollutants.

As mentioned above, a typical approach in cost-benefit analysis is simply to add gains and losses across households. This approach is examined in chapter 7. Using a social welfare function, the relationship between a project's impact on social welfare and its monetary profitability is examined. A positive aggregate consumer surplus is often interpreted as implying that gainers can, at least hypothetically, compensate losers from a proposed project. The circumstances under which this claim holds, and the ethical judgements underlying it, are clarified. The second part of the chapter turns to the intergenerational aggregation problem. The choice of social discount rate in projects affecting several generations is discussed using both conventional growth models and overlapping-generations models. The concepts of transfers in kind and impure altruism are also explored. The final section of the chapter discusses how to deal with altruism in a cost-benefit analysis. It turns out that some types of altruism can be ignored while other types must be accounted for in a cost-benefit analysis.

The effects of a proposed environmental project are often difficult to predict. There is thus a need for cost-benefit rules for a risky world. Chapter 8, which is the first of two chapters on the treatment of risk, derives project evaluation rules which can be used when an environmental investment has uncertain consequences. The chapter also considers the appropriate choice of money measure in cases where risk can be diversified away (is insurable), or is collective.

In some cases, a project affects the probability that a certain event will occur; it shifts the probability distribution. This is typically the case for complex projects aiming at the preservation of endangered species or the reduction of the greenhouse effect. Similarly, projects may affect the probability that human beings will experience one or another health status, including the probability of death. These issues, including results from empirical studies, are dealt with in chapter 9. The chapter also includes a discussion of the value of information. There are both benefits and costs of postponing a project until more is learned about its possibly irreversible consequences, for example. The chapter also contains a discussion of the problems faced – in particular, time inconsistency and credibility – when designing policies in an intertemporal context.

Unfortunately, there seem to be few, if any, cost-benefit analyses of environmental changes that strictly follow the project evaluation rules derived in this book. Alternatively, they are presented in such a sketchy way that it is impossible to infer what rules have been used. Nevertheless, in chapter 10 a few empirical studies are summarized. The first two studies presented are both based on the contingent valuation method, one using continuous responses, the other using both continuous and binary responses. A study explicitly introducing risk is then presented. Next, the possibility of using computable general equilibrium models in cost-benefit analysis is highlighted by summarizing a CGE-based evaluation of environmental regulations. The study by Hammack and Brown (1974) illustrates how optimal control theory and simulation models can be employed in evaluations. Finally, attempts to account for natural resource depletion in national accounts are discussed.

The final chapter of the book is devoted to a presentation of policy instruments that can be used to achieve a socially efficient allocation of environmental resources. These instruments include regulations, emissions charges, and transferable emission permits. The chapter also discusses the evaluation of international environmental problems, i.e. how to assess activities which affect not only the domestic environment but also environmental quality abroad (globally). Policy instruments that can be used to handle such 'international games' are discussed with reference to a recent empirical study.

2　Some basic concepts

This chapter can be viewed as a quick refresher course in microeconomics and welfare economics. The chapter presents some of the tools, such as indirect utility functions, profit functions, definitions of a general equilibrium, Pareto optimality and the social welfare function, that will be used throughout this book. Of necessity, the presentation must be only an outline. The reader interested in detailed investigations is referred to some standard book in microeconomics, such as Kreps (1990) or Varian (1992).

The chapter is structured as follows. Section 2.1 is devoted to the utility maximization problem for a household, while section 2.2 takes a look at the profit maximization problem for a firm. Equilibrium in markets and the meaning of the Pareto-efficiency of a competitive equilibrium are considered in section 2.3. Public goods are introduced in section 2.4, where we derive the condition for the optimal provision of a public good. Sections 2.5 and 2.6 introduce the concept of a social welfare function. The chapter ends with a few comments on the relationship between the social welfare function and social cost-benefit analysis.

2.1　Households

Let us consider a household consuming n different private commodities x_i, where $i = 1, \ldots, n$. These can be bought in non-negative quantities at given, fixed, strictly positive prices p_i. The household supplies k different kinds of labour denoted L_j for $j = 1, \ldots, k$, treating wage rates, denoted w_j, as fixed. The household is viewed as being equipped with an ordinal utility function $U = U(x, L)$, where x is a goods vector of order $1 \cdot n$, and L is a labour supply vector of order $1 \cdot k$. The utility function is assumed to be continuous, increasing in its first argument and decreasing in its second argument, twice continuously differentiable, and 'well-behaved' so as to generate an interior solution to the household's utility maximization problem as well as demand functions having the usual properties.

The economy is assumed to consist of H different households. The problem of utility maximization for household h ($h = 1, ..., H$) can now be written as follows:

$$\max \; U^h(x^h, L^h) \\ \text{s.t.} \quad y^h + wL^h - px^h = 0 \qquad\qquad \forall h \quad \Big\} \quad (2.1)$$

where a superscript h refers to household h, $\forall$ means 'for all', $y^h = Y^h + \Pi^h - \tau^h$ is a lump-sum income, treated as fixed by the household, Y denotes a transfer to the household, τ denotes a tax paid by the household, Π denotes profit income, if any, received by the household, p is a price vector of order $1 \cdot n$, w is a wage vector of order $1 \cdot k$, and any sign referring to transposed vectors is ignored here and throughout. There is also a time constraint saying that working time plus leisure time sum up to 24 hours a day, but this constraint is suppressed in order to avoid unnecessary clutter.

According to (2.1), the household is assumed to act as if it maximizes a well-behaved ordinal utility function subject to a budget constraint. It chooses a bundle of consumption goods and supplies of labour so as to attain the highest possible level of utility subject to the constraint imposed by the budget. First-order conditions for an interior solution to this utility maximization problem are stated in the appendix to this chapter. Solving these conditions for x and L in terms of prices, wages and lump-sum income yields demand functions for goods and supply functions for labour:

$$x^h = x^h(p, w, y^h) \qquad\qquad \forall h \quad \Big\} \quad (2.2) \\ L^h = L^h(p, w, y^h) \qquad\qquad \forall h$$

where $x^h = [x_1^h(p, w, y^h), ..., x_n^h(p, w, y^h)]$ is a vector of goods demands, and $L^h = [L_1^h(p, w, y^h), ..., L_k^h(p, w, y^h)]$ is a vector of labour supplies. The quantity demanded of a commodity and supplied of a labour skill, respectively, are functions of prices, wages and lump-sum income.

Substitution of equations (2.2) into the direct utility function in (2.1) yields the indirect utility function:

$$V^h = V^h(p, w, y^h) = U^h[x^h(p, w, y^h),\; L^h(p, w, y^h)] \qquad \forall h \qquad (2.3)$$

The indirect utility function expresses utility as a function of prices, wages and lump-sum income. Taking the partial derivative of the indirect utility function with respect to the ith price and the jth wage rate, respectively, and invoking the envelope theorem yields:

$$\partial V^h(\cdot)/\partial p_i = -\lambda^h(\cdot) \cdot x_i^h(\cdot) \qquad\qquad \forall h, i \quad \Big\} \quad (2.4) \\ \partial V^h(\cdot)/\partial w_j = \lambda^h(\cdot) \cdot L_j^h(\cdot) \qquad\qquad \forall h, j$$

Thus the partial derivative of the indirect utility function with respect to a price is equal to minus the demand for that commodity multiplied by λ^h. Similarly, differentiating the function with respect to a wage yields the corresponding supply function multiplied by λ^h. In turn, it is easily demonstrated that λ^h, the Lagrange multiplier associated with the budget constraint in (2.1), is the partial derivative of the indirect utility function with respect to lump-sum income:

$$\partial V^h(\cdot)/\partial y^h = \lambda^h(\cdot) = V_y^h(\cdot) \qquad\qquad \forall h \qquad\qquad (2.4')$$

In the light of this result, it is not surprising that λ^h (or V_y^h which is the symbol we will use henceforth) is frequently referred to as the marginal utility of income.

2.2 Firms

The economy is assumed to consist of F different private firms. These are ultimately owned by households, implying that changes in profits constitute an ingredient in a social cost-benefit analysis. For notational simplicity each firm is assumed to produce all the n commodities consumed by households, using k different labour skills as variable inputs. Profits of an arbitrary firm are defined as:

$$\Pi^f = pF^f(l^f) - wL^f \qquad\qquad \forall f \qquad\qquad (2.5)$$

where $F^f(\cdot) = [F^{1f}(L^{1f}), ..., F^{nf}(L^{nf})]$ is a vector containing the fth firm's production functions for the n different commodities, L^{if} for $i = 1, ..., n$ is a vector of labour demands of order $1 \cdot k$, and $\sum_i L_j^{if} = L_j^f$ for $j = 1, ..., k$. The production functions are assumed to be strictly concave, and twice continuously differentiable.

According to (2.5), profits are equal to the difference between sales revenue and wage costs, ignoring here any fixed costs due to a fixed capital stock. The assumed aim of the firm is to maximize its profits, treating all prices and wages as unaffected by the firm's actions. Solving the profit maximization problem (see the appendix) one arrives at the demand functions for labour. Substitution of these into (2.5) yields the profit function:

$$\Pi^f = \Pi^f(p,w) \qquad\qquad \forall f \qquad\qquad (2.6)$$

The profit function is increasing in its first argument and decreasing in its second argument. Taking the partial derivative of the function with respect to p_i and w_j respectively yields:

$$\begin{aligned} \partial \Pi^f(\cdot)/\partial p_i &= x_i^f(p_i,w) & \forall f,i \\ \partial \Pi^f(\cdot)/\partial w_j &= L_j^f(p,w) = \sum_i L_j^{if}(p_i,w) & \forall f,j \end{aligned} \left.\vphantom{\begin{aligned}&\\&\end{aligned}}\right\} \quad (2.7)$$

where $x_i^f = F^{if}(\cdot)$. The partial derivative of the profit function with respect to a price (factor price) is the supply function (demand function) for the corresponding commodity (input). Note that the jth labour skill is used by the firm to produce all n commodities, which explains why we sum across commodities in the second line of equation (2.7).

2.3 Markets, general equilibrium and Pareto optimality

Basically, a market characterized by perfect competition is one in which the individual buyer or seller treats the price as independent of his purchases or sales. This is the assumption we have employed in deriving demand and supply functions for households and firms. In this section we will take a look at competitive markets and their welfare properties. The point of reference is the Pareto criterion. By this criterion a policy change is socially desirable if everyone is made better off (the weak Pareto criterion) or at least some are made better off (the strong Pareto criterion) while no one is made worse off. When the possibilities of making such policy changes are exhausted, we are left with an allocation of commodities that cannot be altered without someone being made worse off. Such an allocation is called *Pareto-optimal* or efficient.

In order to relate our model economy to the Pareto criterion, let us start by defining a market equilibrium. The ith market will be in equilibrium if p_i is such that aggregate supply is equal to aggregate demand:

$$\sum_f x_i^f(p_i,w) = \sum_h x_i^h(p_i,p^-,w,y^h) \qquad \forall i \qquad (2.8)$$

where the vector p^- contains all prices but the ith price, and p^-, w, and y^h, $\forall h$, are fixed at arbitrary positive values. If we fix p_i above the level implicitly given by (2.8), excess supply will result, while there will be an excess demand if the price is fixed below its market-clearing level. It is left to the reader to examine the market for an arbitrary labour skill. The reader should note that the kind of models considered here cannot determine absolute prices. Some particular price must be kept constant, and used as the numéraire. Prices are thus expressed in terms of this numéraire price, i.e. we can only determine relative prices. Alternatively, one defines a price index, but this approach too amounts to fixing one price at an arbitrary level.

We are now ready to define an equilibrium (relative) price and wage vector. This is a vector (p,w) such that all goods and factor markets *simultaneously* are in equilibrium. It is not necessarily true that an equilibrium price vector exists. Alternatively, there may be multiple equilibria in the sense that more than one price vector results in general equilibrium, given the initial distribution of endowments (property rights to firms, etc.). We will not analyse these difficult issues. In this book it is simply assumed that there is a unique equilibrium price vector. The reader interested in existence proofs is referred to Arrow and Hahn (1971) or Varian (1992), for example.

The special feature of the equilibrium price vector can be stated as follows. It *simultaneously* allows all households to maximize utility, and all firms to maximize profits. In other words, given the equilibrium price vector, it is impossible to improve the situation (welfare/profits) of one agent without worsening the situation of some other agent(s), since everybody has already maximized welfare/profits. This result, saying that a competitive equilibrium, if it exists, attains Pareto optimality, is known as the *First Theorem of Welfare Economics*. We will not attempt to provide a proof here, but the reader is referred to Arrow and Hahn (1971), Kreps (1990) and Varian (1992), for example, for detailed proofs. If the equilibrium price vector is unique, given the initial distribution of endowments, all other price vectors would result in market imbalances, implying that at least some agents would face constraints, for example unemployment, over and above those associated with the maximization problems (2.1) and (2.5). These constraints would reduce welfare/profits in comparison with the general equilibrium case.

It is important to stress, however, that if the initial distribution of endowments, for example property rights to firms, were changed, we would end up with a new general equilibrium (price vector). This new equilibrium would correspond to a different distribution of incomes and welfare across households from the one considered above. Some households would gain while others would lose from the change. Given the tools introduced thus far, we are unable to say that one Pareto-efficient allocation is superior to another, since some households will lose if the economy is moved from one Pareto-efficient allocation to another. What is needed is some further ethical criterion for choosing among the efficient allocations. Such a concept, the concept of a social welfare function, will be introduced in a later section.

2.4 Public goods

Thus far we have discussed commodities that follow the principle of exclusivity. The owner of such a good, an orange for example, can exclude others from consuming it. A second property of the commodities discussed above is that they are rival. That is, the production of additional amounts involves some extra costs of production. Goods that possess both properties are known as (strictly) private goods. Goods which are both non-exclusive and non-rival are called (pure) public goods. Once such a good is produced, no one can be excluded from the benefits and additional households may use it at virtually zero marginal costs.

Let us now introduce a pure public good, denoted z. Since it is a pure public good it is consumed in equal amounts by all households, implying that $z^h = z$ for all h. The direct utility function of household h in (2.1) is now augmented by the argument z, while its budget constraint remains unchanged. Any costs for the provision of the public good are covered through tax payments τ^h. The utility maximization problem is specified in the appendix to this chapter. Here we turn directly to the indirect utility function, which now will look as follows:

$$V^h = V^h(p,w,y^h,z^h) \qquad\qquad \forall h \qquad (2.9)$$

Taking the partial derivative of the indirect utility function with respect to z yields:

$$\partial V^h(\cdot)/\partial z^h = V_z^h(\cdot) = \partial U^h[x^h(p,w,y^h,z^h),\ L^h(p,w,y^h,z^h),\ z^h]/\partial z^h \qquad (2.10)$$

This yields the extra utility of a small *ceteris paribus* increase in the provision of the public good. Note that demands for private goods and supplies of labour are functions of z. There are therefore adjustments in purchases and sales following a change in z, but these adjustments 'net out' when prices, wages and incomes are kept constant. This can easily be verified by differentiating the budget constraint of the household. The following should also be noted. Taking the partial derivative of the indirect utility function (2.9) with respect to lump-sum income yields the marginal utility of income. Dividing through (2.10) by the marginal utility of income converts the expression from units of utility to monetary units. The right-hand side expression is then interpreted as the marginal willingness to pay for the public good. This is illustrated in Figure 2.1.

Let us now turn to the Pareto-efficient provision of a public good. There are many different ways in which this problem can be formulated. Here we will follow a route which will provide us with the solution in a fast and straightforward way. The aim is to provide the public good in such an amount that it is impossible to increase the utility for one household without decreasing the utility for some other household, i.e. to attain Pareto optimality. Let us therefore maximize the utility of household 1, while holding the remaining households at prespecified utility levels. We thus have the following maximization problem:

$$\max\ V^1(p,w,y^1,z^1) \qquad\qquad\qquad (2.11)$$
$$\text{s.t.}\quad V^h(p,w,y^h,z^h) = c^h \qquad h \neq 1 \qquad (2.12)$$

where c^h is a constant.

Two additional constraints must be introduced. First of all, there is a (well-behaved) production function for the public good, which is denoted $z = F(x^p, L^p)$, where a superscript p refers to the public sector's demand for inputs. Private goods as well as labour are used to produce the public good. Secondly, the production of the public good must somehow be financed.

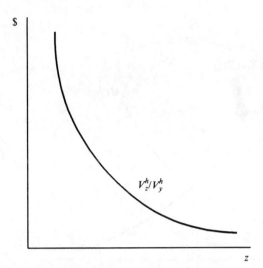

Figure 2.1. Willingness-to-pay curve for a public good.

Let us assume that the government collects lump-sum taxes from the households so as to balance its budget.[1] These two constraints can be written as follows:

$$z^h = F(x^p, L^p) \qquad\qquad\qquad \forall h \qquad\qquad (2.12')$$
$$\sum_h \tau^h = px^p + wL^p \qquad\qquad\qquad\qquad (2.12'')$$

where the fact that $z = z^h$ for all h has been used so as to arrive at equation (2.12'). There are other constraints on the problem, such as market-clearing conditions, but these will be ignored here.

Let us now choose z^h, τ^h, x^p and L^p so as to maximize (2.11) subject to constraints (2.12). After straightforward calculations (see the appendix) one finds that:

$$\sum_h [V_z^h(\cdot)/V_y^h(\cdot)] = p_i/F_i(\cdot) = w_j/F_j(\cdot) \qquad\qquad \forall i,j \qquad\qquad (2.13)$$

where $F_i = \partial F/\partial x_i^p$ and $F_j = \partial F/\partial L_j^p$. The left-hand side expression of (2.13) yields the aggregate marginal willingness to pay for the public good. The remaining terms in (2.13) constitute efficiency conditions, which can be interpreted as yielding the marginal cost of providing the public good. The latter interpretation is most easily obtained by minimizing the cost of producing a specified amount of the public good, i.e. by deriving the public sector's cost function.

Equation (2.13) is the usual Samuelsonian condition for the Pareto-optimal provision of a public good: a public good should be provided in

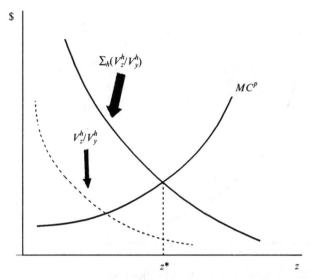

Figure 2.2. Optimal provision (z^*) of a pure public good.

such an amount that the *aggregate* marginal willingness to pay for the good is equal to the marginal cost (MC^p) of providing the good (see Figure 2.2, where z^* denotes the optimal provision of z). This result is in sharp contrast to the corresponding condition for a purely private good. Such a good should be produced in an amount such that the *individual* marginal willingness to pay for the good is equal to the marginal cost; the last unit of the good is consumed (owned) by a single individual, the buyer. The last unit of a pure public good, on the other hand, is consumed by all households.

Underlying the above analysis is an assumption about how much different households must pay for the public good. To highlight the payment and distribution issues, it is useful to introduce a *tax price*. This is the individual household's share of one unit of government revenue. With uniform taxation of H households the uniform tax price is $1/H$. With proportional taxation, the tax price increases with income. In any case, if the tax price is denoted p^h, the tax paid by household h is simply $p^h z$, where z is the amount of the public good provided.

The household can then be viewed as maximizing its utility function (with respect to x, L and z) subject to:

$$y^h + wL^h - px^h - p^h z = 0 \qquad\qquad \forall h \qquad\qquad (2.14)$$

According to the budget constraint (2.14), the household spends its entire income on private and/or public goods. We can thus derive an ordinary demand function for the public good, just as in the case of private goods. Unless the public good is a Giffen good, demand will decrease if the tax price is increased, *ceteris paribus*.

This way of viewing the provision of public goods highlights the fact that there are many different payment schemes, i.e. vectors of tax prices across households, which support a particular z-level. Similarly, shifting from one tax system to another results in a shift in the Pareto-optimal provision of z. In other words, the z-level implicitly defined by (2.13) is sensitive to who pays and how much, unless we make very specific assumptions about utility functions and income distribution in society. The reader interested in further discussion of these issues is referred to, for example, Inman (1987), Mueller (1989) and Stiglitz (1986).

2.5 The social welfare function

We have shown that there are many Pareto-efficient allocations, and that the Pareto criterion is insufficient to rank such allocations. More generally, most real-world projects create both winners and losers. We need more than the Pareto principle to rank such projects. A complete and consistent ranking of social states ('projects') is called a *social welfare ordering*, and is much like a household's preference ordering. If the social welfare ordering is continuous, it can be translated into a *social welfare function*. This is simply a function of the utility levels of all households such that a higher value of the function is preferred to a lower one. Such a function is often called a Bergsonian welfare function, after Abram Bergson, who first used it. Alternatively, it is called a Bergson–Samuelson social welfare function.

The social welfare function is written as follows:

$$W = W[V^1(p,w,y^1,z), \ldots, V^H(p,w,y^H,z)] \tag{2.15}$$

where by assumption $z = z^h$ for all h. Note that we use the specification of the indirect utility functions stated in (2.9). A priori, there is not much we can say about the form a social welfare function takes. The form depends on who is 'behind' the function: it may express the views of parliament or the reader's views, for example. In the literature, however, a social welfare function is generally assumed to have four convenient properties. Firstly, it is assumed to satisfy *welfarism* which means that social welfare depends only on the utility levels of the households, just as in (2.15). Secondly, social welfare is assumed to be increasing with each household's utility level, *ceteris paribus*. The function is thus assumed to satisfy the (strong) *Pareto criterion*, since a *ceteris paribus* increase in the utility of any household increases social welfare. Moreover, if one household is made worse off, then another household must be made better off to maintain the same level of social welfare. Thirdly, the *intensity* of this trade-off is usually assumed to depend on the degree of inequality in society. Social indifference curves are therefore convex to the origin. Fourthly, it is often assumed that it does not matter who enjoys a high or low level of utility. This principle is known as *anonymity*.

If household utility functions are ordinal and non-comparable, then the only possible and consistent social welfare function is a dictatorship. That is, the social welfare function must coincide with the ordinal utility function of some individual regardless of the preferences of the others. This result is known as *Arrow's impossibility theorem* (when dictatorship is precluded by assumption). The reader can check this result by assuming two households consuming two private goods and equipped with Cobb–Douglas utility functions. Define social welfare as the sum of utilities. Next, take the logarithm of one or both utility functions. This is a monotone increasing transformation, and leaves the household's ranking of commodity bundles unchanged. Such a transformation is therefore permitted in an ordinal world. However, the new social welfare function will rank commodity bundles (social states) differently from the initial function, as is easily checked by working through the example for two different commodity bundles; alternatively, consult Johansson (1991, p. 30).

We thus need further assumptions in order to be able to use the concept of the social welfare function. For example, we may assume that utility is fully measurable. In this case the individual household is assumed to be equipped with a unique utility function. In sharp contrast to the case with ordinal utility functions, the social welfare function will now produce a consistent ranking of social states. More generally, full measurability, welfarism and the Pareto principle permit the general Bergson–Samuelson social welfare function (2.15) to rank social states consistently.

One can introduce intermediate or partial measurability and comparability assumptions. For example, utility functions may be cardinal, in the sense that we allow affine transformations ($u^h = a_h + b_h U^h$, where a_h and b_h are constants). Comparability may be partial in the sense that we assume that $b_h = b$ for all households but a_h can differ across households. Such constraints on the information available restrict the set of possible social welfare functions in comparison to the full measurability case considered above. For a fine discussion of this issue the reader is referred to Boadway and Bruce (1984).

Suppose now that we want to maximize social welfare, subject to equations (2.12′) and (2.12″), given that the social planner controls prices, wages, lump-sum taxes and the provision of public goods. The problem (see the appendix) can be used to obtain the following relations:

$$
\left.
\begin{array}{ll}
W_p = 0 \rightarrow x_i^d + x_i^p = x_i^s & \forall i \\
W_w = 0 \rightarrow L_j^d + L_j^p = L_j^s & \forall j \\
W_\tau = 0 \rightarrow W_h V_y^h = a & \forall h \\
W_z = 0 \rightarrow \sum_h V_z^h / V_y^h = dC^p
\end{array}
\right\} \quad (2.16)
$$

where $W_p = \partial W / \partial p_i$, etc., $W_h = \partial W / \partial V^h$, a is the Lagrange multiplier associated with equation (2.12″) and dC^p denotes the marginal cost of providing the public good. Equations (2.16) can be interpreted as follows. Goods prices should be chosen so as to achieve equilibrium in each goods market, and wages should be set so as to achieve equilibrium in each labour market. In arriving at these conditions we have used the fact that households' profit incomes are functions of prices and wages, as can be seen from (2.6) and (2.7). The third line of (2.16) says that incomes should be redistributed until the marginal social utility of income is equal across households. Note that the marginal social utility of income has two ingredients: W_h is the increase in social welfare caused by a marginal increase in the utility of household h, and V_y^h is the marginal utility of income of household h. The product of these two terms must be equal across households in optimum. The final line of (2.16) says that, in optimum, the aggregate marginal willingness to pay for a public good is equal to the marginal cost of providing the good.

2.6 Some illustrations of social welfare functions

In the previous section we introduced the social welfare function. The question arises as to what form this function may have. The choice of a specific form involves a further ethical judgement about how to aggregate individual utilities. In this section, a few commonly employed forms will be presented. The relationship between the distribution of welfare across households and the distribution of income is also discussed.

It is sometimes argued that society's welfare is equal to the sum of the utilities of different individuals. In this case the social welfare function can be written as follows:

$$
W = \sum_h V^h(\cdot) \tag{2.17}
$$

This view is called *utilitarianism*, and was first introduced by Jeremy Bentham in the eighteenth century. In order for changes in the sum of utilities to make sense we assume full (or at least partial) comparability. In a utilitarian society, the social welfare indifference curves W^i are negatively sloped straight lines, as is illustrated in Figure 2.3a. That is, society is willing to give up one unit of household 1's utility for a gain of one unit of household 2's utility. This holds regardless of the degree of inequality in

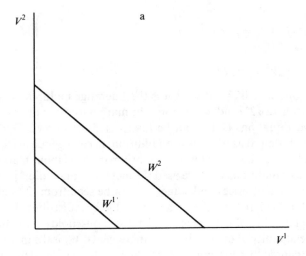

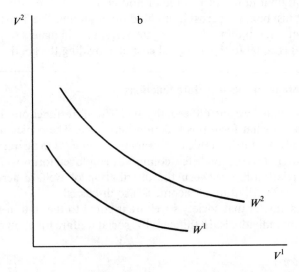

Figure 2.3. Social indifference curves: (a) utilitarian; (b) strictly convex; (c) Rawlsian.

society; the society is completely indifferent to the degree of inequality between households.

Another view of inequality is expressed by the indifference curves in Figure 2.3b. Society should be willing to accept a decrease in the utility of the poor only if there is a much larger increase in the utility of the rich.

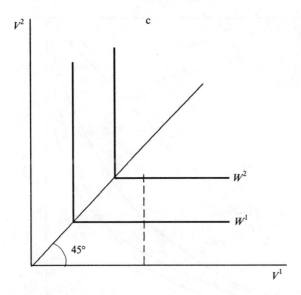

Accordingly, social welfare indifference curves are strictly convex. A simple example is the following:

$$W = \sum_h a(V^h) \cdot V^h(\cdot) \tag{2.17'}$$

where $a(\cdot)$ is a welfare weight that depends on the level of utility attained. Presumably, $a(\cdot)$ is larger the poorer the household is, reflecting the fact that society cares about the poor.

A more extreme position, associated with Rawls (1972), is to argue that the welfare of society depends only on the utility of the poorest household:

$$W = \min\{V^1, \ldots, V^H\} \tag{2.17''}$$

As is illustrated by the broken vertical line in Figure 2.3c, society is better off if the welfare of the poorest household, household 2 in the figure, is improved. Starting from the broken line and moving horizontally to the right, it can be seen that society gains nothing from improving the welfare of the 'richer' household 1.

We now turn to a brief discussion of the relationship between social welfare and the distribution of income. Income distribution is often described as in Figure 2.4. A so-called *Lorenz curve* is obtained by plotting the percentage of total income earned by the various income groups within the population. With complete equality, we would move along the straight positively sloped 45° line in the figure. With a great deal of inequality, as depicted by Lorenz curve A, the poorest 25 per cent have only 2 or 3 per cent of national income. The further to the south-east a Lorenz curve lies, the

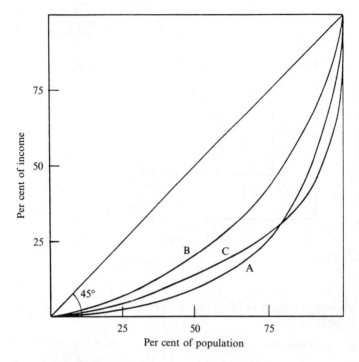

Figure 2.4. Lorenz curves.

more unequal the distribution of income. The Lorenz ordering or ranking of income distribution is partial since if one Lorenz curve crosses another, like curves A and C in the figure, neither can be said to be preferred.

It can be shown that for quite a broad class of social welfare functions, including the utilitarian form as a special case, moving from an income distribution such as A to one such as B in Figure 2.4 will increase social welfare, as was originally shown by Atkinson (1970). See Boadway and Bruce (1984) for a presentation of some extensions of Atkinson's result. The argument is based on the assumption that the total amount of income is independent of its distribution. This ignores the costs of achieving the desired distribution, including the disincentive effect. For example, highly productive people may choose to work less if their incomes are reduced. Moreover, all households need not have the same utility function. One household may derive satisfaction from driving a Mercedes-Benz, while another household may enjoy cheaper leisure activities such as walking in a forest. At a social welfare maximum, as captured by equations (2.16), utility as well as income generally differ across households, although the marginal social utility of income is equalized at the optimum.

2.7 Concluding remarks

The social welfare function ranks all possible social states, including all Pareto-efficient ones. Equations (2.16) select the social state that provides the highest possible social welfare, given the underlying technology and preferences. Thus, given that there is a unique social welfare optimum, equations (2.16) identify this optimum. Moreover, using the social welfare function, we can decide on the social desirability of any project. That is, if we consider a project affecting prices, wages and the supply of public goods (environmental quality), the social welfare function tells us if this project increases or decreases social welfare. In fact, this would be a social *cost-benefit analysis*.[2] A small project can be viewed as the total differential of the social welfare function, denoted dW. The project increases social welfare if $dW > 0$. A large project can be assessed by calculating social welfare with and without the project. The project increases social welfare if $\Delta W > 0$, where ΔW denotes the change in social welfare.

The problem in using the social welfare function approach when assessing projects is that we cannot observe the social welfare function. There are at least two fundamental aspects of this problem to be faced in any application. The first problem is to estimate the welfare weights W_h in equations (2.16). The second problem relates to the unobservability of the individual utility functions. Equations (2.16) indicate, however, that we can collect data on, and estimate, many of the costs and benefits of a project. Moreover, by differentiating the social welfare function, and using conditions such as (2.16), we can see what effects to include in a properly conducted social cost-benefit analysis.

In the next few chapters we will proceed as if there is a single household in the economy under consideration. Alternatively, there are many but identical households. Or we may assume that the welfare distribution is optimal. In both these latter cases we can simply normalize the number of households to one. We want to stick to a single-household economy in order to concentrate on problems in cost-benefit analysis other than the welfare/income distribution issue. If there is just one household in the economy, the social welfare function (2.15) reduces to the utility function of this household. In chapter 7 the aggregation problem, both within and across generations, will be analysed.

Appendix

First-order conditions for an interior solution to the utility maximization problem (2.1) are:

$$\left.\begin{array}{l} \partial U^h/\partial x^h - \lambda^h p = 0 \\ \partial U^h/\partial L^h + \lambda^h w = 0 \\ y^h + wL^h - px^h = 0 \end{array}\right\} \quad (2A.1)$$

where $\partial U^h/\partial x^h = [\partial U^h/\partial x_1^h, \ldots, \partial U^h/\partial x_n^h]$, etc., and λ^h is the Lagrange multiplier associated with the budget constraint in (2.1).

One way to arrive at equations (2.4) and (2.4') is through maximization of the indirect utility function (2.3) subject to the budget constraint:

$$\left.\begin{array}{ll} \max\limits_{\{p,w,y^h\}} & V^h(p,w,y^h) \\[2mm] \text{s.t.} & y^h + wL^h - px^h = 0 \end{array}\right\} \quad (2A.2)$$

Denoting the Lagrange multiplier associated with the budget constraint in (2A.2) λ^h, one obtains the results stated in equations (2.4) and (2.4'). Alternatively, totally differentiate the direct utility function, use the conditions (2A.1) and a totally differentiated budget constraint, to arrive at (2.4) and (2.4').

First-order conditions for an interior solution to the profit maximization problem (2.5) are:

$$p_i \partial F^{if}/\partial L^{if} - w = 0 \quad (2A.3)$$

where $\partial F^{if}/\partial L^{if} = [\partial F^{if}/\partial L_1^{if}, \ldots, \partial F^{if}/\partial L_k^{if}]$. In principle, these conditions can be solved to obtain labour demand functions $L_j^{if} = L_j^{if}(p_i, w)$ for $i = 1, \ldots, n$, and $j = 1, \ldots, k$. Summing across i, one obtains the demand for labour skill j.

The profit function is obtained by substitution of the labour demand functions into equation (2.5):

$$\Pi^f(p,w) = \sum_i [p_i x_i^f(p_i,w) - \sum_j w_j L_j^{if}(p_i,w)] \quad (2A.4)$$

where $x_i^f = F^{if}[L^{if}(p_i,w)]$. Differentiating (2.A.4) with respect to p_i and w_j, respectively, using (2A.3), one arrives at equations (2.7).

If households consume a pure public good, they will maximize:

$$U^h(x^h, L^h, z^h) \quad (2A.5)$$

subject to:

$$y^h + wL^h - px^h = 0 \quad (2A.6)$$

The first-order conditions for an interior solution to this maximization problem look like those stated in (2A.1). The demand and supply functions will now contain z^h as a separate argument:

$$\left.\begin{array}{l} x^h = x^h(p,w,y^h,z^h) \\ L^h = L^h(p,w,y^h,z^h) \end{array}\right\} \quad (2A.7)$$

The maximization problem (2.11) subject to (2.12), (2.12') and (2.12'') yields the following first-order conditions, among others, for an interior solution:

$$\begin{array}{ll} \partial V^1/\partial z^1 - \gamma^1 = 0 & \\ \beta^h \partial V^h/\partial z^h - \gamma^h = 0 & \forall h \neq 1 \end{array}$$

$$\partial V^{1}/\partial \tau^{1} - a \qquad = 0$$
$$\beta^{h}\partial V^{h}/\partial \tau^{h} - a \qquad = 0 \qquad \forall h \neq 1 \qquad\qquad (2A.8)$$
$$\sum_{h}\gamma^{h}\partial F/\partial x^{p} - ap = 0$$
$$\sum_{h}\gamma^{h}\partial F/\partial L^{p} - aw = 0$$

where γ^{h} is the Lagrange multiplier associated with the hth constraint in (2.12'), a is the Lagrange multiplier associated with (2.12''), and β^{h} for $h \neq 1$ is the Lagrange multiplier associated with the hth ($h \neq 1$) constraint in (2.12). In arriving at these conditions, we have put $y^{h} = Y^{h} + \Pi^{h} - \tau^{h}$, with Π^{h} and $Y^{h} = 0$, and $\tau^{h} \gtreqless 0$ for all h. Rearranging (2.A.8) one arrives at equation (2.13).

Maximizing the social welfare function (2.15) subject to (2.12') and (2.12'') one obtains the following first-order conditions for an interior solution:

$$W_{h}V_{y}^{h}(x^{h} - a^{h}x^{s}) - ax^{p} = 0$$
$$W_{h}V_{y}^{h}(L^{h} - a^{h}L^{d}) - aL^{p} = 0$$
$$W_{h}V_{y}^{h} - a \qquad\qquad = 0$$
$$W_{h}V_{z}^{h} - \gamma^{h} \qquad\qquad = 0 \qquad\qquad (2A.9)$$
$$\sum_{h}\gamma^{h}\partial F/\partial x^{p} - ap \quad = 0$$
$$\sum_{h}\gamma^{h}\partial F/\partial L^{p} - aw \quad = 0$$

where $x^{s} = [\sum_{f}x_{1}^{f}, \ldots, \sum_{f}x_{n}^{f}]$, $L^{d} = [\sum_{f}L_{1}^{f}, \ldots, \sum_{f}L_{k}^{f}]$, $a^{h} = [a^{1h}, \ldots, a^{Fh}]$ denote the shares of the F different firms owned by household h, and a and γ^{h} have the same meaning as in (2A.8). Using (2A.9), one arrives at conditions (2.16). Note that households ultimately own the firms. Taking the partial derivative of the indirect utility function of household h in (2.15) with respect to p_{i}, one obtains:

$$\partial V^{h}/\partial p_{i} = -V_{y}^{h}x_{i}^{h} + V_{y}^{h}\sum_{f}a^{fh}x_{i}^{f} \qquad\qquad (2A.10)$$

The final term shows up since the change in p_{i} affects profits ($\partial \Pi^{f}/\partial p_{i} = x_{i}^{f}$), which in turn will affect the income of those owning the firms. If $a^{fh} = 0$, (2A.10) reduces to (2.3).

3 Consumer surplus measures

The benefit side is extremely important in assessing environmental projects. There is a large and growing literature on both the economic theory of environmental benefits and the measurement of such benefits. This is hardly surprising given that many of the services provided by the environment are unpriced. There has therefore been a need to derive money measures of utility changes caused by, in particular, various 'commodities' that can be viewed as public goods or externalities, and to develop procedures for practical measurement of such money measures. This and the next chapter review these two issues.

In this chapter we start by defining money measures of utility change and discussing their properties. The chapter is structured as follows. Section 3.1 derives the two most frequently used money measures, the compensating and equivalent variations. In section 3.2 their properties, for example how they are related to a utility change, are explored. Section 3.3 looks at the posibility of deriving the value of a public good from market data. Then, in section 3.4, we turn to money measures of complex changes that affect prices, income and environmental quality, and discuss the interpretation of such money measures. The final section of the chapter discusses the so-called path-dependency problem, i.e. the problem that the magnitude of a money measure may depend on the order in which prices etc. are changed. We also discuss the problem faced when decomposing total values into use values and non-use values.

3.1 Two money measures of utility change

Consider a household that derives satisfaction from consuming n different private goods and m different public goods. Let us assume that the household possesses a continuous and increasing utility function $U = U(x,z)$, where x is a $1 \cdot n$ vector of private goods and z is a $1 \cdot m$ vector of public goods. The household has an exogenous budget y which is spent on some or all of the n private goods. These can be bought in non-negative quantities at given, fixed, strictly positive prices p_i for $i = 1, ..., n$. We assume that the household is not satiated, implying that the best choice lies on, rather than inside, the budget constraint. How the government finances its expenditures on public goods is not explicitly considered here, but one possibility is to interpret y as an after-tax income, as in the previous chapter. Different tax schemes will be considered in later chapters. Similarly, household supply of labour will be introduced later on.

The household maximizes its utility subject to the budget constraint. The household's indirect utility function can be written as:

$$V = U[x(p,y,z),z] = V(p,y,z) \tag{3.1}$$

where the vector x is interpreted as $x(p,y,z) = [x_1(p,y,z), ..., x_n(p,y,z)]$, i.e. as a vector of demand functions for private goods with quantity demanded being a function of prices, income and the provision or quality of environmental commodities. The indirect utility function is decreasing in prices, and increasing in income and the quality of the environment. Some of the properties of the indirect utility function which are assumed to hold throughout this book are specified in the appendix to this chapter.

Let us now introduce a change in environmental quality. For simplicity, this change is taken to leave all prices as well as household income unchanged. Then, the change in utility is:

$$\Delta V = V(p,y,z^1) - V(p,y,z^0) \tag{3.2}$$

where a superscript 0 (1) denotes initial (final) level values for environmental goods. Since the utility function is not observable, we need a money measure to evaluate the change in utility. Although a great number of measures have been proposed in the literature, attention is focused here on the concepts of compensating and equivalent variation. The reader interested in other, less frequently used measures is referred to McKenzie (1983) and Ng (1979).

Consider first the compensating variation, or CV for short. This is an amount of money such that:[1]

$$V(p,y - CV,z^1) = V(p,y,z^0) \tag{3.3}$$

The compensating variation gives the maximum amount of money that can be taken from the household while leaving it just as well off as it was before an improvement in environmental quality. In other words, CV is the willingness to pay (WTP) for an improvement. If environmental quality deteriorates, CV is the minimum amount of money that must be given to the

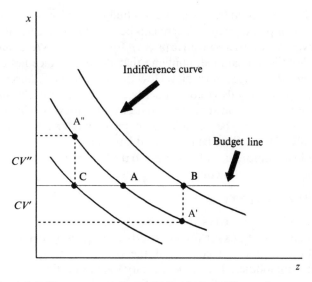

Figure 3.1. The compensating variation for a public good.

household to compensate it for the loss of environmental quality. Thus, CV measures the willingness to accept compensation (WTA) for a deterioration.

This is illustrated for the single private good–single public good case in Figure 3.1 (with $p = 1$). Since the public good or change in environmental quality is supplied free of charge, the budget line is horizontal. In the initial situation the household is at point A. After an improvement in environmental quality the household consumes the combination given by point B, attaining a higher level of utility than previously. Reducing the household's income by an amount CV' will hold the household at the initial level of utility. Combinations A′ and A fall on the same indifference curve, the initial one. Similarly, a reduction in environmental quality given by point C requires a monetary compensation, equal to CV'' in the figure, if the household is to remain at its initial level of utility.

Consider next the equivalent variation (EV). This is an amount of money such that:

$$V(p,y + EV,z^0) = V(p,y,z^1) \tag{3.4}$$

The equivalent variation is the minimum amount of money that must be given to the household to make it as well off as it could have been after an improvement in environmental quality. If environmental quality deteriorates, EV is the maximum the household is willing to pay to prevent that deterioration. These definitions are illustrated in Figure 3.2.

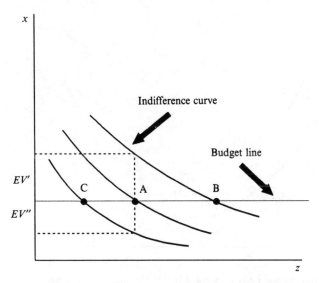

Figure 3.2. The equivalent variation for a public good.

An external effect occurs when the utility of a household depends upon the consumption or production levels of other agents in the economy. Samuelsonian (1954) public goods, i.e. z in our notation, can be interpreted as a type of externality in consumption. For this reason, the consumer surplus measures derived above can be given quite broad interpretations. The measures can be used for an analysis of positive external effects and, with reversed signs, negative external effects such as pollution of the air and water. This is because an externality, like a public good, is usually modelled by including the externality as a separate term in the utility functions of households.

3.2 On the properties of money measures

In general, the CV and EV measures impute different monetary values to a utility change. This is because the monetary valuation of a public good depends on the utility level attained, as will be explained in a moment. Both measures are, however, sign-preserving in the sense that they have the same sign as the underlying change in utility. Substitution of (3.3) and (3.4) respectively into equation (3.2) and use of the intermediate-value theorem reveals that:

$$\left.\begin{aligned} \Delta V &= V_y(p,\bar{y},z^1)\cdot CV \\ \Delta V &= V_y(p,\bar{\bar{y}},z^0)\cdot EV \end{aligned}\right\} \quad (3.5)$$

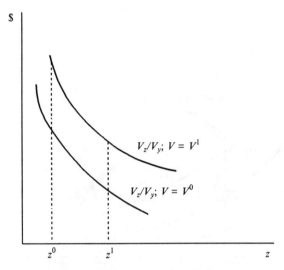

Figure 3.3. Willingness-to-pay curves for initial and final utility levels.

where $V_y(\cdot)$ is the marginal utility of income, i.e. $\partial V(\cdot)/\partial y$, evaluated at some intermediate incomes $\bar{y} \in (y, y - CV)$ and $\bar{\bar{y}} \in (y, y + EV)$, respectively, so as to preserve the equalities between left-hand side and right-hand side expressions in (3.5). Since the marginal utility of income is strictly positive for a non-satiated household, the sign of CV (EV) must be the same as the sign of the change in utility caused by the change in environmental quality. The marginal utility of income converts CV and EV from monetary units to units of utility, so that the left-hand side and right-hand side expressions in (3.5) refer to the same kind of units.

If the underlying utility function is quasi-linear, so that the marginal utility of income is a positive constant, then the two money measures defined in (3.5) must obviously coincide; see the appendix to this chapter. However, a quasi-linear utility function implies that all additional income is spent on a single commodity, i.e. demands for all other private goods are independent of income above some minimum level. This is a questionable description of household behaviour, to say the least. Suppose next that a public good is normal in the sense that the marginal willingness to pay for the good increases with income. The compensated marginal willingness-to-pay curve ('demand' curve) for the good will then shift outwards with the level of utility or income, as in Figure 3.3, where V_z/V_y denotes the compensated marginal willingness to pay for a public good. In this case, $EV > CV$. (If $z^1 < z^0$ both CV and EV take on negative values but EV is closer to zero than CV and hence larger; see the appendix.)

This result has an important implication for applied research in the field. Let us assume that we have collected preference information by asking households how they value some change in the provision of a public good or an environmental service. If the money measure is interpreted as an equivalent variation and the good is normal, we know that the resulting amount of money would be larger than if households had been questioned regarding their compensating variation.

Even though theory, as indicated above, tells us that CV and EV of the same change in general should differ in magnitude, empirical comparisons reveal unexpectedly large differences. The compensation needed in order to accept a loss of a valued commodity often turns out to be ten times as high as the willingness to pay for having the commodity. No simple and completely convincing explanation of such large differences is available. An interesting idea put forward by Hanemann (1991), however, is that the substitution possibilities between environmental goods and other goods ('money') play a crucial role. The more difficult it is to replace a loss of environmental goods with other goods, i.e. the steeper the indifference curves, the higher is the compensation needed in order for the household to accept the loss. In turn, this tends to create a large difference between the compensation or loss measure and the willingness to pay for more environmental goods. On the other hand, if there is a high degree of substitutability between environmental goods and ordinary market goods, then the compensation measure and willingness to pay should be close in value. Several other possible explanations have been suggested. The reader is referred to Gregory (1986) and Harless (1989) for detailed discussions of these explanations.

The next question is whether our money measures can be infinitely large. With regard to an increase in z, the compensating variation is a payment and is hence bounded by income. In the case of a decrease in z, the equivalent variation becomes the WTP-measure and cannot exceed income. Apparently, however, nothing ensures that a compensation requirement falls short of income or even infinity. Suppose, though, that the (for simplicity, single) public good is non-essential in the sense that $U(x, z) = U(x', 0)$, i.e. any bundle including z can be matched by a bundle (x') excluding z. This is a necessary and sufficient condition for the public good always to have a finite consumer surplus regardless of whether the surplus measure is the CV or the EV or some uncompensated money measure; see Willig (1978) for details. Geometrically, this is equivalent to all indifference surfaces intersecting the $z = 0$ hyperplane. Many environmental services such as air to breathe and water to drink are ultimately essential, i.e. it does not make sense to compensate for the complete loss of these goods. Meaningful money measures can be defined for changes in the availability/

quality of such goods and services provided that we do not pass critical levels, though if the availability/quality of essential resources is reduced too much the monetary amount needed in order to compensate for such reductions/ losses may approach infinity.

Sometimes the investigator is interested in ranking several different projects or proposals. By introducing a third vector z^2 corresponding to utility level U^2, it is easy to show that the EV measure ranks any three (any number) of bundles in the same order as the underlying utility function. The EV measure uses z^0 as base bundle in comparing the bundles, i.e.:

$$V(p,y + EV^i,z^0) = V(p,y,z^i) \tag{3.4'}$$

for project i (with $i = 1, 2, \ldots$). Thus, in order to preserve the equality in (3.4') EV has to adjust, since all other left-hand side terms remain constant across projects. As a result, if project 2 (z^2) produces a higher utility than project 1 (z^1), $EV^2 > EV^1$. Proceeding in this way, the reader can use the EV measure to correctly rank any number of projects.

The CV measure, on the other hand, evaluates changes at final z values. Thus, we have:

$$V(p,y - CV^i,z^i) = V(p,y,z^0) \tag{3.3'}$$

The problem in using the CV measure to rank several different projects is that *both* CV and z adjust in the left-hand side expression. This complication implies that CV^2 may exceed CV^1 although the household's utility function ranks z^1 above z^2. It can be shown (see Johansson, 1987) that a quasi-linear utility function ensures that the CV measure ranks an arbitrary number of environmental projects in the same order as the utility function.

It should be stressed that both money measures are suitable for binary comparisons. For the sake of completeness the following should also be noted. If there are two or more initial commodity bundles but only one final bundle, then it is easy to show that the bundles are ranked in the same order by both the CV measure and the household's utility function. This is not necessarily true for the EV measure. For an empirical study (assessing the value of hunting permits) facing this problem in using the EV measure the reader is referred to Johansson *et al.* (1988).

3.3 Environmental quality and market data

Sometimes it is possible to infer the value of a public good by examining the market for a private good. The idea is as follows. Suppose that the private good is non-essential in the sense specified in section 3.2. Then, by increasing its price towards infinity, taking all other prices, income and environmental quality as given, the finite consumer surplus can be deter-

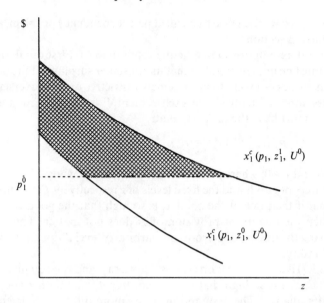

Figure 3.4. The monetary value of a change in the provision of a public good.

mined. If we now repeat the experiment for another level of environmental quality we obtain a new consumer surplus measure, shown in Figure 3.4. The difference in surplus can be attributed to the change in environmental quality, implying that the value attributed to changes in environmental quality can be assessed by examining the market for a private good.

Formally, this result, which is derived in the appendix, can be expressed as:

$$CV_z = -\int_{p_1^0}^{\infty} [x_1(p_1,y-CV(p_1),z_1^1) - x_1(p_1,y-CV(p_1),z_1^0)]dp_1 \qquad (3.6)$$

where all prices but the price of the considered private good (x_1) and all public goods but the considered one (z_1) are suppressed, and the household is held at its initial level of utility through payments $CV(p_1)$ throughout the movement. (These Hicksian demand functions are denoted x_1^c in Figure 3.4.) The right-hand side of (3.6) gives the area to the left of the income-compensated demand curve for the first commodity as it shifts in response to a change in the availability/quality of the public good z_1. In terms of Figure 3.4, CV_z in (3.6) is the shaded area,[2] i.e. the consumer surplus when $z_1 = z_1^1$ less the consumer surplus when $z_1 = z_1^0$ measured in the market for commodity x_1. Alternatively, we could use the equivalent variation measure. It is more complicated to use an ordinary or Marshallian demand function for x_1, since we then face a so-called path-dependency problem, as will be explained in section 3.5.

Two important assumptions underlie the result in (3.6). First of all, the private good must be non-essential so that its consumer surplus is finite, an assumption that does not seem to be extremely restrictive or controversial. The second assumption involved is less self-evident. Formally, the indirect utility function must have the property that:

$$\lim_{p_1 \to \infty} \partial V(p_1, p^-, y, z_1^0, z^-)/\partial z_1 = 0 \tag{3.7}$$

for all $p^- \gg 0$ and $y > 0$, where p^- and z^- are row vectors whose elements are the fixed prices of goods and the fixed levels of z respectively. Condition (3.7) states that if the price of the good x_1 is so high that the good is not consumed, then the quality or provision of z_1 does not matter. Thus, if $x_1 = 0$, improving the quality of z_1 from some arbitrary level z_1^0 does not add to household utility.

Condition (3.7) is a reasonable one if x_1 is a shirt, say, and z_1 its quality. If the price of the shirt is so high that you do not buy it, why bother about (changes in) its quality? The assumption seems more difficult to defend when z_1 is a public good or an external effect. If the condition (3.7) does not hold, i.e. if the household values changes in z_1 even if the private good x_1 is not consumed, the magnitude of the partial derivative in (3.7) will 'jump around' depending on what prices etc. are inserted in the expression. Therefore, in this case the value placed on changes in z_1 cannot be derived from market data. None the less, in many circumstances, the availability of a method that only requires data on demand functions for private goods could prove to be valuable.

Sometimes it is fruitful to view the household as producing, say, recreation, using goods and time as inputs. Thus the household is assumed to be equipped with a production function. In order to illustrate the idea of household production function models, consider the following direct utility function:

$$U = U[x, l^x, f(q, l, z)] \tag{3.8}$$

where l^x is leisure time, $Z = f(\cdot)$ is the recreation 'experience' produced by the household using private goods q, time l, and public goods z as inputs. For example, Z could be a trip to a recreation area which is 'produced' using a car (q), time (l) and roads (z) as inputs. The utility function (3.8) is maximized subject to the budget and time constraints:

$$\left. \begin{array}{l} y + wL - px - pq = 0 \\ l^x + l + L = \bar{l} \end{array} \right\} \tag{3.9}$$

where L is paid working time, $\bar{l}$ is the total time available per period, w is the wage rate, and y, as before, is a lump-sum income.

In principle, the above maximization problem can be solved to obtain demand functions $q = q(p,w,y,z)$ and $l = l(p,w,y,z)$. In turn, these functions can be estimated from market data. However, it is still difficult to assess the monetary value the household imputes to changes in the quantity or quality of public goods z, without directly asking valuation questions, unless we happen to know, or are prepared to make assumptions about, the properties of the household production function $f(\cdot)$. It must hold that the recreation activity Z is non-essential as specified earlier. Furthermore, some marketed input used in the production of Z must be essential, so that Z equals zero if the price of the essential input approaches infinity. Then:

$$\lim_{p_i \to \infty} \partial f[q_i(\cdot),q^-(\cdot),l(\cdot),z_j^0,z^-]/\partial z_j = 0 \qquad (3.10)$$

In words: if the activity Z cannot be produced without input q_i, the amount or quality of the public good input z_j does not matter. If this condition holds and Z is non-essential, one can proceed as in equation (3.6) to value changes in the public good z_j. See Smith (1991) for an excellent review of the household production function approach. See also section 5.1 below.

It should also be mentioned that some goods are mixed public goods or congestible public goods. For example, if too many people simultaneously visit a park this may reduce the utility derived from a trip to the park. Congestion can be introduced by letting the household production function include the number of visitors as a separate argument, for example. More generally, local public goods, e.g. street lights, and club goods, such as swimming pools and golf clubs, are often viewed in this way, i.e. there is an element of congestion. In the next section, rationed private goods appear, a possible interpretation being that these goods are supplied (possibly by the central or local government) at such a low price that congestion (rationing) results.

3.4 Complex changes

A typical feature of many environmental resources is that they provide values of many different types. Following Boyle and Bishop (1985) and Randall (1991), one may distinguish between four more or less distinct values. Firstly, there are *consumptive use values* such as fishing and hunting. Secondly, some resources provide *non-consumptive use values*. For example, some people enjoy bird-watching, while others gain satisfaction from viewing wildlife. Thirdly, a resource may also provide services *indirectly* through books, films, television programmes, and so on. Finally, people may derive satisfaction from the pure fact that a habitat or species *exists*. A change in environmental quality due to, say, pollution of the air may affect the value derived from each of the aforementioned 'commodities'.

Taking these different cases together, the compensating and equivalent variations associated with a large complex change in environmental quality can be written as:

$$V(p^1,w^1,y^1 - P^1X^1 - CV,X^1,z^1) = V(p^0,w^0,y^0 - P^0X^0,X^0,z^0) \atop V(p^0,w^0,y^0 - P^0X^0 + EV,X^0,z^0) = V(p^1,w^1,y^1 - P^1X^1,X^1,z^1) \Bigg\} \quad (3.11)$$

where a superscript 1 (0) denotes final (initial) values, p is a vector of non-negative prices of unrationed services provided by the considered resource, w is a vector of wages, X is a vector of rationed services generated by the resource, P is a vector of prices of rationed services, z is a vector of public goods provided by the resource, and all prices referring to other commodities in the economy are suppressed. The overall compensating variation defined by (3.11) is the sum of money that makes the consumer as well off after a change in 'environmental quality' as he was before the change. The overall equivalent variation is the sum of money that makes the household as well off without the change as it would be with the change in environmental quality. See the appendix for a detailed derivation of (3.11).

Before discussing the various components of expression (3.11) further, three remarks are in order. Firstly, the complications caused by (time and) uncertainty as to the effects of environmental damage are disregarded here; they will be introduced in later chapters. Secondly, the total value of a resource cannot be defined unless the resource is *non-essential*. If life cannot go on in the absence of the resource, it does not make sense to speak of its total value; the loss is immeasurable or infinitely high. Once we recognize that resources include air to breathe, ozone layers, carbon cycles, functioning oceans, etc., it may seem a bit restrictive to assume that resources are non-essential. Nevertheless, if we limit ourselves to (reasonably small) *changes* in 'quality', meaningful money measures can be defined for all kinds of 'resources'. Thirdly, income changes are included in (3.11) through changes in both wage rates and lump sum income y, possibly including profit income. For example, if pollution affects the fishing industry, a household may be affected both as an employee in the industry and as a shareholder in a fishing company.

Environmental damage may affect the use values (including indirect services) derived from an environmental asset through several channels. Three different cases are illustrated in Figure 3.5. Consider first a change in the price of a commodity that is traded in a perfectly competitive market. If environmental damage causes the price of the commodity to increase, the

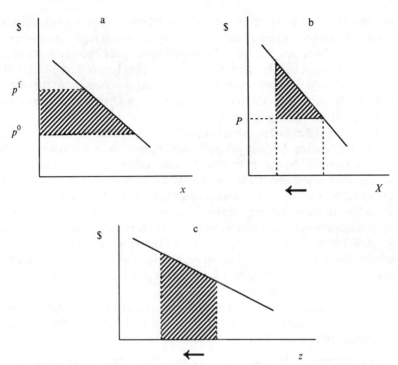

Figure 3.5. Compensating variations associated with changes in (a) a price (b) a ration and (c) a public good.

loss of consumer surplus is given by the shaded area in Figure 3.5a, i.e. is measured as an area to the left of a compensated or Hicksian demand curve. If pollution alters several prices, one has to sum the changes in consumer surplus in each of the markets.

Many environmental services are provided at a low cost or even free of charge. In some cases this will mean that a service is rationed or congested. Such a case is illustrated in Figure 3.5b, where the price is fixed below its market-clearing level so that the individual is compelled to consume less than he would if unconstrained. If pollution causes rationing or congestion, the loss of consumer surplus is shown by the shaded area under the compensated or Hicksian demand curve.

Some non-consumptive uses, e.g. bird-watching, and indirect services, e.g. watching a television programme about a nature reserve, may be thought of as public goods. As shown in Figure 3.5c, at the individual level a decrease in the provision of a public good causes an effect similar to the one following from a reduced supply of an unpriced rationed private commodity; the curve in Figure 3.5c is interpreted as a compensated marginal willingness-to-pay curve. However, at the aggregate level there is a difference, because a change in the provision of a public good affects many individuals, while the change in the private good in Figure 3.5b affects only a single individual. In other words, we must add areas similar to the one in Figure 3.5c for all individuals concerned about the change in the provision of the public good in question.

There is another public-good property of environmental resources that deserves attention. Even if the individual himself does not consume the services provided by the environmental asset under consideration, he may still be concerned about the quality or the existence of the asset. For example, he may derive satisfaction purely from the fact that the asset is available for other people – living now or in the future. This altruistic motive has however been questioned, as will be further explained in sections 7.7 and 7.8. An individual may also take the view that every habitat or species has a right to exist. Therefore, and for this reason alone, he may derive satisfaction from, and be willing to pay for, measures taken to preserve endangered species.

Boyle and Bishop (1985, p. 13), following Bishop and Heberlein (1984), suggest five altruistic motives for what can be labelled *existence value*. According to Boyle and Bishop these motives are:

(a) *Bequest motives*. As Krutilla (1967) argued many years ago, it would appear quite rational to will an endowment of natural amenities as well as private goods and money to one's heirs. The fact that future generations are so often mentioned in debates over natural resources is one indication that their well-being, including their endowments of natural resources, is taken seriously by some present members of society.

(b) *Benevolence towards relatives and friends*. Giving gifts to friends and relatives may be even more common than making bequests to them. Why should such goals not extend to the availability of natural resources?

(c) *Sympathy for people and animals*. Even if one does not plan to personally enjoy a resource or do so vicariously through friends and relatives, he or she may still feel sympathy for people adversely affected by environmental deterioration and want to help them. Particularly for living creatures, sympathy may extend beyond humans. The same emotions that lead us to nurse a baby bird or stop to aid a run-over cat or dog may well induce us to pay something to maintain animal populations and ecosystems.

(d) *Environmental linkages*. A better term probably exists here. What we are driving at is the belief that while specific environmental damage such as acidification of Adirondack lakes does not affect one directly, it is symptomatic of more widespread forces that must be stopped before resources of direct importance are also affected. To some extent this may reflect a simple 'you've got to stop 'em somewhere' philosophy. It may also reflect the view that if 'we' support them in maintaining the environment, 'they' will support us.

(e) *Environmental responsibility*. The opinion is often expressed that those who damage the environment should pay for mitigating or avoiding future damage. In the acid rain case, there may be a prevalent feeling that if 'my' use of electricity is causing damage to ecosystems elsewhere, then 'I' should pick up part of the costs of reducing the damage.

Even if one does not agree with all the above claims and arguments, they are arguments that are commonly used to explain the concept of existence value. Where an existence value is admitted, this value is often modelled by including the stock of the resource as an argument in the utility functions (see chapter 6 for discussion of this issue). In the case of assets such as air and water, one may instead use visibility measures and water quality indices respectively. The use of such measures highlights the fact that existence is not always treated as a binary variable. Instead, it is generally assumed that the marginal existence value is positive but declines with the size of the stock or quality of the resource (although it is not obvious that this holds for all 'resources', e.g. mosquitoes). This also means that areas under a compensated marginal willingness-to-pay curve can be used to assess a change in 'existence value', just as in Figure 3.5c.

In evaluating (3.11), it should be noted that the overall compensating variation (equivalent variation) is equal to the sum of the changes in compensating variations (equivalent variations) in the 'markets' where prices, quantity constraints or the supply of public goods change, i.e. we can add the shaded areas in Figures 3.5a–c. This assumes, however, that each change is evaluated subject to all previously considered changes and holding utility throughout at its prespecified level, as is shown in the next section. The practical implication of this is that one cannot simply ask a respondent about his willingness to pay for the opportunity to fish in a polluted lake that is cleaned up, then ask about his willingness to pay for the scenic beauty provided by the restored lake, and then sum these amounts and hope to obtain the total value of the lake. Instead, one must proceed by asking for the maximum willingness to pay for fishing, disregarding any scenic values, and then ask for the respondent's maximum willingness to pay for the scenic values provided by the lake, subject to what he has paid for the change in fishing. This 'order of integration', just like the reverse or any intermediate 'order of integration', yields the overall compensating variation and hence incorporates the individual's budget constraint. Alternatively, one may simply ask for the total willingness to pay for the improvement in fishing *and* scenic beauty. The reader is also referred to section 5.4, where an empirical study in which benefits are incorrectly aggregated is discussed.

Finally, the reader should note that the ranking properties of the money measures defined in (3.11) are the same as those for the measures defined in section 3.2: see the discussion following equations (3.4′) and (3.3′) in that section. In short: if there is just a single initial bundle (denoted by a superscript 0 in equation (3.11)), then the *EV* measure ranks any number of changes or projects in the same order as the household's utility function. This is not necessarily true for the *CV* measure. This outcome is reversed if there are several initial bundles but just a single final one to compare. However, for binary comparisons, as in equation (3.11), both money measures are sign-preserving, i.e. have positive signs only if the project increases household welfare.

3.5 On path-dependency of money measures

In this final section the path-dependency problem is briefly considered. There are three reasons for doing this. Firstly, in the previous section we simply assumed that the order in which prices etc. are changed has no impact on the overall willingness to pay. Secondly, the path-dependency problem has some bearing upon the cost-benefit rules derived in later chapters of this book. Thirdly, it can be used to illustrate what theory can teach us about the possibility and meaningfulness of decomposing money measures into use values and non-use values as proposed in section 3.4.

Let us begin by totally differentiating the indirect utility function (3.11), adjusting lump-sum income through a payment/compensation dS so as to keep the utility level constant:

$$dV/V_y = xdp - Ldw + (V_z/V_y)dz + dy - dS = 0 \qquad (3.12)$$

where $dX = dP = 0$ for simplicity, all terms have been multiplied by $1/V_y$, the inverse of the marginal utility of income, (V_z/V_y) is a vector of marginal monetary valuations of public goods, dL is a vector of labour supplies, dS is the amount of money which keeps the household at its initial level of utility, and any sign indicating transposed vectors is suppressed. (See the appendix for details.)

Equation (3.12) can be viewed as a cost-benefit analysis of a small environmental project. The direct benefits are given by (V_z/V_y), and the project has some spillover effects on wages, prices and lump-sum income. The net willingness to pay for the project is given by dS. We will come back to the interpretation of equation (3.12) in section 5.2.

In equation (3.12) it does not matter whether we use Marshallian or Hicksian demand concepts since these coincide. In Figure 3.6 this is illustrated for two private goods. A utility-maximizing household would consume the ('Marshallian') bundle x_1^*, x_2^*.

Obviously, given the current prices of these goods, the least-cost bundle that the household can consume to attain utility level $\bar{U}$ in the figure is the

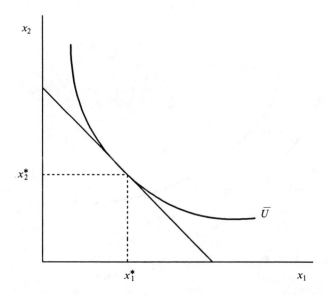

Figure 3.6. A utility maximizing and cost minimizing commodity bundle.

('Hicksian') bundle x_1^*, x_2^*. However, a change in a price or environmental quality affects Marshallian and Hicksian demands in different ways, since in the latter but not in the former case the household's income is adjusted through S so that it remains at the original utility level, i.e. $\bar{U}$ in Figure 3.6. Hence, in assessing large changes or projects, one must decide which concept to base the analysis upon. It is here that the path-dependency problem enters the picture.

The argument is illustrated in Figure 3.7. The demand curves in the figures are Marshallian or ordinary ones. Assume p_i is lowered from p_i^0 to p_i^1 with all other prices etc. fixed. The change in consumer surplus in the ith market is given by area A in Figure 3.7a. The change in p_i shifts the position of the demand curve in the jth market to the right (left) if goods i and j are complements (substitutes). However, if income, environmental quality and all prices but the ith price are fixed, the total change in consumer surplus is still given by area A in the figure. Recall that $xdp = x_i dp_i$ in (3.12) if $dp_j = 0$ for all $j \neq i$, implying that we need only bother about the ith market. Thus the shift in the demand curve of the jth good in Figure 3.7b does not have any significance *per se* when calculating a money measure of the utility change associated with a *ceteris paribus* change in the price of good i.

If we now also lower the price of the jth good, the change in consumer surplus in the market for this good must be evaluated bearing in mind the fact that we have already reduced the price of the ith good. Thus the

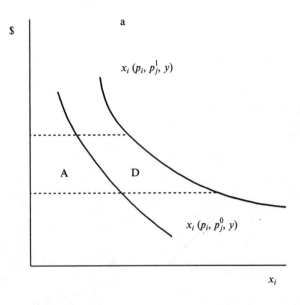

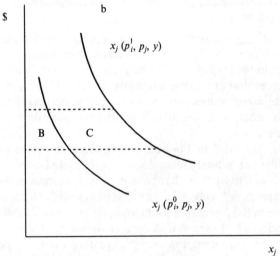

Figure 3.7. The path-dependency problem.

relevant change in consumer surplus in the market for the jth good is equal to area $B+C$ in Figure 3.7b. The money measure S of the utility change caused by the combined fall in p_i and p_j is equal to area $A+B+C$ in the figure.

Assume that we instead lower p_j before p_i. The change in consumer surplus in the jth market is now measured to the left of the demand curve drawn for $p_i = p_i^0$, i.e. is equal to area B in Figure 3.7b. As the price of good j is lowered, the demand curve for the ith good may move leftward or rightward. In any case, the change in consumer surplus in market i must be evaluated to the left of the 'final' demand curve obtained for $p_j = p_j^1$, i.e. is equal to area A + D in Figure 3.7a.

In general, the paths of price adjustment considered here impute different dollar gains or total consumer surpluses to the underlying unique change in utility, i.e. area A + B + C need not be equal to area B + A + D in Figure 3.7. Intuitively, the shift in the demand curve for good i as the price of good j is changed need not be equal to the shift in the demand curve for good j as p_i is changed, implying that area D need not be equal to area C in the figure.

It has been shown (Johansson, 1987) that most utility functions generate path-dependent Marshallian consumer surplus measures. In fact, if rationed variables change, it seems as if a quasi-linear utility function is the only utility function which ensures path-independence. On the other hand, if the analysis is based on the Hicksian demand concept, there is no path-dependency problem, provided one assumes that the expenditure function is twice continuously differentiable (in some set of prices etc.). This is a standard assumption employed in microeconomics and ensures symmetry of the relevant cross-derivatives; see the appendix. This means that analysis of large projects affecting significantly more than a single price or quality attribute must be based on the Hicksian demand concept. Basing the analysis on the Marshallian concept would mean that, in principle, a large project's monetary social profitability may range between minus infinity and plus infinity depending on the choice of the path of integration.

Figure 3.7 can also be used to illustrate the fact that decomposing total values into use values and non-use values, as we did in the previous section, is ultimately an arbitrary procedure. Suppose, for example, that existence value in equation (3.11) is defined conditional on all prices remaining at their initial levels. In this case we obtain one compensated money measure of existence value. If we derive the compensated monetary existence value conditional on all prices being at their final levels, however, it will differ from the initial one. Thus if more than one parameter is changed, it is not in general possible to obtain unique compensated money measures of the individual changes,[3] although the total change is uniquely defined (i.e. path-independent). This result also illustrates the fact that the consistency of the questionnaire technique, to be presented in the next chapter, cannot be checked by letting one sample pay for change A and then for change B, while a second sample is asked the reverse sequence of questions, to see if both samples value A and B in the same way. In general, the samples should value the individual changes differently. If the questions are asked in the correct conditional way, however, the two samples should report the same overall willingness to pay. At least, this is what theory tells us.

Appendix

The household in section 3.1 maximizes a strictly quasi-concave and at least twice continuously differentiable utility function:

$$U = U(x,z) \qquad\qquad (3A.1)$$
$$\text{s.t. } y - px = 0 \qquad\qquad (3A.1')$$

Necessary conditions for an interior solution are:

$$\left.\begin{aligned} U_x &= \lambda p \\ y - px &= 0 \end{aligned}\right\} \qquad (3A.2)$$

where $U_x = [\partial U/\partial x_1, \ldots, \partial U/\partial x_n]$, $p = [p_1, \ldots, p_n]$, λ is the Lagrange multiplier associated with the budget constraint, and any sign denoting transposed vectors is suppressed (here and in what follows).

In principle, equations (3A.2) can be solved to yield:

$$\left.\begin{aligned} x &= x(p,y,z) \\ \lambda &= \lambda(p,y,z) \end{aligned}\right\} \qquad (3A.3)$$

where $\lambda\ (=V_y)$ is the marginal utility of income. (We assume throughout the book that all functions, such as those in (3A.3), are well-behaved, e.g. continuous and at least once continuously differentiable on some set Ω of $p \gg 0$, $y > 0$ and $z \gg 0$, and attention is restricted to this set.)

Substitution of the demand functions in (3A.3) into (3A.1) yields the indirect utility function in (3.1). However, let us differentiate totally the direct utility function using the necessary conditions for an interior solution. This yields:

$$dU = \lambda p dx + U_z dz \qquad\qquad (3A.4)$$

where $U_z = [\partial U/\partial z_1, \ldots, \partial U/\partial z_m]$, and $dz = [dz_1, \ldots, dz_m]$. Totally differentiating the budget constraint and substituting the resulting expression into (3A.4) yields:

$$dU = -\lambda x dp + \lambda dy + U_z dz \qquad\qquad (3A.5)$$

The properties of the indirect utility function (3.1), i.e. $V = V(p,y,z)$, then become transparent:

$$\left.\begin{aligned} \partial V/\partial p_i &= -\lambda x_i(p,y,z) & \forall i \\ \partial V/\partial y &= \lambda(p,y,z) \\ \partial V/\partial z_j &= \partial U[x(p,y,z),z]/\partial z_j & \forall j \end{aligned}\right\} \qquad (3A.6)$$

Or, in vector form:

$$\left.\begin{aligned} V_p &= -\lambda x(p,y,z) = V_p(p,y,z) \\ V_y &= \lambda(p,y,z) = V_y(p,y,z) \\ V_z &= \partial U[x(p,y,z),z]/\partial z = V_z(p,y,z) \end{aligned}\right\} \qquad (3A.6')$$

The expenditure function corresponding to the maximization problem (3A.1) is stated here for convenient reference:

$$e(p,z,\bar{U}) = \min_x \{px \mid U(x,z) \geq \bar{U}\}$$
$$= px^c(p,z,\bar{U}) \tag{3A.7}$$

where a superscript c refers to a Hicksian or income-compensated demand function. Suppose that we want to evaluate the compensating variation of a *ceteris paribus* change in p_1 from p_1^0 to p_1^1. Then:

$$CV = e(p_1^0,p^-,z^0,U^0) - e(p_1^1,p^-,z^0,U^0) = -\int_c [\partial e(\cdot)/\partial p_1]dp_1 = -\int_c [x_1^c(\cdot)]dp_1$$
$$= \int_c [V_{p_1}(p,y - CV(p_1),z)/V_y(p,y - CV(p_1),z)]dp_1 \tag{3A.8}$$

where c is the path from p_1^0 to p_1^1, and $CV(p_1)$ is such that the household remains at the prespecified (initial) utility level throughout as p_1 changes. Equation (3A.8) reveals that we can either calculate compensated money measures using the expenditure function or, as is usually the case in this book, using the indirect utility function.

A public good is said to be normal if:

$$\partial(V_{z_1}/V_y)/\partial y > 0 \tag{3A.9}$$

so that the marginal willingness to pay for the good, i.e. V_{z_1}/V_y, increases with income. This means that the compensated willingness-to-pay curve referring to utility level U^1 falls outside (inside) a corresponding curve referring to utility level U^0 if $U^1 > U^0$ ($U^1 < U^0$).

A utility function is called quasi-linear if it takes the form:

$$U = u(x_1, \ldots, x_{n-1},z) + ax_n \tag{3A.10}$$

where a (>0) is a constant. The reader can easily verify that this function yields:

$$\left. \begin{array}{l} x_i = x_i(p,z) \qquad \forall i \neq n \\[2mm] x_n = y - \sum_{i=1}^{n-1} p_i x_i \\[2mm] \lambda = a/p_n \end{array} \right\} \tag{3A.11}$$

so that all extra income (above some minimum level) is spent on the nth good.

In order to illustrate the result stated in equation (3.6), let us use the expenditure function (3A.7) suppressing all prices but p_1 and all public goods but z_1. The condition (3.7) can then be written as:

$$\lim_{p_1 \to \infty} \partial e(p_1,z_1^0,U^0)/\partial z_1 = 0 \tag{3A.12}$$

while non-essentiality of x_1 implies that:

$$\lim_{p_1 \to \infty} e(p_1,z_1^0,U^0) = k \tag{3A.13}$$

where k is a strictly positive constant. Now CV_z in equation (3.6) can be obtained from:

$$CV_z = e(p_1^0, z_1^0, U^0) - e(p_1^0, z_1^1, U^0)$$
$$= [e(p_1^0, z_1^0, U^0) - e(p_1^\infty, z_1^0, U^0)] \tag{3A.14}$$
$$- [e(p_1^0, z_1^1, U^0) - e(p_1^\infty, z_1^1, U^0)]$$

where p_1^∞ means that p_1 approaches plus infinity, and $e(p_1^\infty, z_1^1, U^0) = e(p_1^\infty, z_1^0, U^0)$ because of assumptions (3A.12) and (3A.13). Equation (3.6) is simply the two integrals implicitly defined by the expressions within brackets in (3A.14). Compare also equation (3A.8).

The household in equation (3.11) maximizes:

$$U = U(x, \tilde{X}, L, z) \tag{3A.15}$$

s.t. $\quad y + wL - px - P\tilde{X} = 0 \tag{3A.16}$

and $\tilde{X} = X \tag{3A.17}$

where the vector X represents binding constraints on the consumption of goods $\tilde{X}$ and L is a vector of labour supplies. After substitution of (3A.17) into (3A.16) and (3A.15), one obtains the following first-order conditions for an interior solution to the maximization problem:

$$\left. \begin{array}{l} U_x = \lambda p \\ - U_L = \lambda w \\ y + wL - px - PX = 0 \end{array} \right\} \tag{3A.18}$$

which, in principle, can be solved to yield:

$$\left. \begin{array}{l} x = x(p, w, y - PX, X, z) \\ L = L(p, w, y - PX, X, z) \\ \lambda = \lambda(p, w, y - PX, X, z) \end{array} \right\} \tag{3A.19}$$

Substitution of $x(\cdot)$ and $L(\cdot)$ into (3A.15) yields an indirect utility function:

$$U[x(\cdot), L(\cdot), X, z] = V(p, w, y - PX, X, z) \tag{3A.20}$$

where $X = \tilde{X}$.

Totally differentiating (3A.20) or proceeding as when obtaining (3A.5) yields:

$$dV = - V_y x dp + V_y L dw + V_y dy - V_y (X dP + P dX) + V_x dX + V_z dz \tag{3A.21}$$

Suppose that the household pays an amount of money such that utility in (3A.21) remains constant. Subtracting an amount dS ($S = 0$, say, initially) from y in (3A.20) and including $V_y dS$, with dS in (3A.21) such that $dV = 0$, achieves this target. Dividing through by V_y converts the measure (3A.21) from units of utility to monetary units.

The expenditure function corresponding to (3A.20) is:

$$e(p, w, P, X, z, \bar{U}) = \min_{x, L} \{px + PX - wL \mid U(x, X, L, z) \geq \bar{U}\}$$
$$= px^c(p, w, X, z, \bar{U}) + PX - wL^c(p, w, X, z, \bar{U}) \tag{3A.22}$$

where a superscript c means 'compensated'.

The conditions under which a line integral is independent of the path of adjustment remain to be investigated. Consider a line integral:

$$\int_{\bar{c}} \sum_{i=1}^{n} f_i(q_1, \ldots, q_n) dq_i \tag{3A.23}$$

where $\bar{c}$ is some path between initial and final q-vectors, and assume that all f_i have continuous first derivatives in a (pathwise) simply-connected open set R of space. Accordingly, a set, for example a convex set, where any two points can be joined by a path lying in R, and any two paths in R with the same end points, can be deformed into each other without moving the end points and without leaving R.

The value of the line integral (3A.23) is independent of the particular choice of path $\bar{c}$ (a simple oriented arc) in R and determined solely by the end points of $\bar{c}$ if and only if (iff) the mixed derivatives are symmetric, i.e.

$$\frac{\partial f_i}{\partial q_j} = \frac{\partial f_j}{\partial q_i} \text{ for all } i,j \tag{3A.24}$$

It is important to notice that conditions (3A.24) are necessary for, and almost suffice to ensure, path-independence. They become sufficient if we add the assumption, stated above, concerning the geometrical properties of the region in space in which (3A.23) is considered (see Courant and John, 1974, pp. 95–106).

Throughout this book it is assumed that all the functions used, whether indirect utility functions, expenditure functions or profit functions, are such that the path-independency conditions hold, unless explicitly stated otherwise. For example, (3A.24) means that $\partial^2 e/\partial p_i \partial z_j = \partial^2 e/\partial z_j \partial p_i$ is assumed to hold for the expenditure function (3A.22) on some set of strictly positive prices, quantity constraints and environmental quality.

4 Valuing public goods: practical methodologies

In the case of a commodity that is traded in the market, buyers and sellers reveal their preferences directly through their actions. In the case of public goods and 'bads', on the other hand, no such direct revelation mechanism is available. This raises the question of how to overcome the problem of preference revelation. Several different practical methods which can be used to measure the willingness to pay for public goods (bads) have been suggested in the literature. This chapter presents the most frequently used and/or suggested methods: survey techniques, estimation of demand and utility functions, travel cost methods, and hedonic approaches. The chapter ends with an interpretation of willingness-to-pay measures in terms of a demand curve for the private or public good under consideration.

4.1 The contingent valuation method

The contingent valuation method (CVM) is the modern name for the survey method (since the answers to a valuation question are contingent upon the particular hypothetical market described to the respondents). The method was first used by Davis (1964) who used questionnaires to estimate the benefits of outdoor recreation. In their excellent book on the contingent valuation method, Mitchell and Carson (1989) list more than 100 US studies based on this technique, while in a recent survey Green et al. (1990) list 26 UK studies. Since these lists were made, a large number of new studies based on the contingent valuation technique have undoubtedly been completed. There is also a large experience with the technique in other countries, e.g. in Scandinavia. The survey technique is thus widely used for the estimation of environmental benefits in particular, and there is a large body of knowledge on the method's advantages and disadvantages. See also the recent survey of European studies by Navrud (1992).

Roughly speaking, the CVM collects preference information by asking households how much they are willing to pay for some change in the

46

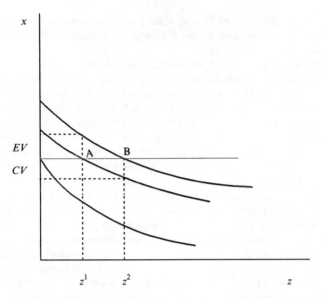

Figure 4.1. Two money measures associated with a change in the provision of z.

provision of a public good, or for the minimum compensation households require if the change is not carried out. For example, the following questions may be asked of the respondent:

(CV) Suppose the provision of z is increased from z^1 to z^2. What is the most you would be willing to pay for this increase?

(EV) Suppose the government refrains from increasing the provision of z. What is the minimum compensation you would need in order to be as well off as after an increase in z?

These concepts are illustrated in Figure 4.1, where an increase in z from z^1 to z^2 moves the respondent from point A to point B.

In most empirical applications, the central valuation question is much more detailed than the above examples suggest. The following describes the procedure adopted in a Norwegian study aimed at determining the willingness to pay for improved air quality in a heavily polluted industrial area.[1] More than 1,000 randomly chosen people out of 68,000 adults living in the area were interviewed. The interviews were based upon pictures depicting visibility ranges. Picture A shows the selected area on a day with heavy haze; roughly every tenth day is that hazy. Picture B depicts the same area on an average day. In order to make the interviewees familiar with the considered hypothetical change in the environment, they were asked to estimate the number of days per year which are as hazy as pictures A and B, respectively. Then the following question was asked.

It is impossible to eradicate all of the fog since part of it is caused by natural conditions. However a reduction in the discharge of industrial waste would undoubtedly lead to much cleaner air.

A reduction in the discharge of industrial waste may be financed by the company itself, the local population, society in general or by all three categories on a joint basis. In order to establish whether a further reduction in air pollution is desirable, it is essential to examine the effect of cleaner air on the welfare of the local population. One measure of this improvement in welfare is the maximum amount that an individual is willing to pay in order to receive a given improvement in visibility, provided that the local population and local companies are themselves required to meet a substantial share of the costs involved. In this study we are interested in finding out how *individuals* themselves evaluate the advantages of cleaner air. Let us assume that it is possible to halve the number of days of type (A) and instead have a level of visibility approximating to type (B). It is further assumed that a proportion of the expenditure on the reduction of air pollution is financed jointly by means of a general income tax on all income-earners in the district. It is not easy to determine in advance the actual level of expenditure required by these improvement measures.

Would they themselves be prepared to pay (   ) per cent of their income towards such a project in the coming years if all of the other income-earners in the area were also prepared to do the same thing? It should be noted that a 1 per cent tax for an individual who earns 100,000 NEK per annum is equivalent to 1,000 NEK per annum or 2.74 NEK per day. Similarly a 5 per cent tax is equivalent to 5,000 NEK per annum or 13.70 NEK per day.

The respondent may either accept or reject the proposal to pay the suggested tax increase, say 1 per cent of annual income. If he refuses to pay that much, the bid is lowered; if he accepts, the bid is raised, say to 2 per cent. If the respondent still accepts, the bid is increased further; while if he refuses to pay 2 per cent, the bid is reduced to, say, 1.5 per cent. The highest tax increase accepted by the respondent is considered to be his bid (CV), the basic idea of this iterative bidding approach being that it is claimed to be much simpler for a respondent to come to a yes–no decision when faced with a specified bid than to locate directly his maximal willingness to pay for the considered change.

There are, however, a number of pitfalls and problems in using the contingent valuation method. Table 4.1 (from Mitchell and Carson, 1989) briefly describes many of the principal biases that may appear in a contingent valuation study. A few remarks regarding Table 4.1 will be made, but the reader interested in details is recommended to read Mitchell and Carson's 463-page examination of the contingent valuation method.

The best-known problem is the *free-rider problem* (Table 4.1, 1A). This may be expressed as follows. If consumers have to pay according to their stated willingness to pay, they may try to conceal their true willingness to pay in order to qualify for a lower price. On the other hand, if respondents believe that the price or the tax charged is unaffected by their response, they may have an incentive to overstate their willingness to pay in order to secure a large supply of the public good. However, the available evidence from a number of empirical studies and experiments seems to indicate that strategic bias is a minor problem in contingent valuation studies. It can occur if the valuation question is sufficiently 'biased' but should not pose a great problem for a skilled investigator.

It is difficult to locate one's maximum willingness to pay for a proposed project. In order to simplify the task, a respondent may try to use some pieces of information provided by the researcher as cues to the project's 'correct value'. For example, the respondent may interpret a starting bid as providing some information about the project's benefits, which will thereby influence his answer to the valuation question. In fact, many studies, including the Norwegian one cited above, report a positive relationship between the size of the starting bid and the maximum willingness to pay. Similarly, using a payment card with a large number of amounts may induce the respondent to use the range of these amounts as a frame of reference in estimating his own WTP.

A respondent may not fully understand the scenario specified by the researcher. Scenario misspecification occurs when the respondent incorrectly perceives one or more aspects of the contingent market and the good to be valued. For example, it is well known that even small changes in wording can cause large differences in responses. Also, the respondent may view the proposed project as symbolic of a larger policy package, and report his WTP for this larger package. When asked to value improved air quality in a small area, the respondent may view this as symbolic for improved national air quality unless the valuation question clarifies exactly what is to be valued. Similarly, it may be difficult to value subcomponents of a policy package. To illustrate, even if you know your WTP for a charter trip to the Bahamas, it may be difficult to specify the WTP for the weather, the WTP for the hotel, and so on; it is the package, not a number of subcomponents, that you buy.

In closing, it should be noted that investigators are of course aware of these and other problems associated with the questionnaire technique. An important part of ongoing applied research within the field, therefore, is to improve our understanding of how the question format, the payment vehicle, and so on, affect a person's willingness to pay for a good or service. In particular, it should be stressed that there seems to be no strong case for the assumption that people act strategically in order to bias the outcome of willingness-to-pay questions. Moreover, it could be argued that many of the 'biases' associated with the contingent valuation method are quite natural. For example, there is no reason to believe that people are

Table 4.1. *Typology of potential response effect biases in contingent valuation studies*

1 Incentives to misrepresent responses

Biases in this class occur when a respondent misrepresents his or her true willingness to pay (WTP).

A. *Strategic bias:* where a respondent gives a WTP amount that differs from his or her true WTP amount (conditional on the perceived information) in an attempt to influence the provision of the good and/or the respondent's level of payment for the good.

B. *Compliance bias*

　i. *Sponsor bias:* where a respondent gives a WTP amount that differs from his or her true WTP amount in an attempt to comply with the presumed expectations of the sponsor (or assumed sponsor).

　ii. *Interviewer bias:* where a respondent gives a WTP amount that differs from his or her true WTP amount in an attempt to either please or gain status in the eyes of a particular interviewer.

2 Implied value cues

These biases occur when elements of the contingent market are treated by respondents as providing information about the 'correct' value for the good.

A. *Starting point bias:* where the elicitation method or payment vehicle directly or indirectly introduces a potential WTP amount that influences the WTP amount given by a respondent. This bias may be accentuated by a tendency to yea-saying.

B. *Range bias:* where the elicitation method presents a range of potential WTP amounts that influences a respondent's WTP amount.

C. *Relational bias:* where the description of the good presents information about its relationship to other public or private commodities that influences a respondent's WTP amount.

D. *Importance bias:* where the act of being interviewed or some feature of the instrument suggests to the respondent that one or more levels of the amenity has value.

E. *Position bias:* where the position or order in which valuation questions for different levels of a good (or different goods) suggest to respondents how those levels should be valued.

3 Scenario misspecification

Biases in this category occur when a respondent does not respond to the correct contingent scenario. Except in A, in the outline that follows it is presumed that the *intended* scenario is correct and that the errors occur because the respondent does not understand the scenario as the researcher intends it to be understood.

A. *Theoretical misspecification bias*: where the scenario specified by the researcher is incorrect in terms of economic theory or the major policy elements.

B. *Amenity misspecification bias*: where the perceived good being valued differs from the intended good.

  i. *Symbolic*: where a respondent values a symbolic entity instead of the researcher's intended good.

  ii. *Part-whole*: where a respondent values a larger or a smaller entity than the researcher's intended good.

    a. *Geographical part-whole*: where a respondent values a good whose spatial attributes are larger or smaller than the spatial attributes of the researcher's intended good.

    b. *Benefit part-whole*: where a respondent includes a broader or a narrower range of benefits in valuing a good than intended by the researcher.

    c. *Policy package part-whole*: where a respondent values a broader or a narrower policy package than the one intended by the researcher.

  iii. *Metric*: where a respondent values the amenity on a different (and usually less precise) metric scale than the one intended by the researcher.

  iv. *Probability of provision*: where a respondent values a good whose probability of provision differs from that intended by the researcher.

C. *Context misspecification bias*: where the perceived context of the market differs from the intended context.

  i. *Payment vehicle*: where the payment vehicle is either misperceived or is itself valued in a way not intended by the researcher.

  ii. *Property right*: where the property right perceived for the good differs from that intended by the researcher.

  iii. *Method of provision*: where the intended method of provision is either misperceived or is itself valued in a way not intended by the researcher.

  iv. *Budget constraint*: where the perceived budget constraint differs from the budget constraint the researcher intended to invoke.

  v. *Elicitation question*: where the perceived elicitation-question fails to convey a request for a firm commitment to pay the highest amount the respondent will realistically pay before preferring to do without the amenity. (In the discrete-choice framework, the commitment is to pay the specified amount.)

  vi. *Instrument context*: where the intended context or reference frame conveyed by the preliminary non-scenario material differs from that perceived by the respondent.

  vii. *Question order*: where a sequence of questions, which should not have an effect, does have an effect on a respondent's WTP amount.

Source: Mitchell and Carson (1989, pp. 236–7).

indifferent to the choice of payment vehicle, i.e. who pays and how. After all, we know that many people are concerned about distributional issues, implying that they may view the payment vehicle as a part of the policy package. Similarly, it is quite natural that the stated willingness to pay for a public good is conditional on the amount and quality of the information provided. This should be no more surprising than the fact that advertising may affect the willingness to pay for a Mercedes-Benz. For a recent review of many of the issues discussed above and other problems in using the survey technique, the reader is once again referred to Mitchell and Carson (1989).

4.2 Closed-ended techniques

The valuation techniques in which a respondent is asked for his maximal willingness to pay for a particular change are often referred to as open-ended techniques. An alternative, the closed-ended approach, confronts each respondent with a single bid or tax increase, which he has to accept or reject.[2] The important point, however, is that different subsamples are confronted with different bids. To illustrate, in the study referred to in section 4.1, a respondent in subsample 1 is asked if he is willing to pay 1 per cent of his income, a respondent in subsample 2 is confronted with a bid corresponding to 2 per cent of his income, and so on. The resulting relationship between the proportion of the total sample (or the population from which the sample is drawn) that accepts a particular tax increase in exchange for better air quality may be of the form depicted in Figure 4.2. Almost 100 per cent are prepared to accept a small tax in order to obtain the specified improvement in air quality, but the higher the tax, the lower the proportion of the respondents prepared to vote 'yes'. Using the figure, one can locate the *median voter*, i.e. the voter who accepts a tax, τ^1 in the figure, such that 50 per cent of the voters would accept a higher tax and 50 per cent would be prepared to accept only a lower tax in exchange for the considered improvement in air quality. In other words, there is a 50:50 chance that the tax τ^1 would be accepted in a majority-voting referendum. The results can thus be interpreted in terms of a median voter.

A typical formulation of the underlying choice problem is the following. Suppose the household is offered an improvement in environmental quality in exchange for a payment of S. The proposal is accepted if:

$$\Delta V = v(y - S, z^1) - v(y, z^0) + \eta > 0 \tag{4.1}$$

where a superscript 0 (1) refers to initial (final) environmental quality, and η is a random variable whose expected or mean value is equal to zero. The particular assumption behind this formulation is that the household knows its utility function with certainty, but from the point of view of the

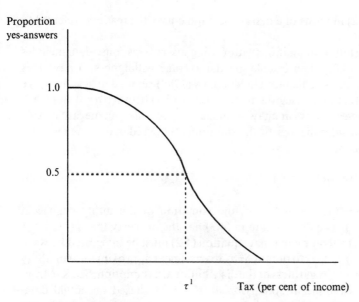

Figure 4.2. A bid curve.

investigator it contains some unobservable elements. In other words, on average the investigator is right, i.e. $V = v(y,z)$ since the expected value of η is zero, but in the individual case the investigator is wrong because of unobservable and seemingly stochastic variations in tastes for instance. These latter components generate the stochastic structure of the model.

A cumulative distribution function (c.d.f.) can be used to calculate the average or expected willingness to pay. Usually a c.d.f. is defined as a function $G(S)$ yielding the probability that the respondent is willing to pay less than S, i.e. vote 'no' to paying S. Thus, the downward sloping curve in Figure 4.2 is equal to $F(S) = 1 - G(S)$ since it yields the probability that the respondent is willing to pay S or more. Now, if we denote the probability that the respondent is willing to pay exactly S by $\pi(S)$, the average or expected willingness to pay can be written as:

$$S^E = \int_a^b S\pi(S)dS = -\int_a^b G(S)dS + G(b)b - G(a)a$$
$$= \int_0^b [1 - G(S)]dS - \int_a^0 G(S)dS$$
$$= \int_0^b F(S)dS - \int_a^0 [1 - F(S)]ds \qquad (4.2)$$

where $a \leq 0$ and $b > 0$ are the lower and upper limits of integration, respectively, $G(b) = 1$, $G(a) = 0$, and the first line equality is obtained using integration by parts (note that $G'(S) = \pi(S)$). For an interpretation of equation (4.2) in terms of a market demand curve, the reader is referred to section 4.6.

It is important that an investigator using discrete response data includes all terms in (4.2) when calculating the average willingness to pay. This should be emphasized, since Hanemann's (1984) seminal article may give the impression that it is legitimate to evaluate (4.2) between $a = 0$ and $b > 0$. To many investigators it may seem natural to rule out negative bids. However, consider the logistic distribution, often used in discrete response data experiments:

$$F(S) = 1/(1 + e^{-\Delta V}) \tag{4.3}$$

with $\Delta V = v_z - v_y S$, i.e. a linear approximation of the utility change in equation (4.1). The distribution in (4.3) has the property that $F(-\infty) = 1$ while $F(+\infty) = 0$, implying that equation (4.2) must be integrated between $a = -\infty$ and $b = +\infty$ to obtain S^E. (Given a linear approximation of utility change, $S^E = v_z/v_y$ regardless of the distributional assumption. See Kriström (1990).) An example in Johansson et al. (1989), based on actual data, produced $S^E = \$220$, while setting $a = 0$ yielded a 'mean' equal to \$430, i.e. a considerable difference which might have far-reaching consequences for the outcome of a cost-benefit analysis.

On the other hand, suppose that $\Delta V = v_z - \ln S$, as in the example discussed by Hanemann (1984). Negative bids are then ruled out so that (4.2) should be integrated between zero and plus infinity. There are also other possibilities open to the investigator who wants to rule out negative bids, as shown by Kriström (1990) for example. The important point to make here, however, is that there seems to be a considerable uncertainty about the 'shape' of the tails of the distribution obtained in empirical studies, and the assumptions made in this respect seem to have a considerable impact on the magnitude of the estimated mean willingness to pay. The example referred to above confirms this. In fact, there is no guarantee that the integral in (4.2) converges. For example, Bishop and Heberlein (1979) face this 'infinitely high mean WTP problem'. The conclusion that emerges is that the investigator must invest a lot of time in designing the bid vector, and possibly use a pilot study to test its properties. A finite 'mean' willingness to pay can always be achieved by some cunning truncation, e.g. by ruling out negative bids and limiting b to income, but this is a completely arbitrary procedure, which casts doubt on the results of a study.

In the simple linear model used below equation (4.3), the mean and the median (S^*) coincide. Choosing S in such a way that $\Delta V = 0$ in (4.3), the acceptance probability becomes 0.5, i.e. the probability is one-half that the respondent agrees to pay an amount S^*. Because $\Delta V = v_z - v_y S$ it follows immediately that $S^* = S^E = v_z - v_y$. However, in more complicated (non-linear) models the two measures need not coincide. The question of which money measure to use in applied studies therefore becomes important.

If the ultimate goal is to undertake a cost-benefit analysis, the mean seems to be the relevant concept. In such an analysis the total willingness to pay for a project is compared with its total costs (setting aside here matters of equity and income distribution). Given that there are H households, the total willingness to pay is simply $H \cdot S^E$. Therefore, of the two money measures considered, S^E is the natural one to employ in cost-benefit analysis.

On the other hand, if the goal is to interpret the results in terms of the outcome of a referendum, S^* is the more interesting concept. (See also Cameron (1988) for a discussion.) Basically, S^* can be interpreted as an amount such that 50 per cent of the people would vote 'yes' and 50 per cent would vote 'no' to a proposed project, if it costs S^* per household. However, it is well known that such a median voter approach does not in general produce a Pareto-efficient outcome. The median voter generally prefers more (or less) public expenditure than is consistent with Pareto efficiency. (In addition, the outcome is very sensitive to the choice of reversion level, i.e. z^0 in our terminology. See Inman (1987) for an excellent discussion.) This means that the median must be used with great care in contingent valuation studies. It is primarily a pedagogical device that may help the investigator to explain to the general public the basis of willingness-to-pay experiments.

4.3 Utility functions and demand equations

Another approach sometimes used in order to estimate the valuation of public goods/'bads' is to assume that the utility functions take a particular form, and estimate complete demand systems. McMillan (1979) has used the translog utility function (see equation (4.4) below) to establish a system of demand equations for housing characteristics. In a sense, McMillan's approach consists of two steps. Households first decide on how much they will allocate to housing, and then they decide on the combination of housing characteristics they want to acquire. Hedonic prices are used to create a system of budget share equations for housing characteristics so that the demand for environmental characteristics can be estimated within the housing budget constraint.

Polinsky and Rubinfeld (1975) estimate willingness to pay for changes in air quality assuming a Cobb–Douglas utility function within each considered income group. However, once a particular form of utility function is assumed, the change in utility can be calculated directly, so that it seems superfluous to estimate money measures which in general are not proportional to the change in utility.

In order to illustrate this point, and also some of the methods discussed in chapter 3, let us examine a study by Shapiro and Smith (1981). They applied a slightly different method from that of Bradford–Hildebrandt–Mäler–Willig, described in section 3.3, to data characterizing twenty-eight counties in the southern half of California and obtained implicit prices for four 'environmental' goods: rainfall, temperature, public expenditures and pollution.

The indirect utility function used by Shapiro and Smith is similar to the translog function, except that variables are not taken in their log form:

$$V\left(\frac{p}{y},z\right) = -\sum_i a_i \hat{p}_i - \sum_i \sum_j \beta_{ij} \hat{p}_i \hat{p}_j - \sum_i \sum_k \gamma_{ik} \hat{p}_i z_k \tag{4.4}$$

where $\hat{p}_i = p_i/y$, and z_k denotes an environmental quality variable ($k = 1, \ldots, m$). Using (4.4) and assuming $\beta_{ij} = \beta_{ji} = 0$ for all i and j, which makes preferences homothetic in the market commodities, one can easily derive expenditure share equations:

$$\frac{p_i x_i}{y} = (a_i p_i + \sum_k p_i \gamma_{ik} z_k)/(\sum_j a_j p_j + \sum_j \sum_k \gamma_{jk} p_j z_k) \tag{4.5}$$

Estimation of this expenditure share system (or the demand equations) yields parameter values that may be used to calculate the implicit prices of environmental quality variables:

$$\frac{(\partial V/\partial z_k)}{V_y} = \sum \gamma_{ik} p_i / \sum (a_j p_j + \sum \gamma_{jk} p_j z_k) \tag{4.6}$$

Hence, the calculation of implicit prices depends only upon the parameters which can be estimated using the expenditure share system (4.5). The estimation of the prices of environmental goods was carried out in two stages using maximum likelihood techniques. First, parameter estimates were obtained from ($n-1$ of) the market share equations (4.5). These estimates were then used to estimate the prices of environmental goods using equations (4.6). Obviously, the parameter estimates can also be used to estimate the indirect utility function, and hence can be used to calculate the change in utility of changes in prices, income and environmental goods.

In spite of the use of extremely aggregated data (only three classes of private goods were employed to estimate the implicit prices, for example), Shapiro and Smith found several indications that the analysis might be on the right track (Shapiro and Smith, 1981, pp. 116–19). For a recent application of this approach to the value of improved air quality, the reader is referred to Shechter (1991).[3]

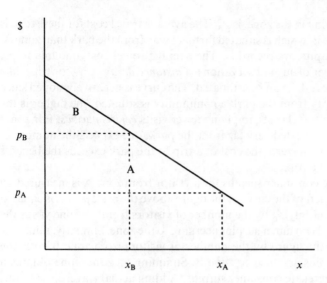

Figure 4.3. The travel cost method.

4.4 The travel cost method

The services of a recreation site are usually provided at a low price. Although this is efficient in the absence of congestion, it makes estimation of demand functions difficult. However, every user pays a price measured by his travel costs. Suppose the estimated relationship between visit rates x and travel cost p is given by $x = x(p)$. Then the change in consumer surplus resulting from, say, a polluted stream which is cleaned up to permit its use for sport fishing is:

$$S = -\sum_j n_j \int_{p_j^0}^{p_j^1} x(p)dp \qquad (4.7)$$

where n_j is the population in zone j, p_j^0 is the travel cost for fishing trips from zone j to streams situated farther away, and p_j^1 is the new travel cost. This method, proposed by Hotelling in a letter in 1947, was first used by Clawson (1959). For a recent survey of the method, the reader is referred to Fletcher et al. (1990).

The basic idea of the travel cost method is illustrated in Figure 4.3. Suppose, for simplicity, that there is a single park that can be reached by individuals living in a particular area. Let us divide the area into a number of zones or communities according to travel distance from the park. The number of trips originating from zone A, expressed as a multiple of the total population living in the zone, is x_A. The average travel cost for these trips is p_A. From zone B, which is situated farther away from the park than zone A, x_B trips per capita are recorded. The average travel cost amounts to p_B. Given a number of such observations, a *distance decay curve* for trips, like the one in Figure 4.3, can be estimated. The curve is negatively sloped since the farther away from the park a community is situated, the higher is the price paid (the travel cost), implying fewer visits *ceteris paribus*. For zones or communities located very far from the park, one expects the number of visits to be equal to zero; the cost of a trip to the park exceeds the benefits derived from the trip.

The average consumer surplus for a visitor from zone A is measured by the area to the left of the curve in the figure above the price p_A, i.e. is equal to area A + B. Multiplying by the number of visitors from the zone yields the total (ordinary) consumer surplus accruing to the zone. Similarly, multiplying area B in the figure by the number of visitors from zone B gives the consumer surplus assigned to zone B. Summing all zones, one obtains a measure of aggregate consumer surplus. Adding actual travel costs to this surplus yields a measure of the total aggregate willingness to pay for the park.

In an actual application of the travel cost method one would of course have to estimate a more complicated demand function for trips than the one used in the above example. For example, one might collect information on the following: home area, means of travel, travel costs, length of stay, main activities during the stay, valuation of the trip to the area as well as the area itself, alternative recreation sites and household disposable income. Using this kind of information, more complete and reasonable demand functions (or distance decay functions) can be estimated. One may even estimate a system of demand functions, with a separate demand function for each available recreation site, as in Burt and Brewer (1971) and Cicchetti *et al.* (1976). The reader interested in a broad discussion of the problems one faces in estimating such extended (systems of) demand functions is referred to Fletcher *et al.* (1990).

An alternative approach would be to use the household production function method described in section 3.3. The household is assumed to 'produce' trips using time and various marketed goods as inputs. Under conditions stated in section 3.3, it is possible to recover the household's valuation of a trip to a recreation site. Yet another approach is to use the discrete choice model outlined in section 4.2. Reinterpreting the amount S in equation (4.1) as the travel cost, the household will visit the site if the subjective valuation of the trip at least covers the travel cost. Similarly, assuming a logistic distribution, equation (4.3) yields the probability that a household facing a travel cost of S will undertake the trip. Estimating this equation produces the parameter values that are needed in calculating the willingness to pay for a trip. The approach can easily be extended so as to cover multiple sites, i.e. where the household can choose among several alternatives. For an application to Atlantic salmon fishing, the reader is referred to Morey et al. (1991).

The travel cost method uses people's *actual* behaviour, in sharp contrast to the contingent valuation method. In spite of this attractive feature of the travel cost method, it has been subject to much criticism. Firstly, the method captures only 'use values'. If people derive benefits from the park on altruistic grounds – derive satisfaction simply from the fact that others can enjoy the park – such benefits are not captured by this method. Secondly, planned future visits are not captured by the method (unless a representative sample of the population is explicitly questioned about its travel plans). Thirdly, there may be large variations in tastes, availability of substitute parks, incomes, etc., across the population zones used to estimate the distance decay curve in Figure 4.3. Although one can deal with these complications with econometric techniques, the data needed and the costs of using the method increase dramatically. Fourthly, many public goods and 'bads', such as acid rain, are such that it is hard to imagine how travel costs can be used to reveal demand.

4.5 Hedonic prices

There has been a growing interest in using property values as a source of information on the benefits provided by public goods and on measures taken to reduce externalities such as air pollution. The most popular approach is probably the hedonic price technique developed by Griliches (1971) and Rosen (1974). This is a method used to estimate the implicit prices of the characteristics which differentiate closely related products. In order to illustrate the approach in the simplest possible manner, let us consider two units of housing which are identical with one exception: one unit is affected by air pollution. One would expect their prices to differ. If people place a value on clean air, the difference in market price between the two units should, *ceteris paribus*, express the willingness to pay for an improvement in air quality. Thus, in certain circumstances, one can use the information contained in market prices to reveal how people value a public good or 'bad'.[4] In practice, houses differ with respect to such features as the square footage of the home, number of bathrooms, fireplaces and neighbourhood characteristics. However, if data on such characteristics and market prices are available, it is possible to isolate the contribution of various factors to the market price through the use of econometric techniques. Hence, one can sometimes use the market price of a private good to estimate the value of a public good.

In order to further illustrate this method, let us introduce a (well-behaved) hedonic or implicit house-price function:

$$P = f(z) \tag{4.8}$$

where P is the price of a house, and z is a vector of characteristics such as the square footage of a home, number of bathrooms, air quality, and so on. Inserting the characteristics of a particular house in this function should ideally produce this particular house's market price. Thus, equation (4.8) is interpreted as yielding market equilibrium housing prices for a particular city or region.

Next, suppose a representative household maximizes a well-behaved utility function:

$$U = U(x,z) \tag{4.9}$$

subject to its budget constraint:

$$y = px + f(z) \tag{4.9'}$$

where x is a composite commodity representing all consumption but housing.

Consider the first-order condition for utility maximization with respect to characteristic z_i. Assuming an interior solution, this condition can be written as:

$$f_i(z) = U_i(x,z)/\lambda(x,z) = g(y - P,z) \tag{4.10}$$

where $f_i = \partial f/\partial z_i$, $U_i = \partial U/\partial z_i$, λ is the Lagrange multiplier associated with (4.9'), and the budget constraint has been used to eliminate x from the right-hand side expression. According to (4.10), the household consumes z_i in such an amount that its marginal implicit price is equal to the household's marginal willingness to pay for z_i. Inserting the optimal levels of z_i for all i into the rent function (4.8) yields the rent or price paid by this particular household.

Suppose that a (non-linear) version of (4.8) has been estimated for housing in an area. The question is whether $\partial P/\partial z_i = f_i$ can be interpreted as an inverse demand function for the characteristic z_i. The answer is positive if all households have identical utility functions and incomes. These assumptions ensure that all households have identical demand functions, implying that all observations in Figure 4.4 must lie on the same (inverse) demand curve.

If households are not alike, the supply side of the housing market must be considered. If the supply of houses with given bundles of characteristics is

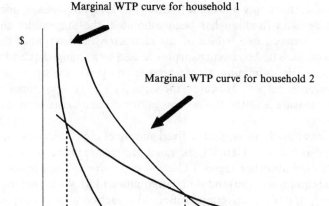

Figure 4.4. The property value method.

perfectly elastic, then the implicit price of a characteristic is exogenous to the individual household. Since we can observe z_i for each household and the implicit price can be calculated, a regression of observed quantities of z_i against implicit prices and other independent variables, such as income and other socioeconomic characteristics, should identify the demand function for z_i.

On the other hand, if the supply of a characteristic is fixed, individuals can be viewed as bidding for the characteristic in question. We can then use $\partial P/\partial z_i = f_i(\cdot)$ to calculate the implicit price paid by each household, and regress this variable on observed quantities of z_i and various socioeconomic variables. As a result, the inverse demand curves for different households do not generally coincide, implying that $f_i(\cdot)$ cannot be interpreted as an inverse demand curve unless households are identical in every respect. This is illustrated in Figure 4.4, where the marginal willingness-to-pay curves of two different households are shown.

In the intermediate case, where supply adjusts, but not infinitely rapidly, a simultaneous equation approach must be used. We must therefore specify equations for the supply side as well as for the demand side, and estimate these simultaneously.

Thus no simple conclusion emerges, apart from the possibly trivial one that in empirical studies using the property-value approach, one must carefully examine the supply side of the housing market. Nevertheless, once the (inverse) demand function has been estimated, the area under the demand curve between two values of the characteristic determines the change in uncompensated consumer surplus caused by a changed quantity of the characteristic. Summing across households yields the aggregate change in consumer surplus. However, the same (lack of) proportionality between this measure and the underlying utility change exists as in the previous chapter.

In an empirical application, with a fixed supply of characteristics, one would proceed as follows. (Here it is assumed that we are interested in the valuation of air pollution in a region.) The first step is to estimate a hedonic housing-value equation of the kind stated in equation (4.8). We would then calculate $\partial P/\partial z_i = f_i(\cdot)$ for the average household in each community or part of the considered region. Next we would regress f_i on a set of independent variables such as community average income and pollution levels, i.e. we would estimate some variation of equation (4.10). Finally we would integrate this equation between initial and final pollution levels. This would yield an area under an inverse demand curve between the two considered levels of air pollution, i.e. the willingness to pay for the considered change.

The property-value approach has its deficiencies, like the approaches outlined in the previous sections. For example, if the supply of houses in an area adjusts to changes in prices, then the interpretation of the hedonic price of a characteristic becomes more complicated than the above discussion suggests. More generally, there are a lot of technical problems associated with the use of the hedonic property-value method, but it would take us too long to review and discuss these here. Moreover, the method is of no relevance when dealing with many types of public goods, e.g. defence, national parks, endangered species, nationwide air pollution and so on, since no prices are available. The reader is referred to Freeman (1979) for further discussion of these issues.

4.6 A useful interpretation of WTP measures

As noted in section 4.2, it has become increasingly popular to use binary types of question in willingness-to-pay experiments. The theoretical foundations for this approach were provided by Hanemann (1984). Basically, Hanemann added a stochastic term to the household's utility function. The interpretation is that the household knows its utility function, but that it contains some elements which are unobservable from the point of view of the investigator. These elements generate the stochastic structure of the model. Given an assumption on the distribution of yes/no bids, the model can be estimated and the average willingness to pay for a proposed project can be calculated.

This section, which is much inspired by Suen (1990) and Mäler (1974), presents an interpretation of willingness-to-pay measures, including measures based on binary responses, in terms of a demand curve. Hopefully, this interpretation is useful as a complement to the interpretations supplied in most other textbooks on welfare economics and environmental economics.

Let us consider a household which consumes different private commodities and values 'environmental quality'. The household is asked about its willingness to pay for a proposed change (improvement) in environmental quality. The maximal willingness to pay is implicitly defined by the following equation:

$$V(y - CV, 1) = V(y, 0) \qquad (4.11)$$

where $V(\cdot)$ is the indirect utility function, y is a lump-sum income, CV is the compensating variation, 1 (0) denotes environmental quality with (without) the proposed project, and prices of private goods have been suppressed.

Suppose there is a continuum of households with different valuations of the proposed project. In order to simplify the interpretation, without any loss of generality, the number of households is normalized to one. The valuation of the project is described by a continuous distribution function $F(p) = \text{prob}[CV \leq p]$, where p is the bid ('market price'). Thus, $F(p)$ yields the number of households that are willing to pay no more than p for the project. Since a household either 'purchases' the project or not, aggregate or market demand for the proposed project is given by:

$$D(p) = 1 - F(p) \qquad (4.12)$$

where $D(p)$ is the aggregate demand curve, i.e. it yields the number of households that are willing to pay at least p for the project. The consumer surplus can be interpreted as the area to the left of a demand curve, provided the lowest possible price is non-negative. Integrating equation (4.12) between the lowest possible and the highest possible p-values yields the aggregate consumer surplus.

It need not be the case that everyone is willing to pay a non-negative sum of money for the project. If the project provides a pure public good which is consumed by everyone, the total willingness to pay is given by area A in Figure 4.5a and by area A less area B in Figure 4.5b. In the latter case, some households need a compensation to voluntarily accept the project. In terms of equation (4.2), area B corresponds to the integral from a to 0. If the project provides a priced private service, say a medical treatment, the consumer surplus is equal to the area to the left of the demand curve above the market price for the treatment, provided participation in the treatment is voluntary.

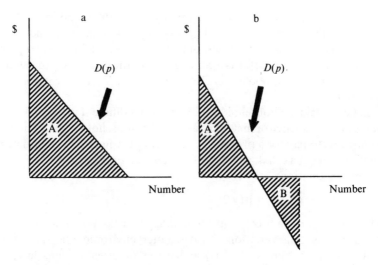

Figure 4.5. Willingness to pay for a discrete commodity.

If an open-ended bid question is used in a study, one can simply plot the individual maximum bids to obtain the market demand curve, as in Figure 4.5. Still, it may be of interest to use regression techniques to examine what factors determine the location of the curve. If the study uses a closed-ended valuation question, one must estimate the function $F(p)$ in equation (4.12). One of the most commonly used functions in such studies is the logistic one; see section 4.2. In any case, once the function is estimated, the consumer surplus is calculated in the way explained above. This shows that it is not necessary to start from a utility function and make complicated derivations to arrive at an expression to estimate. The market demand curve approach described here seems simpler and more intuitively appealing.

A final example may help to further highlight the advantages of the approach. Suppose there is uncertainty (with respect to prices, incomes, or the consequences of the proposed project as in chapters 8 and 9). If households are asked for their maximum non-contingent willingness to pay, we can still use the approach described above. All of the interpretations presented continue to hold. We just replace CV by CV^e, where CV^e denotes the maximal non-contingent willingness to pay.

In closing, it should be noted that the compensated demand curve defined by equation (4.12) and the ordinary demand curve coincide. This is due to the assumption that you either participate or you do not. In other words, you purchase one unit of the good or you purchase none.

5 General equilibrium cost-benefit rules

Thus far we have concentrated on money measures which can be used to assess households' monetary valuation of environmental quality. However, private sector firms also affect and are affected by the current level of environmental health. In the absence of policy instruments which affect firms' behaviour, firms' activities which affect the environment do not show up in their annual accounts (unless firms respond to consumer reactions and voluntarily take action to reduce environmental 'spillover' effects). Instead, these effects show up in household utility functions and can be assessed in the way discussed in chapter 3. However, firms are also affected by pollution or the level of environmental quality, for example. This is obviously true for a downstream fishery affected by firms or households upstream polluting the river.

In this chapter, we start by examining how changes in environmental quality affecting a firm can be evaluated. That is, money measures or producer surplus measures are derived. Ultimately, firms are owned by households. This is true even if the direct owner of a firm is a pension fund or the government, for example, since there are households behind these institutions. Changes in profits caused by pollution, for example, therefore affect household welfare, and must be accounted for in an assessment of a project's – say a new pollution treatment plant's – total effects on the whole of society. In section 5.2, general equilibrium cost-benefit rules for a small or marginal environmental project are derived. In sections 5.3 and 5.4 these rules are generalized so as to cover large projects as well, i.e. projects which significantly affect the economy's prices etc. Then various distortions such as taxes, other than lump-sum ones, and price rigidities causing unemployment are introduced. Project evaluation rules relevant for such distorted economies are presented.

5.1 Producer surplus measures

Let us consider a profit-maximizing firm producing a single output using a number of priced inputs L and an environmental asset whose quality is denoted z. This asset is assumed to be a public good, say air quality, which affects the output the firm can produce from given amounts of other inputs. The firm's profit function, which is derived in the appendix, is written as:

$$\Pi(p,w,z,K) = px(p,w,z) - wL(p,w,z) - K \tag{5.1}$$

where p is output price, $x = F[L(p,w,z),z]$ is output, with $F[\cdot]$ denoting the well-behaved production function; w is a vector of input prices, L is the corresponding vector of inputs, K is a fixed cost, the dependence of x and L on the fixed stock of capital is suppressed, and any notation denoting transposed vectors is suppressed. The reader may wish to interpret x as a vector of outputs, p as a vector of output prices, and z as a vector of environmental inputs. Thus, according to (5.1), profits are equal to the difference between revenues and variable plus fixed costs. Taking the partial derivative of the profit function with respect to a price yields the corresponding supply or demand function, as shown in the appendix to this chapter. It is assumed that the profit function is twice continuously differentiable in all of its arguments on some set of prices and environmental quality. By restricting the analysis to this set, one encounters no path-dependency problem in assessing multiple price changes, for example.

By definition, fixed costs, such as the cost of buildings and machines, are independent of the level of production the firm chooses in the short run. In general, therefore, interest is focused not on profits, but on quasi-rent, or producer surplus. This is the difference between revenues and variable production costs. There are various ways to illustrate the concept of producer surplus graphically. In Figure 5.1a it is represented as the difference between output price and average variable costs multiplied by the profit-maximizing output level x^0. Alternatively, as in Figure 5.1b, it is the area to the left of the supply curve between the ruling market price p^0 and the choke price $\bar{p}$ where the firm ceases to produce since it is unable to cover even its variable costs if the price falls below it. Thus, one has:

$$PS = \Pi(p^0,w^0,z^0,K) + K = \Pi(p^0,w^0,z^0,K) - \Pi(\bar{p},w^0,z^0,K)$$
$$= \int_0^{p^0} x(p,w^0,z^0)dp \tag{5.2}$$

where PS denotes producer surplus, a superscript 0 denotes current levels of prices, etc., $\Pi(\bar{p},w^0,z^0,K) = -K$ since the firm ceases to produce if $p \leq \bar{p}$, and $\partial\Pi/\partial p = x(\cdot)$. The latter fact explains why the right-hand side expression,

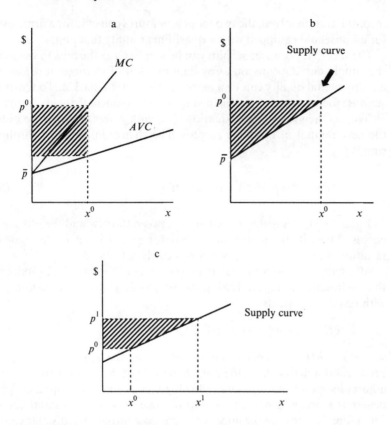

Figure 5.1. Producer surplus measures.

i.e. the area to the left of the supply curve, equals the producer surplus. We integrate between *zero* and the current market price simply because supply is equal to zero for $p \leq \bar{p}$ i.e. integrating between zero and $\bar{p}$ does not add to or detract from the producer surplus.[1]

Similarly, the change in producer surplus caused by a change in the output price from p^0 to, say, p^1 is simply the area to the left of the supply curve between initial and final prices; equation (5.2) is now integrated, not between 0 and p^0, but between p^0 and p^1. This is illustrated in Figure 5.1c for an increase in output price. Basically, the change in producer surplus in Figure 5.1c is the maximum amount of money the firm would be willing to pay for an increase in its output price from p^0 to p^1. It is also the minimum compensation the firm needs in order to willingly accept that the price is not increased from p^0 to p^1. Thus one can interpret producer surplus measures in terms of compensating and equivalent variations. Since there are no income effects involved, the two money measures coincide for a firm, just as for a household equipped with a quasi-linear utility function.

The fact that producer surplus can be identified as the area to the left of the supply curve means that any combination of changes in prices and environmental quality can be assessed in the output market. To illustrate, suppose there is a *ceteris paribus* change in environmental quality from z^0 to z^1. We can then re-evaluate equation (5.2) with z^0 replaced by z^1 to obtain the new amount of producer surplus. The change in producer surplus is simply:

$$\Delta PS = \int_0^{p^0} [x(p,w^0,z^1) - x(p,w^0,z^0)]dp \qquad (5.3)$$

In Figure 5.2a, this is the shaded area between the new and the old supply curves. Thus, if the quality of the environmental input is changed, the resulting change in producer surplus is easily calculated.

Alternatively, one could calculate the value of the marginal product of the environmental input. Taking the partial derivative of equation (5.1) with respect to z yields:

$$\partial \Pi(\cdot)/\partial z = p\,\partial x(\cdot)/\partial z = pF_z[L(p,w,z),z] \qquad (5.4)$$

where $F_z = \partial F[\cdot]/\partial z$. This result is derived in the appendix. Using the production function, as in the right-hand side of (5.4), shows that the firm adjusts its use of other inputs following changes in z: the optimal factor demands L are, in general, functions of prices *and* environmental quality. Therefore, in assessing the impact on producer surplus of a discrete change in environmental quality, the expression defined by equation (5.4), and not the value of the marginal product of z (VMP_z for short) for fixed levels of inputs L, must be used. Applying the le Chatelier principle (see Samuleson (1972)) the area under the VMP_z curve between $z = z^0$ and $z = z^1$ provides a lower (upper) bound for the change in producer surplus if $z^1 > z^0$ ($z^1 < z^0$). This is so because the VMP_z curve assumes that the firm cannot adjust input levels so as to maximize profits. The 'demand function' defined by (5.4), on the other hand, allows the firm to select profit-maximizing input combinations throughout the movement from z^0 to z^1. These profit-maximizing input combinations can, but certainly need not, coincide with the initial one, implying that the firm can in general increase profits by adjusting $L(\cdot)$ to changes in z. The associated change in producer surplus is given by the shaded area in Figure 5.2b. The reason that we obtain an area below and not to the left of the curve is that environmental quality, by assumption, is available free of charge and in 'amounts' that are exogenous to the firm.

The question arises whether changes in producer surplus due to shifts in

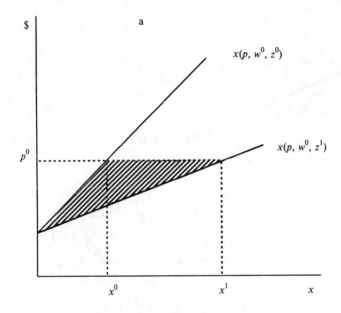

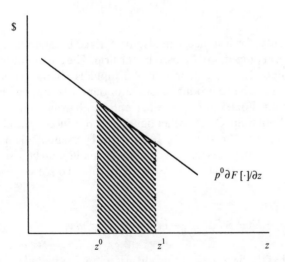

Figure 5.2. Two ways of calculating the change in producer surplus when z is changed.

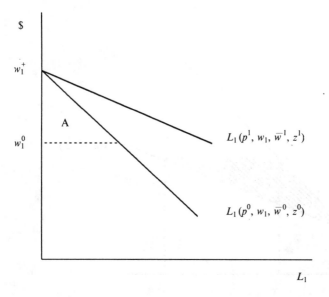

Figure 5.3. Producer surplus as an area to the left of a derived demand curve for a factor.

environmental quality, for instance, can also be derived by examining the market for an arbitrary input, say L_1, used by the firm. The answer depends on whether the input is essential or not. An input is characterized as essential if the firm is unable to produce positive amounts of output without the input in question. For example, a paper mill can hardly continue to produce paper without pulp. On the other hand, pulp produced specifically from birch is not essential to the firm. If an input is essential, then any combination of changes in prices and environmental quality can be assessed by examining the derived demand curve for that input. To see why, note that:

$$\Pi(p^0, w^0, z^0) - \Pi(p^0, \bar{w}_1^+, \bar{w}^0, z^0) = \int_{w^0}^{\infty} L_1(p^0, w_1, \bar{w}^0, z^0) dw_1 \qquad (5.5)$$

where w_1^+ is such that the firm ceases to produce if $w_1 \geq w_1^+$, $\bar{w}^0 = [w_2^0, \ldots, w_k^0]$, and $\Pi(p^0, \bar{w}_1^+, \bar{w}^0, z^0) = -K$, so that the left-hand side difference in (5.5) is equal to the producer surplus earned from the combination (p^0, w^0, z^0). Producer surplus earned for (p^0, w^0, z^0) can thus be obtained by calculating the area to the left of the derived demand curve for an essential input, as shown by area A in Figure 5.3. Repeating the experiment for some other combination of prices and environmental quality yields another amount of producer surplus. Comparing the two producer surpluses, as in equation (5.3), yields the change in producer surplus caused by the change in p, w and z.

If the input under consideration is not essential, one faces the problem that the firm's profits exceed minus the fixed cost K, i.e. $\Pi > -K$, even if the factor price approaches infinity. The firm simply switches to some other input. Therefore the equality in (5.5) breaks down, i.e. one cannot completely recover producer surplus by considering the market for a non-essential input. In turn this means that unless we consider a *ceteris paribus* change in the own-factor price, w_1, changes in producer surplus cannot be calculated by examining this market in isolation. This is also true for a non-essential environmental input used by the firm, i.e. curves like the one depicted in Figure 5.2b cannot be used to assess combined changes in z and prices if z is a non-essential input. Finally, it should be mentioned that whenever a firm produces several outputs, the market for an essential output can be used to assess any change in prices and environmental quality. In the single output case, this output is trivially essential. See Just *et al.* (1982) for details.

The reader interested in empirical methods which can be used to assess changes in profits due to environmental factors is referred to section 10.4. See also Varian (1992), who discusses how to use econometric methods to estimate profit functions, for example.

5.2 General equilibrium cost-benefit rules

Firms are ultimately owned by households. In the single-household economy considered in this chapter, all profits must accrue to this single household. The assumption of a single household allows us to derive cost-benefit rules for small and large projects with a minimum of notational clutter. The important issue of how a project affects the distribution of welfare and income across households is discussed in chapter 7.

The indirect utility function of the economy's single (or representative) household is written as:

$$V = V[p,w,Y + \Pi(p,w,z) - \tau,z] \tag{5.6}$$

where Y is an exogenous income, and τ is a lump-sum tax collected by the government. In order to simplify exposition, no reference is made to individual goods, prices or firms. We thus proceed as if there is a single firm producing a single good. However, the reader may also interpret p as a vector of prices and Π as the sum of firms' profits. All results derived below hold in either case. We can therefore safely consider the rules derived below as general equilibrium ones. In what follows, it is assumed that the household considers profit income as independent of its own actions. However, from the point of view of the economy, a change in a price, say, will affect the household's income through its impact on profits. A neat implication which the reader may want to check by using equations (2.16) is as follows. If the welfare function (5.6) is differentiated with respect to prices and the resulting expressions are set equal to zero, one finds that in order to maximize welfare, prices should be chosen so as to equate supply and demand in all markets, i.e. so as to achieve general equilibrium. This can also be seen from equation (5.7) below.

In what follows we will use (5.6) to derive a set of cost-benefit rules. Given this purpose there is no loss of generality in assuming that the government controls the variable z, which is interpreted as an indicator of environmental quality. The magnitude of z can be changed, though an increase in z requires the use of real resources such as labour and produced goods, while a decrease in z releases resources for other uses. Let us consider a small change in environmental quality. If prices adjust continuously so as to clear markets, the change in z, however small, will cause adjustments in possibly all prices. Suppose that the direct monetary cost, calculated at initial prices, for inputs to the project is dC and that we are looking for a contribution dCV from the household over and above dC such that the household remains at its initial level of utility. The cost-benefit rule can then be written as:

$$dV/V_y = (x^s - x^d)dp + (L^s - L^d)dw \\ + [(V_z/V_y)dz + pF_z dz - dC - dCV] = 0 \tag{5.7}$$

where V_y denotes the marginal utility of exogenous income evaluated at initial levels of prices etc., and a superscript s (d) denotes supply (demand); see the appendix for a derivation of this result. If prices adjust so as to equate supply and demand, the first two terms in the middle expression of (5.7) vanish (since $x^s = x^d$ and $L^s = L^d$). Thus, even if the project affects all (relative) prices in the economy, we can still concentrate on the terms within brackets in (5.7). Household supply and demand functions in (5.7) can be interpreted as either ordinary ones or compensated ones since they coincide for given prices etc., as was shown in section 3.5.

According to equation (5.7), the general equilibrium cost-benefit rule for a small project can be stated as
(i) The monetary value of an improvement in environmental quality is equal to the sum of households' direct monetary valuation of the improvement and its direct impact on firms' profits.
(ii) This aggregate monetary value can be measured as the sum of direct project costs dC and a maximum payment dCV, net of direct project costs. Alternatively, setting $dC = 0$ in (5.7), the maximum payment would measure the monetary value of the project.

(iii) Changes in profits (and project costs) due to changes in prices should not be counted, since price changes 'net out' from (5.7) if prices adjust so as to create equilibrium in markets.

(iv) Any inputs used by the project under consideration should be valued at ruling (initial) market prices.

The maximum contribution (dCV) which the household is prepared to make in exchange for an improvement in environmental quality may or may not be positive. If project costs are sufficiently high, dCV in (5.7) becomes negative and is then interpreted as the minimum compensation that the household needs in order to be indifferent to the project. Obviously, the project is socially profitable only if $dCV > 0$ in equation (5.7). Note also that if environmental quality deteriorates ($dz < 0$) so that utility falls, then dCV would be interpreted as a compensation such that the household stays at its initial level of utility.

Alternatively, we can base the cost-benefit analysis on the equivalent variation measure. The equivalent variation dEV is an amount of money such that the household is indifferent between accepting dEV or the project. The equivalent variation is thus equal to the sum of all terms except dCV in the middle expression in (5.7). In other words, $dCV = dEV$ for a small project. In fact, and as discussed in section 3.5, we can also use the ordinary or uncompensated willingness-to-pay concept in evaluating a small project. In what follows we will (arbitrarily) use CV as our money measure.

It is important to emphasize that changes in profits due to price changes caused by the project do not show up in the cost-benefit equation. Including an estimate of such profit changes would produce an erroneous project evaluation. In other words, one cannot calculate household willingness to pay for an environmental change given prices and profits and then add a separate estimate of the change in total profits. This approach produces a nonsense estimate of the project's benefits. This is one of many useful insights produced by a general equilibrium approach. Another is the following one. Interpret p as a price vector, including the prices of any goods and services purchased as part of households' 'defensive' expenditures to protect their environment. It follows immediately that any adjustments in such expenditures due to the postulated change in z vanish or net out from the cost-benefit rule (5.7) since they only show up in the first term in the middle expression of (5.7). The same holds true for any measures taken by firms to protect themselves from environmental pollution. In other words, the rule in (5.7) holds also in the presence of defensive expenditures by households and firms.

The reader should also note that welfare can be increased by changing z so long as $dCV \neq 0$. At an interior social welfare optimum, assuming here and throughout that the appropriate second-order conditions are satisfied, the project's marginal social revenue must be equal to its marginal social cost, as in equations (2.16). See Brown (1991) and Starrett (1988) for discussions of the problems that ensue when non-convexities serve to generate multiple solutions to the necessary conditions. More generally, equations like (5.6), possibly including more complicated tax schemes as in section 5.5, can be used to derive conditions for the optimal provision of public goods, optimal tax rates, etc., by maximizing the welfare function with respect to the different control variables. This result will be further elaborated upon in section 6.5 of the next chapter when we discuss optimal project rules and sustainable development.

In closing, a comment on the project cost dC is in order. Suppose that the government uses x and L as inputs when producing environmental quality: $z = F(x^p, L^p)$ as in chapter 2. For example, if we consider a pollution treatment plant, labour as well as finished products may be needed for its operation. Then $dC = pdx^p + wdL^p$, where a superscript p refers to the pollution treatment plant. Inputs are thus valued at current (initial) market prices. Terms like $x^p dp$ and $L^p dw$ show up in the first two terms in the middle expression in (7) and hence vanish from the cost-benefit rules. In turn, this means that the direct project cost dC is different from a lump-sum tax $d\tau$ collected to finance the project since $d\tau$ must also cover the price change terms. Note also that leisure time at the margin is valued at the ruling market wage. Thus if the project recruits labourers who would otherwise be outside the labour force, their time, i.e. the opportunity cost for leisure time foregone, is valued at ruling market wages w. The ruling equilibrium wage rate for a particular kind of labour is such that, at the margin, people are indifferent between working an extra hour and using that hour for leisure activities.

5.3 Assessing large projects

In this section, the discussion of general equilibrium project evaluation rules is continued. Here, however, the focus is on large projects. In principle, one can also use equation (5.7) to assess large projects. If prices adjust continuously so as to equate demand and supply, the two price change terms in (5.7) will also vanish if the evaluated project is large or non-marginal. Therefore, integrating the remaining four terms between initial and final z-levels produces the desired cost-benefit rule. This assumes, however, that compensated demand and supply functions are used in order to avoid the path-dependency problem.

However, let us start by defining the welfare change caused by a change in environmental quality from z^0 to z^1:

$$\Delta V = V(p^1, w^1, Y^1 + \Pi^1 - \tau^1, z^1) - V(p^0, w^0, Y^0 + \Pi^0 - \tau^0, z^0) \quad (5.8)$$

where prices are interpreted as general equilibrium prices before (superscript 0) and after (superscript 1) a change in environmental quality, $\Pi^i = \Pi(p^i, w^i, z^i)$ for $i = 0,1$, $\tau^1 = p^1 x^p + w^1 L^p$, and $\tau^0 = 0$. The project possibly also affects the lump-sum income Y, as seen in (5.8).

Either the compensating variation or the equivalent variation could be used to evaluate the project. The former concept is used here. The compensating variation CV is an amount of money such that the household remains at its initial level of utility following the change in prices etc. specified by equation (5.8). The final term in (5.8) can therefore be replaced by an indirect utility function expressed in final prices etc., and a payment CV such that the household stays at the initial utility level. The change in utility can thus be expressed as:

$$\Delta V = V(p^1, w^1, Y + \Pi^1 - \tau^1, z^1) - V(p^1, w^1, Y + \Pi^1 - \tau^1 - CV, z^1)$$
$$= \bar{V}_y \cdot CV \qquad (5.9)$$

where $\bar{V}_y$ is the marginal utility of income evaluated at some intermediate income as explained in section 3.2. The monetary welfare change measure defined by (5.9) is obviously a sign-preserving measure of utility change and can be interpreted as suggested in section 3.4, the main difference being that this money measure also covers changes in profits and lump-sum taxes. We shall return to this interpretation below.

In order to elucidate the willingness-to-pay question to which CV is the answer, it is useful to use (5.7) and (5.9) to restate the money measure as follows:

$$CV = \int_{z^0}^{z^1} \{p(z)F_z(\cdot) + [V_z(\cdot)/V_y(\cdot)] - C'(z)\}dz \qquad (5.10)$$

where any change in lump-sum income Y is suppressed, p is written as a function of z in order to highlight the fact that the general equilibrium output price varies with z, and $C'(z) = p(z)(\partial x^p/\partial z) = w(z)(\partial L^p/\partial z)$ denotes real project costs evaluated at general equilibrium prices throughout the movement from z^0 to z^1. The remaining terms also depend on equilibrium prices etc. as explained further by equation (5A.10) in the appendix.

In order to interpret the right-hand side of equation (5.10), let us start by assuming that the environmental project considered has a negligible impact on equilibrium prices. The project can then be assessed as follows:

(i) The value to a firm of the change in z is equal to the area between the new and the old supply curves, as in Figure 5.2a. Alternatively, the gain can be calculated as an area below a value of the 'demand' curve for z between initial and final z-levels, as in Figure 5.2b.

(ii) Add (i) and the households' direct compensated monetary valuation of the change in environmental quality so as to obtain the project's total benefits.

(iii) If total benefits exceed direct project costs, with inputs valued at ruling market prices, the project is socially profitable, i.e. $CV > 0$ in equation (5.10).

Thus, if the project leaves prices more or less constant, the large-project evaluation rule is a straightforward generalization of the marginal project cost-benefit rule stated in section 5.2. If, on the other hand, the project has a significant impact on prices, it is extremely difficult to apply the cost-benefit rule (5.10). There seems to be no simple device which can be used to place upper or lower bounds on the different terms in equation (5.10). In a partial equilibrium context such bounds can sometimes be obtained. If prices fall, for example, valuing benefits at initial prices provides an upper bound for their 'true' value, while evaluating them at final prices provides a lower bound, and vice versa. However, there is no strong reason to assume that a project has a uniform impact on general equilibrium prices. Some prices may increase while others decrease following a project, making it more or less fruitless to try to develop rules of thumb suggesting that initial or final prices produce an upper or lower bound for a project's social profitability.

It should be noted here that the integral in equation (5.10) is not evaluated sequentially in the way proposed in section 3.5. In terms of equation (5.7), the equality between supply and demand in markets is preserved throughout the movement from z^0 to z^1 if supply and demand at each point of the movement are evaluated at the corresponding general equilibrium prices, which can be viewed as functions of z; see (5A.10). Proceeding sequentially, one would start by changing, say, p from p^0 to p^1 and then w_1 from w_1^0 to w_1^1. The problem with this approach is that the price change terms in the middle expression of (5.7) do not vanish since we create disequilibria in markets. The different terms of the resulting line integral would therefore be very difficult to interpret.

Unfortunately, a similar problem is associated with equation (5.10). Household demand and supply functions are compensated ones. Equilibrium prices should therefore be interpreted as prices which equate these compensated household functions with the corresponding firm functions. Now, however, (p^1, w^1) is not the general equilibrium price vector for the project, but rather the general equilibrium vector for the project conditional on households remaining at initial utility levels. Thus (p^1, w^1) in (5.8) and (5.9) is different from that implicitly used in assessing the right-hand side expression in (5.10), implying that CV in (5.10) need not coincide with CV in equation (5.9).

In other words, equations (5.9) and (5.10) represent two different ways of assessing a large project. In the former case, we simply try to convert the actual utility change ΔV in equation (5.8) into monetary units. In the latter case, the household pays/receives money so as to remain at the initial or pre-project utility level throughout the movement from (p^0,z^0) etc. to z^1 and the associated 'compensated' general equilibrium price vector. The specific problem with this latter approach is that the 'compensated' equilibrium prices are unobservable and must somehow be computed using compensated demand and supply functions. Moreover, the sum CV in (5.10) must somehow be extracted from the economy if positive (or injected if negative) for the household to remain at the prespecified utility level. We will come back to a comparison of these two money measures in section 7.3.

5.4 Some further interpretations

In equation (5.10) a large project was evaluated in terms of its different benefits and costs. This approach turned out to be difficult to use in real-world applications. It is important to note, however, that the (single) household's answers to the hypothetical willingness-to-pay questions behind equations (5.9) and (5.10) provide single-number estimates of the project's social profitability. The number CV provides all the information necessary to take a decision on the proposed environmental project since CV is a sign-preserving measure of the underlying utility change. It would therefore be erroneous to add to this number the project's impact on private sector profits, for example. This would simply cause a double counting of some of the project's effects.

A main message of the above exercise, therefore, seems to be that it is extremely important that the investigator clarifies what information a willingness-to-pay question contains. Otherwise, the project evaluation may be seriously flawed in the sense that some benefits or costs are not counted at all while others are counted twice. To further illustrate this, and also in order to relate the CV-measure to that presented in section 3.4, let us reformulate the willingness-to-pay question. Suppose that the household is asked for its willingness to pay for the project disregarding any effects on lump-sum income, profit incomes and taxes. The total willingness to pay CV, as defined by equation (5.9), and the new partial one, denoted CV^p, are then given by:

$$V(p^1,w^1,Y^1 + \Pi^1 - \tau^1 - CV,z^1)$$
$$= V(p^1,w^1,Y^0 + \Pi^0 - \tau^0 - CV^p,z^1) = V^0 \qquad (5.11)$$

where V^0 refers to the level of utility attained without the project as specified in equation (5.9). The difference between the left-hand side expression and the middle expression refers only to income terms. Thus the difference between the two willingness-to-pay measures is simply:

$$CV = CV^p + \Delta Y + \Delta \Pi - \Delta \tau \tag{5.12}$$

where $\Delta Y = Y^1 - Y^0$, $\Delta \Pi = \Pi^1 - \Pi^0$, and $\Delta \tau = \tau^1 - \tau^0$.

Therefore if the household has been asked for its willingness to pay CV^p for the project disregarding any effects of the project on incomes and taxes, the project's social profitability is obtained by adding to CV^p:

(i)   any change in the household's lump-sum income Y due to the project;
(ii)   any change in private sector profits, calculated as profits if the project is undertaken less profits if the project is not undertaken, i.e. $\Pi(p^1,w^1,z^1) - \Pi(p^0,w^0,z^0)$;

and subtracting:

(iii) any change in taxes, i.e. $\Delta \tau = p^1 x^p + w^1 L^p$, if $\tau^0 = 0$ for simplicity.

In turn, the CV^p measure can be given broadly the same interpretation as that suggested in section 3.4. That is, the measure covers use values and various non-use values provided by the project. The addition of income changes caused by the project yields its social profitability.

The above exercise shows that it is extremely important that the investigator makes clear both to himself and to interviewees exactly what they are supposed to include in their monetary valuation of a project. Otherwise, an interviewee may report, say, his CV measure while the investigator believes it is a CV^p measure and erroneously adds income changes to arrive at the project's social profitability. An example may be useful in this context. Suppose that the project affects human health. In many countries, workers are covered by paid sick-leave. Therefore, the question is whether they should include gross or net income losses when they report their willingness to pay. To the entire society, loss of production is the relevant measure, while a household, viewing taxes/insurance payments as unaffected by the project, may look just at its disposable income. Specifying what the household is supposed to value in the valuation question would solve the problem and avoid unnecessary uncertainties when assessing the project's social profitability. Another useful lesson that can be learned from the above exercise is that one can, at least sometimes, simplify the calculation of a cost-benefit analysis by asking the 'right' valuation questions. In other words, the need for supplementary information is, broadly speaking, a function of what information the valuation questions generate.

A similar danger relates to the use of existing valuation data in a cost-benefit analysis of a large project. The basic problem can be illustrated by means of a simple example. Suppose a person in one study is asked for his willingness to pay (WTP) for a Jaguar, in a second study for his WTP for a Mercedes-Benz, and in a third study for his WTP for a Volvo. Obviously, one cannot sum these three unconditional amounts of money and interpret

Table 5.1. *Benefits of water pollution control regulation in the US* *($ billions (1985))*

Category	Range	Most likely point estimate
Recreation		
Freshwater fishing	0.7–2.1	1.5
Marine sports fishing	0.1–4.5	1.5
Boating	1.5–3.0	2.2
Swimming	0.3–3.0	1.5
Waterfowl hunting	0.0–0.5	0.2
Subtotal	2.6–13.1	6.9
Non-user benefits		
Aesthetics, ecology and property value	0.7–5.9	1.8
Commercial fisheries	0.6–1.8	1.2
Diversionary uses		
Drinking water/health	0.0–3.0	1.5
Municipal treatment costs	0.9–1.8	1.3
Households	0.2–0.7	0.4
Industrial supplies	0.7–1.4	0.9
Subtotal	1.8–6.9	4.1
Total	5.7–27.7	14.0

Source: Freeman (1990, p. 123).

the result as the person's total WTP for cars. Either we must proceed sequentially in the way explained in sections 3.4 and 3.5, i.e. ask for the WTP for a car conditional on what has already been spent on cars in previous questions, or ask for the total WTP for cars. Unfortunately, using existing valuation data in a cost-benefit analysis is often equivalent to the former approach in the sense that the investigator adds unconditional WTPs collected from different studies. The outcome of such a study is difficult to interpret at best.

This is further illustrated by Table 5.1, which contains Freeman's (1990) estimate of the aggregate benefits of a water pollution control regulation in the US. Freeman also provides an estimate of the corresponding costs, thus undertaking a social cost-benefit analysis. However, for reasons explained above, summing benefits collected from different sources as in the table is an incorrect procedure, at least if the project is non-marginal. Hence one must conclude that Freeman's cost-benefit analysis is questionable, to say the least. A similar warning is in order when using cost-benefit analysis to rank different projects. The general problem is using the CV and EV measures in ranking large projects was analysed in section 3.2. All the conclusions obtained there carry over to the general equilibrium context of this chapter. One must therefore be very careful in the choice of money measure to use in a cost-benefit analysis of which the aim is to rank two or more proposed projects, at least if they are large (non-marginal).

Another issue that should be raised is the following. Large projects which have a significant impact on the economy's prices are naturally extremely difficult to evaluate for an individual household. What we demand is basically that the household should evaluate the complicated integral in equation (5.10), or break down the project's consequences as in equation (5.12). This is by no means an easy task. At the same time, a democratic society often requires its citizens to take decisions (e.g. through referenda) on issues so complicated that no welfare economist would even dream of designing and evaluating such scenarios on his own. If the average citizen is considered too uninformed to make decisions on complicated issues, who is competent, and in what sense?

There are not many alternatives available, however. In the previous chapter, different methods which can be used to assess changes in environmental assets were reviewed. Most of these methods, however, are developed and used for the evaluation of a *ceteris paribus* change in the availability/quality of an asset. The most useful tools for the evaluation of large projects are probably computable general equilibrium models, possibly combined with questionnaire techniques. CGE models can be used to see how the project's effects spill over to other sectors of the economy, and whether these spillover effects are considerable or not, relative to the direct effects. Possibly, such studies can also be used to provide background information to households asked for their willingness to pay for the project. We will come back to these issues later. Here it should just be mentioned that available evidence on the importance of spillover effects is inconclusive. As one would expect, some studies find that evaluating a project at initial prices, i.e. disregarding any general equilibrium effects, is an acceptable approximation, while in other cases this approach turns out to produce large errors. See, for example, Bergman (1991), Jorgenson (1990) and Kokoski and Smith (1987) for some evidence as well as further discussion of this issue.

A final issue to be raised is the following one. The social profitability of a project is expressed in terms of the *difference* between benefits and costs, as can be seen from (5.7), for example. Nevertheless, practitioners sometimes prefer to use the benefit–cost *ratio* (or its inverse) as the decision criterion.

This is perfectly legitimate if we consider a single project in isolation. It is, however, dangerous to use ratios in order to rank the desirability of two or more projects. To see why, it is sufficient to consider a project z whose size can be varied continuously. Let $B(z)$ and $C(z)$ denote benefits and costs, respectively, as continuous and differentiable functions of the size of the project. By differentiating $R(z) = B(z)/C(z)$ with respect to z, the reader can easily verify that the ratio can fall even if marginal benefits exceed marginal costs. In other words, and more generally, $R(z^0)$ may exceed $R(z^1)$, even where the benefits obtained by adding $\Delta z = z^1 - z^0$ to z^0 exceed the associated increase in costs. This shows in a simple way the danger of using ratios to rank projects. For a further discussion of this issue, including the circumstances under which ratios can be used to rank projects, the reader is referred to McKean (1958).

5.5 The treatment of taxes

Thus far it has been assumed that there are no distortions such as income taxes and value-added taxes in the economy under consideration. In order to arrive at project evaluation rules that can be used to assess projects in real-world economies, it is necessary to introduce distorting taxes. In this section we extend the general equilibrium cost-benefit rules derived in previous sections to an economy with three different taxes (plus lump-sum taxes). Firstly, there is a value-added tax, i.e. an *ad valorem* tax on all finished products sold in markets. For notational simplicity the assumption of a single produced commodity is maintained here, but commodity-specific taxes, subsidies and a tax on profits are introduced in the appendix. Secondly, the government taxes labour. There is an *ad valorem* tax on market wages which is paid by employers. This tax is collected as social security contributions. Finally, households pay an income tax which is proportional to their wage incomes.

Let us now re-evaluate our environmental project, assuming that the government is free to change any tax rates it wishes and can also use lump-sum taxes so as to balance its budget. Moreover, the government subsidizes the project under consideration. If the project is small, its social profitability can then be evaluated as follows:

$$dCV = pF_z dz + (V_z/V_y)dz - pdx^p - [w(1+\alpha)/(1-\theta)]dL_1^p$$
$$- w(1-\tau_w)dL_2^p + d\tau_R \tag{5.13}$$

where $p = p^s/(1-\theta)$ is the consumer price, p^s is the producer price, θ is the value-added (plus any commodity-specific) tax, α is social security contributions paid by employers, τ_w is a proportional tax on labour income, dL_1^p refers to workers drawn from the private sector to the project, dL_2^p refers to workers drawn from leisure activities, and $d\tau_R$ is a residual tax as explained in the appendix; $d\tau_R = 0$ if, for example, the considered project leaves the supplies of all kinds of labour constant. See the appendix for details.

The above project evaluation rules for a tax-distorted economy can be interpreted as:

(i)   The marginal product of environmental quality to firms should be valued at consumer prices, i.e. inclusive of VAT and any commodity-specific taxes.

(ii) Produced inputs purchased for the project should be valued at consumer prices, i.e. inclusive of VAT and any commodity-specific taxes.

(iii) Workers drawn to the project from private sector firms should be valued at market wages plus social fees plus value-added taxes (and any commodity-specific taxes), so as to reflect the value consumers place on the commodities foregone or displaced.

(iv) Workers drawn from leisure activities should be valued at their reservation wages. If labour markets clear, the reservation wage is equal to the after-tax wage rate. This is the lowest amount of money inducing an individual to switch, at the margin, from leisure time to work time.

(v)   Subsidies to the project do not affect its social profitability. Therefore, subsidies should not be included in the evaluation. Subsidies are like transfers (and taxes on profits), i.e. they net out in the aggregate.

It should be emphasized once again that the formulation of the project evaluation rule in (5.13) is one among several possibilities. By playing around with the terms one can break down revenues and costs in the way one finds most useful for one's own purposes. Also, the interpretation of equation (5.13) is based on the assumption that the 'residual' τ_R remains constant. As can be seen from equation (5A.12′) in the appendix, this assumption need not hold. The assumption that the government can ultimately rely on lump-sum taxation is also questionable. However, it would take us too far to try to develop rules for cases in which the government cannot use lump-sum taxes. See Drèze and Stern (1987) for a discussion of this issue.

If the investigator lacks data on alternative uses of labour and other production factors used up by the project, the following approach can be used. A kind of *upper bound* for the project's costs is obtained by assuming that all resources in the economy are fully employed. Our project then completely crowds out other production activities. Using points (ii) and (iii) above to value labour and produced inputs used by the project, one arrives at this 'complete crowding-out' case. A kind of *lower bound* for costs is obtained by assuming that only leisure time is crowded out. Labour used up by the project is then valued according to point (iv) above. Similarly, produced inputs should be valued at real marginal costs: workers are valued at their reservation wages, and any commodity-specific taxes and VAT are excluded. The reason is that no other user, whose valuation is reflected by prices inclusive of taxes, is crowded out since production increases by dx^p. The complete set of cost-benefit rules to be used in these two cases can be found in equations (5A.13) in the appendix. It is suggested that the investigator supplies the decision-maker with upper bounds and lower bounds for the project's costs. In section 6.3 these bounds are used in an empirical cost-benefit analysis.

It should be noted that any tariffs should be deducted from imported inputs used by the project. Imports should in all other respects be treated as domestic inputs since we are ultimately interested in consumers' valuation of resources drawn from domestic uses to the export sector to 'finance' the new imports. This result holds under fixed and flexible exchange rates so long as the country faces no borrowing constraints; see the appendix to chapter 6. If it does, one must try to locate the displaced user and calculate this user's marginal valuation of the displaced imports. See Cuddington *et al.* (1984) for details.

As explained in section 5.4, the kind of information that must be collected for a project evaluation depends in part on what approach is used. If a questionnaire is used to ask valuation questions, for example, it is important to clarify exactly what a respondent is bidding upon. At the same time, this provides the investigator with an opportunity to be selective in the information sought. For example, if a lot of information is already available on the project's costs, its impact on private sector profits, etc., the relevant household valuation question is probably something like the CV^p question defined by equation (5.11). Calculating the different terms in equation (5.12) one then arrives at an expression for the (large or small) project's social profitability. Thus depending on the circumstances, one may choose to use (a possibly modified version of) (5.12) or (5.13) to assess a project.

Much attention has been devoted to the concept of the *marginal cost of funds* in a tax-distorted economy, i.e. the welfare cost of a marginal tax dollar. In particular, a lot of authors have simulated results from computable general equilibrium models. Here it should just be noted that our cost-benefit rules for a tax-distorted economy cover the marginal cost of funds. In fact, equation (5.13) can easily be rewritten so as to yield an explicit formula for the marginal cost of funds. This exercise will not be performed here, but the reader can check equations (6) to (8) in Mayshar (1991) to see the close correspondence between our cost-benefit rules and the definition of the marginal cost of funds. It would thus be a kind of double-counting to adjust the cost-benefit rules in equation (5.13) so as to cover the welfare cost of the marginal tax dollar.

5.6 Unemployed resources

We now turn to the question of how to value the services of workers who before the project were unemployed. If the gains in jobs can be counted as a benefit of the project, its social profitability increases. We hinted at a possible answer in the previous section when introducing the concept of a worker's reservation wage. This is the lowest wage that would induce a person to accept a job offer. The social cost of hiring a person who before the project was unemployed is his reservation wage. There is no loss of production in other sectors of the economy since the person hired is drawn from the pool of unemployed, not from the production of goods and services. Therefore, if there is a social cost, it must be in the form of a loss of valued 'leisure' time.

It is sometimes argued that the reservation wage may overstate the true social cost of using unemployed labour. The unemployed lose self-respect, their working skills atrophy and their working habits degenerate. Therefore, it is argued, the true social cost of hiring an unemployed worker is zero or even negative. In evaluating these arguments, however, a distinction must be made between short-term unemployment and long-term unemployment. An unemployment rate of, say, 5 per cent in a society may be due to either a few people being unemployed for 6–8 months each or many people being unemployed for a week or two each. One would expect the duration of unemployment spells to be of some importance for the social cost of unemployment; the longer the spell, the higher the social cost. A disturbing point raised by many economists, however, is why unemployed labourers do not drive down the market wage rate so as to achieve full employment.

We will not even attempt to argue in favour of one or other of the above positions. Instead, let us use Figure 5.4 to illustrate the usual partial equilibrium view of the cost of hiring an unemployed person. The wage rate in the figure is fixed above its market-clearing level so that there is an excess supply of labour. If the firm in question hires workers from this market, they are directly or indirectly drawn from the pool of unemployed. The firm's cost for an extra worker is w^1, but the social cost is (conditional on the reservations introduced above) given by the worker's reservation wage w. The firm's wage cost thus overstates the social cost by an amount equal to $w^1 - w$ for each unemployed worker it hires. This assumes that the jobs are allocated to those who have the lowest reservation wages. It is of course questionable whether the employment exchange can pick out these people. The reservation wages of those actually hired may therefore exceed (or even

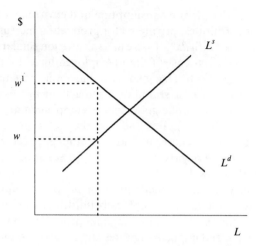

Figure 5.4. Disequilibrium in a labour market.

fall short of) w, implying that the social cost would be understated (overstated) if it is evaluated at w per unemployed worker.

A further problem is that the levels of employment in other firms may be affected by the impact of the project under evaluation. For example, if private sector firms expand output due to the favourable effect of improved environmental quality on productivity ($pF_z > 0$), the equilibrium output price will fall, *ceteris paribus*. In fact, via complicated adjustments in relative prices, the small project under consideration may cause aggregate unemployment to increase. If so, the true social cost of an unemployed worker hired by the project exceeds the wage cost, as is shown in the appendix to this chapter. The perhaps somewhat surprising implication is that when the economy suffers from unemployment, profitability calculated at market prices is not sufficient to ensure that a small project is socially profitable. This is in sharp contrast to the perfect market economy with full employment, where profitability calculated at market prices guarantees that a small project is socially desirable.

The project may cause crowding-out effects even in a situation with *Keynesian unemployment*. Such unemployment is due to deficient total demand in society: firms operate at less than full capacity because they are unable to sell all the output they are willing to sell at ruling prices. Any effects of the project on private sector output must therefore go through one of two channels. Firstly, the project's demand for finished goods will stimulate aggregate demand and hence also demand-constrained private sector production. Basically, we have the famous balanced-budget theorem in operation, i.e. there is a 1:1 relationship between the expansion in aggregate output and the project's demand for goods. Secondly, depending on whether households consider private consumption and environmental quality as complements or substitutes, private sector production increases or decreases. In the former case (with $dx^p = 0$), we have a situation similar to the one described above; the social cost of the unemployed hired by the project may exceed the wage cost. One can also, however, visualize situations in which the project has a stimulative impact on aggregate demand. If the project provides a public good that is complementary to some private good (e.g. roads–cars), demand for the latter good is stimulated. In this case, the project causes a kind of multiplier effect that adds to the project's social (but not private) profitability. See Johansson (1986) for a derivation of these results.

The above analysis clearly shows the inadequacy of the partial equilibrium view found in many textbooks and graphically illustrated in Figure 5.4. This view treats all labour employed in a marginal project as coming from the pool of unemployed, and implicitly ignores any effect on employment in other sectors of the economy. The problem with the alternative ('general equilibrium') view discussed above is how the cost-benefit practitioner should determine the net effect of a project on aggregate unemployment. In many instances an examination of the sectors directly affected by a project can give valuable information regarding the nature of market imbalances. In some countries, disaggregated econometric macromodels are available and can be used to assess the effect of a project on aggregate employment.

Appendix

The firm maximizes its profits, i.e.

$$\Pi = pF(L,z,K) - wL - 1 \cdot K \tag{5A.1}$$

where $L = [L_1, \ldots, L_k]$, the production function is assumed to be at least twice continuously differentiable in all arguments, the price of capital is set equal to unity, and any notation referring to transposed vectors is suppressed.

Necessary conditions for an interior solution to the maximization problem are:

$$\partial \Pi / \partial L_i = p \partial F(\cdot) / \partial L_i - w_i = 0 \qquad \forall i \tag{5A.2}$$

i.e. the value of the marginal product of an input must equal its price. See Varian (1992), for example, for necessary and sufficient conditions for profit maximization. In principle, equations (5A.2) can be solved to yield:

$$L_i = L_i(p,w,z) \qquad \forall i \tag{5A.3}$$

where the dependence on K is suppressed.

Substitution of (5A.3) into the production function (with K suppressed) yields the supply function:

$$x(p,w,z) = F[L(p,w,z),z] \tag{5A.4}$$

Throughout, it is assumed that supply and demand functions are well-behaved (for example, they have finite derivatives), for $p > 0$, $w,z \gg 0$.

Totally differentiating (5A.1) using (5A.2) produces:

$$dΠ = xdp + [p(\partial F/\partial L) - w]dL - Ldw + p(\partial F/\partial z)dz$$
$$= xdp - Ldw + p(\partial F/\partial z)dz \tag{5A.5}$$

This explains the properties of the profit function, i.e. the fact that taking the partial derivative with respect to output price yields the supply function, while the partial derivative with respect to a factor price, say w_1, yields (minus) the demand function for L_1. This result is known as Hotelling's lemma.

An input, say L_1, is characterized as essential in section 5.1 if:

$$\lim_{w_1 \to \infty} Π(p,w_1,\bar{w},z) = -K \tag{5A.6}$$

for $p > 0$ and $\bar{w},z \gg 0$.

To arrive at the indirect utility function (5.6), assume that the household consumes (a vector of) private goods x^d, supplies k different kinds of labour $L^s = [L_1^s, ..., L_k^s]$ and values environmental quality z. Then:

$$V(p,w,Y+Π-τ-CV,z) = \max_{x^d,L^s} \{U(x^d,L^s,z) \mid Y+Π+wL^s-τ-CV$$
$$-px^d = 0\} \tag{5A.7}$$

The household thus treats $Π$, $τ$ and CV as exogenous. The direct utility function in (5A.7) is assumed to be such that the indirect utility function exists and to have the usual well-behaved properties, e.g. differentiability, generally assumed in the literature. Setting $CV = 0$ yields (5.6).

Totally differentiating the indirect utility function yields:

$$dV = -V_y x^d dp + V_y L^s dw + V_y dY + V_y dΠ - V_y dτ + V_z dz - V_y dCV = 0 \tag{5A.8}$$

where

$$dΠ = x^s dp - L^d dw + p(\partial F/\partial z)dz \tag{5A.9}$$

from (5A.5). Substituting (5A.9) into (5A.8) and rearranging terms yields equation (5.7). Note that all derivatives in (5A.8) are evaluated at (say) p^0,w^0, Y^0, $τ^0$, CV^0, z^0, and that one price is assumed to be fixed, since models like the one considered here determine only relative prices.

In assessing large changes in z it should be noted that in equation (5.10):

$$\left.\begin{array}{l}
p(z)F_z = p^*F_z[L(p^*,w^*,z),z] \\
V_z = V_z[p^*,w^*,Y^*+Π^*-τ^*-CV^*,z] \\
V_y = V_y[p^*,w^*,Y^*+Π^*-τ^*-CV^*,z] \\
C'(z) = p^*\partial x^p/\partial z - w^*\partial L^p/\partial x
\end{array}\right\} \tag{5A.10}$$

where $p^* = p(z)$, $w^* = w(z)$, $Y^* = Y(z)$, $Π^* = p^*x(p^*,w^*,z) - w^*L(p^*,w^*,z)$, $τ^* = p^*x^p(z) - w^*L^p(z)$, and $CV^* = CV(z)$ is such that the household stays at its initial level of utility throughout the movement from z^0 to z^1. Note that Y is treated as being constant ($Y^1 = Y^0$) in equation (5.10).

If the wage rate for type i labour is fixed above its market-clearing level so that there is unemployment, equation (5A.7) would look like:

$$V = V(p, w^-, Y + \Pi + w^i \bar{L}^i - \tau - CV, \bar{L}^i, z) \tag{5A.7'}$$

where $\bar{L}^i = L^{di} + L^{pi}$ is the perceived constraint in the market for type i labour; $\bar{L}^i$, in equilibrium, is equal to demand for that kind of labour; and w^- is a vector of all wages but the ith wage. See also equations (3A.15)–(3A.21) on p. 44.

Differentiating (5A.7') with respect to $\bar{L}^i$ one finds that:

$$dV/dL^i = V_y \cdot w^i + V_{\bar{L}} \tag{5A.7''}$$

where $V_{\bar{L}}$ is the marginal utility of work (≤ 0). As long as the household is compelled to work less than it would like to, $dV/dL^i > 0$. Only at an interior optimum is $dV/dL^i = 0$ since then the marginal disutility of work is equal to the wage rate (times the marginal utility of income). In equation (5A.8) $V_y L^{si} dw^i$ would be replaced by the right-hand expression in (5A.7''). Then, the *general equilibrium cost-benefit rule* stated in equation (5.7) will read:

$$dV/V_y = (V_z/V_y)dz + pF_z dz - pdx^p - wdL^p + (w^i - w^i_R)d\bar{L}^i - dCV = 0 \tag{5.7'}$$

where $w^i_R = -(V_{\bar{L}}/V_y)$ is the reservation wage. Thus, if the considered project reduces aggregate employment, $d\bar{L} < 0$, there is a project cost in addition to the direct labour cost, i.e. wdL^p. Conversely, if the project increases employment, the project's direct labour cost should be reduced by the 'correction factor' $(w^i - w^i_R)d\bar{L} > 0$. Similar results can be derived for tax-distorted economies.

To arrive at equation (5.13), note that:

and
$$\left. \begin{array}{l} \Pi = p(1-\theta)F(L,z) - w(1+\alpha)L^d - K \\ -\tau = \theta px^s + \alpha wL^d + \tau_w L^s - px^p - wL^p \end{array} \right\} \tag{5A.11}$$

Note that subsidies to the project under consideration have been netted out from the tax expression (and it is implicitly assumed that at least one good or factor is untaxed, i.e. we need a numéraire here as before).

Using these expressions in (5A.7) and replacing w in the indirect utility function by $w(1 - \tau_w)$ so as to arrive at after-tax wages, and totally differentiating the function, one obtains, after straightforward but tedious calculations:

$$dCV = pF_z dz + (V_z/V_y)dz + p\theta F_L dL^d + wadL^d + w\tau_w dL^s - pdx^p - wdL^p \tag{5A.12}$$

If we define $dL^p = dL_1^p + dL_2^p$, $dL_1^p = -dL_1^d$, and $dL_2^p = dL_2^s$, where dL_1^p is labour drawn from the private sector and dL_2^p is labour drawn from leisure activities, (5A.12) can be written as:

$$dCV = pF_z dz + (V_z/V_y)dz + pdx^p - [w(1+\alpha)/(1-\theta)]dL_1^p \\ - w(1-\tau_w)dL_2^p + d\tau_R \tag{5A.12'}$$

where $d\tau_R = w[(\alpha + \theta)/(1-\theta)](dL^d + dL_1^p) + w\tau_w(dL^s - dL_2^p)$.

Note that if labour supplies are constant, then $dL^p = dL_1^p = -dL^d$ in the above expressions, while if $dL^s = dL^p$, then $dL^d = dL_1^p = 0$. Also note that tax changes, e.g. $d\theta$, net out from the expressions due to market clearing and the assumption that the government is free to use lump-sum taxation at the margin so as to balance its budget.

In addition, if the economy produces many different commodities, some of which are subject to value-added taxation and some of which are also subject to specific taxes (just like labour), then θ can be interpreted as a vector in (5A.12) with elements $\theta^i = \bar{\theta} + \theta^{si}$, with $\bar{\theta} = $ VAT, and $\theta^{si} \geq 0$ being a commodity-specific tax on commodity i. The reader can easily verify that a tax on profits nets out from $\Pi - \tau$ in (5A.11) and hence leaves (5A.12') unchanged.

In section 5.5, we defined upper and lower bounds for the project's costs. The complete evaluation rules for these two cases can be stated as follows:

$$
\left.
\begin{aligned}
dCV &= pF_z + (V_z/V_y)dz - pdx^p - [w(1 + a)/(1 - \theta)]dL_1^p \\
dCV &= (V_z/V_y)dz - w(1 - \tau_w)[dL^d + dL_2^p]
\end{aligned}
\right\} \quad (5A.13)
$$

where the first line yields the upper bound and the second line yields the lower bound. In the second line, $w(1 - \tau_w)dL^d$ is the marginal cost of producing x^p when labour is valued at the reservation wage.

6 Cost-benefit rules, national income accounts and sustainable development

Thus far we have dealt exclusively with project evaluations in single-period models. This chapter is the first of a sequence dealing with intertemporal problems. In developing the theory it is as well to discuss the simplest considerations first. For this reason the assumption that agents do not face any uncertainty is retained throughout this chapter. In fact, it is assumed that agents have perfect foresight, i.e. know or can calculate all present and future equilibrium prices etc.

Section 6.1 extends the single-period model described in the previous chapter to cover optimization for T-period horizons. Overall or lifetime consumer surplus measures are briefly discussed. Such overall measures, however, require huge amounts of information and may be difficult to calculate and estimate. Therefore, so-called instantaneous consumer surplus measures are introduced, and the question of whether the present value of such surpluses can be used as a proxy for lifetime surplus measures is investigated. Section 6.2 presents intertemporal cost-benefit rules for environmental measures which affect household utility as well as firms' production possibilities. Section 6.3 outlines a cost-benefit analysis of a plant producing ethanol to be used as a motor fuel. The purpose is to illustrate in a simple way how to use the evaluation rules derived in this and the previous chapter. Section 6.4 introduces natural resources and indicates what the cost-benefit rules look like in an economy harvesting both non-renewable and renewable natural resources. The final section of the chapter is devoted to trade-offs between the interests of the current generation and future generations. A dynamic growth model is used to take a closer look at issues such as cost-benefit rules, national income accounts and sustainable development.

6.1 An intertemporal model

Let us begin by considering a household with a T-period horizon. The household consumes private as well as public goods and supplies labour in each period. Borrowing and lending any amount is allowed at the prevailing interest rate, i.e. capital markets are perfect. Moreover, it is assumed here that the household does not plan to leave its heirs assets or debts, though this assumption will be dropped later on in the chapter. The household maximizes its utility subject to a lifetime budget-constraint. If the household considers all prices, interest rates and period incomes as exogenous, the solution to the optimization problem parallels the solution of the single-period optimization problems in chapters 2 and 3.

We turn directly to the indirect utility function; details of this can be found in the appendix to this chapter. This function can be written as:

$$V(p,w,y,z) = U[X_{11}(p,w,y,z), \ldots, L_{kT}(p,w,y,z), z] \qquad (6.1)$$

where x_{it} is the demand for commodity i, $i = 1, \ldots, n$ in period t, L_{jt} is the supply of factor j, $j = 1, \ldots, k$ in period t, prices and wages are now expressed as present values using the market rate of interest as discount rate, $p = [p_{11}, \ldots, p_{nT}]$ is a vector of present value prices, $w = [w_{11}, \ldots, w_{kT}]$ is a vector of present value wages, $y = \sum \gamma^{t-1} y_t$ is the sum of fixed income during T periods, discounted to the initial period using the market rate of interest as the discount rate, i.e. $\gamma = (1 + r)^{-1}$ with r denoting the (for simplicity, constant) interest rate, $z = [z_{11}, \ldots, z_{mT}]$, and primes that denote transposed vectors are suppressed. Thus, according to (6.1), in each period the household consumes n private goods, supplies k different kinds of labour, and values m different environmental assets/services.

From (6.1) it can be seen that the effects of changes in prices, lump-sum income or environmental quality in this intertemporal model must be very similar to the effects obtained in the atemporal models investigated in the previous chapters. In fact, most results carry over to the intertemporal model, provided one replaces the words 'prices' and 'incomes' with the phrase 'the present value of prices and incomes'.

Similarly, one may define the compensating variation (and, of course, the equivalent variation). Using equation (6.1):

$$V(p^1, w^1, y^1 - CV, z^1) = V(p^0, w^0, y^0, z^0) \qquad (6.2)$$

where a superscript 1 (0) denotes final (initial) level values, and CV is the overall compensating variation, i.e. the present value of the lump-sum income that can be taken from (must be given to) the household while leaving it just as well off as it was before a change in present-value prices, exogenous present-value income, and environmental quality in different periods. All of the results concerning path-independency and ranking properties carry over from the atemporal models discussed in earlier chapters to the simple intertemporal model used in this section. For example, provided that the indirect intertemporal utility function is well-behaved in the sense discussed in the appendix to chapter 3, the CV measure implicitly defined by equation (6.2) is path-independent, i.e. the order in which prices etc. are changed does not affect the magnitude of the overall measure.

The overall CV measure can be decomposed into use and non-use values in the way illustrated in chapter 3, the difference being that we can now explicitly distinguish between *current values* and *future values*. For example, a household which at present is not using an environmental resource devotes no current use value to it, as illustrated in Figure 6.1 for the case of a public good. Nevertheless, in some future period t the household may plan to use the resource and therefore reports a positive present-value willing-ness to pay (or use value) in response to a suggested increase in the availability/quality of the commodity.

The reader should also note that if an asset is 'completely' depleted or destroyed in some future period, then all of its values vanish from that period onwards. Depending on whether the asset is essential or not as defined in chapter 3 above, meaningful CV and EV measures may be formulated for such cases. If it is essential, mankind ceases to exist after the critical period, implying that no meaningful analysis can be performed for periods beyond that period. Still, one can evaluate measures taken to delay 'doomsday' using the simple model outlined here. That is, one can meaningfully define the willingness to pay for having the destruction of some essential asset delayed from a period t to some later period $t + s$. Thus, the intertemporal model, although similar to the atemporal ones in previous chapters, provides a richer menu when it comes to policy applications.

The consumer surplus measures discussed thus far may be called overall, or lifetime, measures. Suppose, however, that the consumer surplus is instead calculated at each point in time, as would probably be the procedure in an empirical study because of the obvious problems entailed in calculat-ing a lifetime measure. Drawing on Blackorby *et al.* (1984), we should ask whether the present value of these instantaneous consumer surpluses has the same sign as the overall utility change.

The lifetime utility-maximization problem assumes that the household is free to borrow and lend any amount of money at the prevailing market rate of interest. The instantaneous (or 'annual') indirect utility functions, on the other hand, assume that the household is constrained by its instantaneous income, just as in previous chapters. The household is thus prevented from reallocating its consumption expenditures over time by borrowing and lending. In general, this means that the discounted value of the sum of instantaneous utility levels falls short of the maximum lifetime utility level as defined by equation (6.1), assuming that the utility function is separable in order to ensure that instantaneous preferences (utility functions) exist.

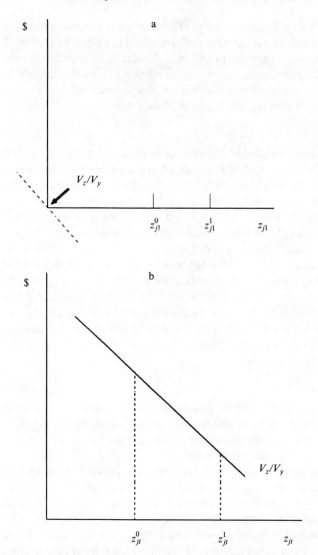

Figure 6.1. Illustration of the case in which willingness to pay for a good is zero today (a) but positive in some future period (b).

As before, the overall compensating variation is the maximum amount of present-value income or wealth that the household is willing to give up to secure a proposed change in prices etc. Similarly, the instantaneous compensating variation is the present-value income in period t that can be taken from the household while leaving it just as well off as before a proposed change in that period. It can be shown that:

$$CV \geq \sum_t \gamma^{t-1} \tilde{CV}_t = \sum_t CV_t \qquad (6.3)$$

where $\tilde{CV}_t$ is the *current-value* period t compensating variation, $\gamma = 1/(1+r)$ is the discount factor, and r is the (for simplicity, constant) market rate of interest. Equation (6.3) indicates that $\sum CV_t$, the sum of *discounted* instantaneous compensating variations, can, but need not, have the same sign as the overall measure CV. However, if $\sum CV_t \geq 0$, then it must be the case that $CV \geq 0$. In this case, the discounted sum of instantaneous compensating variations ranks the alternatives in the same order as the overall measure.

The present-value criterion does not work when $\sum CV_t < 0$. Even if the sum of discounted instantaneous compensating variations is negative, the overall compensating variation may be positive. In order to obtain a rule for project rejection, we must use the equivalent variation instead, i.e. the minimum amount the household would accept in lieu of the change from initial to final level values in prices and/or environmental quality, for instance. It can be shown that:

$$EV \leq \sum_t EV_t \qquad (6.3')$$

Hence, if the discounted sum of instantaneous equivalent variations is negative, then the overall equivalent variation EV must also be negative. This means that the sum of discounted instantaneous EVs can be used to check whether a project should be rejected.

In short, if the discounted sum of compensating variations (equivalent variations) is positive (negative), then lifetime welfare has increased (decreased). However, ambiguous results occur when the present value of compensating variations is negative and the present value of equivalent variations is positive. This is demonstrated by Blackorby *et al.* (1984). Nevertheless, in many cases the sum of the discounted consumer surplus should be a useful concept. Assume that we have estimated compensated demand functions for one or more periods. Even if these demand functions, like the demand functions in previous chapters, only reflect instantaneous utility maximization, some conclusions can be drawn. Firstly, if the sum of the discounted instantaneous compensating variations associated with a project is positive, the project is certainly worthwhile. Secondly, if $\sum CV_t < 0$, we should compute the discounted sum of instantaneous equivalent variations. If this discounted sum is negative, the project must be rejected. Although there remains a zone of indeterminacy ($\sum CV_t < 0$ while $\sum EV_t > 0$), the discounted-sum approach greatly simplifies the calculations in the many cases for which definite conclusions emerge.

6.2 Intertemporal cost-benefit rules

In this section, cost-benefit rules which can be used to assess small projects in an intertemporal context are outlined. These rules are in a sense straightforward generalizations of those rules derived in chapter 5, but there are important differences. Most importantly, firms' capital stocks can no longer be treated as fixed, implying that an explicit treatment of investment decisions is needed. Moreover, later on in the discussion of sustainable development and similar issues, changes in capital and resource stocks will play an important role.

In this chapter, the market rate of interest is treated as a constant. One way to motivate this assumption is as follows. Let us view the economy under investigation as a small open economy. This economy can lend and borrow 'unlimited' amounts of a single internationally traded bond at the prevailing rate of interest. Because of the small open economy assumption it is not necessary for our purposes to explicitly distinguish between traded and non-traded goods or to introduce the balance of payments. We can therefore ignore any signs indicating the country of origin and destination of a particular commodity, and all prices can be interpreted as denominated in the currency of the country under investigation. The reader is referred to Dixit and Norman (1980), Cuddington et al. (1984) and Dinwiddy and Teal (1990) for details. See also the appendix to this chapter.

Given the small open economy interpretation, the exchange rate is assumed to be fixed, but as shown by Cuddington et al. (1984) and Johansson and Löfgren (1989), the kind of project evaluation rules derived here are robust with respect to the treatment of the exchange rate mechanism. Alternatively, the reader can interpret the model developed below as a closed economy model, and add a bond market which determines the interest rate. See Stokey and Lucas (1987) for such a closed economy general equilibrium model. Our cost-benefit rules for small projects will be the same regardless of which of the above interpretations is employed.

Let us begin by considering the firm analysed in section 5.1. Its profit in period t is equal to the difference between revenues from sales less labour costs and capital costs. If the firm is unconstrained in capital markets, the market rate of interest can be used to express period t profits as a present value at the beginning of the first period. The sum of present-value net cash flows for all T periods is the value of the firm:

$$\Pi^v = \sum_t [p_t F^t(K_t, L_t, z_t) - w_t L_t - \hat{q}_t I_t] \tag{6.4}$$

where $F^t(\cdot)$ is the concave and twice continuously differentiable period t production function, $w_t = [w_{it}, \ldots, w_{kt}]$ is a vector of present-value wages in period t, L_t is the corresponding vector of labour demands, $\hat{q}_t$ is the present-value price of investment goods in period t, I_t is investment in new capital goods in period t, and a prime that denotes a transposed vector is suppressed.

The firm maximizes (6.4) subject to a constraint indicating that there is a connection between the capital stock and the rate of investment. The constraint is:

$$K_{t+1} = (1 - \delta)K_t + I_t \tag{6.5}$$

This says that the capital stock in period $t + 1$ is equal to the capital stock in period t less depreciation, which is assumed to be exponential at rate δ, plus gross investment.[1]

Maximizing (6.4) subject to (6.5), one obtains the following (and other) necessary conditions for an interior solution:

$$p_t F_k^t = (\delta + r)\hat{q}_t = q_t \qquad \forall t > 1 \tag{6.6}$$

where $F_k^t = \partial F^t(\cdot)/\partial K_t$, r is the market rate of interest, assumed to be constant over time, and any effect due to changes in the price of capital goods (capital gains) is suppressed. Thus, according to equation (6.6), at each point of time the firm selects a capital stock such that the value of the marginal product of capital is equal to the cost of capital. This cost is equal to the interest charge on $\hat{q}_t$ plus the depreciation charge incurred because a proportion δ of the unit of capital has depreciated in the period. In the absence of adjustment costs or irreversibilities there is no well-behaved investment function, a problem which is ignored here. See Nickell (1978) for details. The reader is also referred to section 9.7 where the firm faces price uncertainty, and investment decisions are irreversible.

Let us now consider a public sector whose aim is to improve future environmental quality. Suppose that the government orders a social cost-benefit analysis of a proposed small pollution treatment plant. In the first period, the plant is constructed, and it then produces current benefits and costs for a number of years. As in chapter 5, the project is assumed to improve household utility as well as firms' production possibilities. In order to simplify notation, we proceed as if there is a single household and a single firm. Adding profit income and deducting lump-sum taxes from equation (6.1), we have an intertemporal extension of the atemporal model in section 5.2 used to derive cost-benefit rules.

Proceeding as in chapter 5, the general equilibrium project evaluation rule for a small project can be written as:

$$dCV = -dI^p + \sum_t [p_t F_z^t + (V_z^t/V_y) - C'(z_t)]dz_t \qquad (6.7)$$

where $dI^p = p_1 dx_1^p + \hat{q}_1 dI_1^p + w_1 dL_1^p$ is the initial investment (requiring ordinary produced goods, capital goods and labour) in the considered plant, p_t is the present value of the period t output price, $F_z^t = \partial F^t(p_t, w_t, q_t, z_t)/\partial z_t$, $V_z^t = \partial V(\cdot)/\partial z_t$, $V_y = \partial V(\cdot)/\partial y$, $C'(z_t) = p_t(\partial x_t^p/\partial z_t) + w_t(\partial L_t^p/\partial z_t)$, and $t = 2, ...,$ T. The project is thus associated with an investment cost in the first period. Then, in succeeding periods, the project produces annual benefits and costs (including maintenance), as covered by the terms within brackets in (6.7). Any final-period scrap value should be counted as a benefit, though it has been suppressed in equation (6.7).

The small-project evaluation rule defined by (6.7) looks very similar to the rule defined by equation (5.7). Flexible prices ensure that all markets are in simultaneous equilibrium at each point in time, explaining why excess demand terms do not show up in, or rather vanish from, atemporal as well as intertemporal general equilibrium cost-benefit rules. The fact that private sector investment, and hence capital stock changes, are now allowed does not change the basic interpretation of the project evaluation rule. Note, however, that the value of the marginal product of environmental quality to firms is now calculated on the assumption that firms have invested so as to achieve the optimal or profit-maximizing capital stock at each point in time.

In short, the small environmental project in equation (6.7) can be assessed in the following way:

(i) Any initial (first-period) investment cost is evaluated at current prices, i.e. equipment installed and labour used are valued at market prices.

(ii) The project's benefits, assumed to accrue from the second period and onwards, equal the sum over time of the present value of the marginal product of environmental quality to firms in different periods, plus the sum over time of households' monetary valuation of the project's direct impact on utility in different periods.

(iii) The project's operating costs are evaluated at current market prices and expressed as present values at the beginning of the first period.

(iv) The market rate of interest is used as the social discount rate in calculating present values.

(v) Taxes and unemployment should be accounted for in the way specified in sections 5.5 and 5.6, respectively.

All benefits and costs are discounted to the first period since the project is assumed to be implemented in that period. The project's real social profitability is not changed if we instead prefer to express all prices as present values in an arbitrary period t. Similarly, the time profile of the project may be different from the one specified in equation (6.7). For example, it may take several periods before the project becomes operative.

Or we may look for the optimal point in time at which the project should be undertaken. Equation (6.7) can easily be rewritten so as to handle these and other scenarios. However, a discrete-time model is not well suited for analysis of the optimal timing of a project. See Porter (1984) for a continuous-time model used for such an analysis of environmental projects.

We have used our model to derive cost-benefit rules for a particular project. However, it is easy to apply the rules to other kinds of projects/activities. To illustrate this, consider a private sector activity which has a harmful impact on (present and/or) future environmental quality. Then $dz < 0$ in equation (6.7), while $C'(\cdot)dz = 0$ so long as no measures are taken to reduce the harmful impact. If the activity is such that households but not firms are harmed, then $p_t F_z^t = 0$ in (6.7). This shows that one can use the terms in (6.7) for the evaluation of a broad class of projects/activities.

In closing this section, it should be mentioned that there are two ways of handling inflation in project assessments. The first alternative is to allow prices to change over time owing to inflation/deflation. We then use the *nominal* market rate of interest as the social discount rate in equation (6.7). Alternatively, a price index is constructed and used to convert prices to prices in some base year, e.g. the first-period price level. The *real* market rate of interest is then used to discount future prices. Both approaches produce the same present-value social profitability. If the annual inflation rate is $\dot{p}$ per cent, one has $(1 + i)/(1 + \dot{p}) = (1 + r)$, where i is the nominal and r the real interest rate. Thus, using the nominal interest rate in equation (6.7) instead of the real one would be equivalent to multiplying real prices by a factor $(1 + \dot{p})$ so as to convert them from real to nominal ones. But the factor $(1 + \dot{p})$ apparently nets out from the expression so that whether we use real prices and the real interest rate, or nominal prices and the nominal interest rate, does not matter. For further discussion of the choice of discount rate, the reader is referred to sections 7.5 and 7.6. Gramlich (1990) provides much useful advice for the choice of discount rate in empirical studies.

6.3 An illustration of a cost-benefit analysis

Since the seventies there has been much discussion in Sweden about how to reduce dependence on imported petrol. A recent suggestion is to produce ethanol from domestic wheat. Ethanol can be mixed in small quantities with petrol to obtain gasohol. This fuel does not have any major effect on the properties of a car engine. Alternatively, ethanol can be used in buses, for example, that have been modified so as to run on ethanol. In what follows we will present an outline of a cost-benefit analysis of an ethanol plant. The basic idea is to illustrate the cost-benefit rules derived in this and the previous chapter, not to produce a detailed CBA. The data refer to a

Table 6.1. *Benefits and costs of*
producing ethanol as a complement
to petrol ($ per litre in 1985)

Benefits	
Value of ethanol	0.20
Side products	0.45
Environmental values	0–0.10
Costs	
Capital	0.10–0.13
Labour	
upper bound	0.19
lower bound	0.05
Energy, chemicals	0.27–0.33
Wheat	0.90
Net loss per litre	0.57–0.90

small plant built in the mid-eighties and producing around 5,000 m^3 of ethanol per year. The cost estimates are probably also relevant for large plants since the variable wheat cost is the dominant cost factor.

Benefits and costs per litre of ethanol are given in Table 6.1. Since ethanol is assumed to replace petrol, we use the world market price of petrol as our benefits measure. Ethanol has a lower energy content than petrol, implying that we overestimate benefits, but if we restrict the analysis to a small addition of ethanol to petrol then our approach is reasonable. The (late 1985) world market price ($0.16) has been converted to a domestic consumer price by multiplying by $1/(1 - \theta)$ where θ is VAT, here set equal to 0.20. The idea is that resources released from the export sector when imports decrease will produce commodities which domestic consumers value at $1/(1 - \theta)$ per unit 'world market' price. The plant also yields 'side products' such as fodder, whose domestic market value is included as a benefit. Note that benefits provided by a public sector project through products sold in markets were ignored in the cost-benefit rule stated in equation (6.7).

In Sweden a value is attributed to the open agricultural landscape. Closing down a farm often means that the land is converted to forests. This yields a much more uniform and boring landscape than previously. According to a recent contingent valuation study (Drake, 1992), the average Swede's annual willingness to pay for the preservation of 50 per cent of the open landscape is about $125. In terms of the land area used for the project under examination this corresponds to $0.1 per litre of ethanol.

It is of course highly questionable whether one can use figures from different studies in this way, as was explained in section 5.4 of the previous chapter. Moreover, a large part of the WTP in Drake's study is attributed to altruistic motives. As is shown in section 7.8, it is not self-evident that altruistic values should be included in a cost-benefit analysis. For these reasons, we let these environmental benefits range between zero and $0.1.

No other environmental benefits or costs have been included in the analysis. Adding small quantities of ethanol, say 2–5 per cent, to petrol will not have any noticeable impact on health and the environment. Matters are different if ethanol is used to run converted buses or trucks, but no estimates of the willingness to pay for the associated reduction in emissions are available.

The investment cost for the plant is not presented in the way suggested by equation (6.7). Instead it has been converted to a capital cost per litre of ethanol. The economic lifetime of the plant is estimated to be fifteen years. An annual fixed cost is obtained by calculating $dI^p = \sum a(1+r)^{-t}$, where a is the annual cost (annuity), and r is the real interest rate. The choice of a discount rate is a problematic issue in cost-benefit analysis, and one can find different suggestions in the literature, ranging from 2–3 per cent to 12–15 per cent. Here we use an estimate of a risk-free interest rate as the discount rate. The idea is to adjust separately for risk, though that correction is not undertaken here. See the discussion in section 8.4. Using government bonds as a proxy for risk-free assets, it seems reasonable to put r equal to 3–4 per cent. This yields a capital cost of $0.1 per litre of ethanol (net of VAT).

The firm's labour cost inclusive of social security contributions is $0.15 per litre of ethanol. The upper bound for the social labour cost as defined in section 5.5 is about $0.19 while the lower bound, assuming that $a = 0.4$ and $\tau_w = 0.5$, is about $0.05. Probably, some of those employed by the plant would otherwise be unemployed, at least for shorter periods. As discussed in section 5.6, it is far from self-evident that the social cost of labourers in the presence of unemployment falls below the market wage. For this reason, and in the absence of detailed information on local labour markets, the 'reservation wage', i.e. $0.05, is also used as lower bound in the presence of unemployment in the economy.

Labour used in the construction of the plant should be evaluated in the same way as that employed by the firm. Owing to lack of data, this correction is difficult to undertake. We therefore use $1/(1 - \theta)$ times the fixed cost, i.e. $0.13, as an upper bound for capital costs and treat $0.1 as the lower bound. The same valuation procedure is used for operating costs other than labour and wheat (mainly electricity and chemicals).

In an official Swedish government report (SOU 1986:51), the plant was evaluated using world market prices to calculate the cost of wheat. If the plant is compelled to use domestically produced wheat this approach underestimates the social cost. Because of subsidies, domestic farmers receive prices which are 50–60 per cent higher than those on the world market. Still, they have difficulties in covering their real marginal cost of production. The latter cost therefore yields a reasonable lower bound estimate of farmers' long-run value in other production activities. The social cost of wheat, inclusive of VAT, is estimated to be $0.9 per litre of ethanol.

The plant under study is apparently very unprofitable to society; the interval in the final line of Table 6.1 yields reasonable upper and lower bounds for its social profitability. To get a picture of its overall profitability one must try to forecast prices for the planning horizon (15 years). The net present value formula (6.7) can then be used to calculate the profitability of the plant. The advantage in using the procedure behind Table 6.1 is that we base our CBA on actual market prices. This makes the analysis less shaky than if it is based on forecast prices. Moreover, the chosen approach highlights the fact that only one price really matters: the real petrol price. This price would have to increase dramatically and sustainably, far above its level during the Gulf war, to make the evaluated plant socially profitable. Finally, it should be mentioned that the Swedish government decided not to support a proposed large-scale programme for the production of ethanol. The farmers' association, however, has far from surrendered. They continue to try (seemingly successfully) to convince members of parliament to support the project.

6.4 Natural resources

The project evaluation rules derived thus far do not include natural resources, though we touched upon the issue in the previous section. In this section, the optimal use of renewable and non-renewable resources is briefly discussed, and the set of project evaluation rules is broadened so as to include the use of natural resources. The discussion also provides a necessary input for the analysis of the concept of sustainable development in the next section.

The renewable resource problem is illustrated in Figure 6.2. The stock of the resource is drawn as a function of the annual growth of the resource. A bell-shaped growth function is perhaps not very realistic (except for some bacteria) but is appropriate for our purposes. Starting from the stock R^1 the annual growth is g^1. Harvesting this amount would maintain the resource stock constant over time. A harvest falling short of growth would add to the stock. In the complete absence of harvests, the resource stock would eventually reach size R^M, where natural growth ceases. A resource such as a

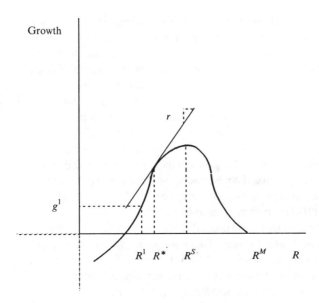

Figure 6.2. Growth of a renewable resource.

fish population does not expand indefinitely, since natural conditions (food) set a limit to expansion. On the other hand, once again starting from resource stock R^1 but now moving to the left, i.e. harvesting more than growth, would ultimately cause the depletion of the resource. In fact, as the growth curve has been drawn, there is a threshold level. If the stock falls below this level, the resource will eventually be depleted, since its growth is negative so that the stock diminishes over time.

The maximum sustainable yield resource stock in Figure 6.2 is denoted R^S. This stock, however, is in general different from the economically optimal one. To see why, let us consider a very simple T-period optimization problem. Suppose a firm owning (having property rights to) a resource can harvest it without facing any harvesting costs. The optimization problem is to maximize:

$$\Pi^R = \sum_t p_t^R h_t - \sum_t \mu_t [R_t - f(R_{t-1}) - R_{t-1} + h_t] \tag{6.8}$$

where p_t^R is the present-value price of the harvested output, h_t is the quantity harvested at the end of period t, R_t is the stock at the end of period t, $g = f(\cdot)$ represents the growth of the resource in a period as a function of the stock at the end of the preceding period with $\partial f / \partial R \gtreqless 0$ and $\partial^2 f / \partial R^2 < 0$, and μ_t is a Lagrange multiplier. The constraint in equation (6.8) simply says that the harvest in period t plus what is left to period $t+1$ equals what was left over from the previous period plus the growth of the stock in period t. Also note that the terminal value of the resource discounted to the initial period should be included as a part of the value of the firm in equation (6.8). However, as T tends to infinity, the present value of the 'scrap value' tends to zero. This is why this value has not been included in expression (6.8). It should also be remembered that the management of natural resources is ultimately a long-run issue.

Let us focus on a steady-state situation, where the firm harvests the growth in each period so that the stock remains constant over time. Under certain conditions (see the appendix to this chapter) this means that the profit-maximizing firm selects a stock such that its marginal growth rate equals the market rate of interest. The basis of this well-known result is quite simple. If the firm reduces the stock by one unit in period t, it can earn a once-and-for-all revenue which equals $p_t^R \cdot 1$. On the other hand, the firm loses all future revenues from the harvest of the natural growth of this unit of the stock. If the marginal growth of the resource $\partial f / \partial R$ falls short of the interest rate r, it is profitable to decrease the stock, i.e. to transfer resources to the investment opportunity that gives the highest rate of return. If the marginal growth rate exceeds the market rate of interest, it pays to increase the stock of the resource. Hence, the optimal stock is the one for which the marginal growth rate equals the market rate of interest. As can be seen from Figure 6.2, this optimal stock R^* falls short of the stock R^S which gives the maximum sustainable yield. It should be emphasized, however, that in more complicated models the optimal stock may exceed the maximum sustainable yield stock. See, for example, Baumol and Oates (1988), Clark (1976), Dasgupta and Heal (1979) and Johansson and Löfgren (1985) for details.

Turning now to non-renewable resources, natural growth in equation (6.8) is equal to zero. It can be shown (see the appendix) that a profit-maximizing firm would deplete the resource immediately if its price is expected to increase at a rate which falls short of the market interest rate, while it would not deplete it at all if price grows faster than the interest rate. The intuition behind this result is simply that if you can place your money in either of two banks, you will prefer the one offering the highest return on your money. This is also the strategy applied by the resource-extracting firm. Only if the resource price continuously increases at a rate equal to the interest rate will the firm extract during a number of periods. This result is known as Hotelling's rule; see Hotelling (1931).

Suppose now that the project assessed in section 6.2 demands renewable and non-renewable resources as inputs to its production process. These inputs should be valued at market prices, as with produced inputs and labour. There is thus no reason to adjust the cost-benefit rule so as to explicitly recognize the use of natural resources. This is also true for household consumption of services produced by such resources. These rules hold so long as firms harvesting renewable or non-renewable resources keep to the optimal extraction paths outlined above. Harvesting an extra unit today means that this unit, plus its growth (if renewable), is lost in the future. But today's gain exactly balances the present value of the future loss:

$$p_t^R - p_{t+1}^R\{1 + [\partial f(R^*)/\partial R]\} = 0 \qquad (6.9)$$

Thus, as long as firms extract optimally, terms like the ones in equation (6.9) net out or vanish from the cost-benefit rule.[2] However, if actual harvest patterns deviate from their optimal ones, the equality in (6.9) will not hold, implying that the difference between the two terms enters the project evaluation rule. In such cases, consuming an extra unit today will have future consequences which must be accounted for explicitly in the project evaluation. Similarly, households may place a value on the stock of a resource, an existence value, say. This value, or at least any change in it caused by the considered project, must then be included as a part of the assessment. This is implicitly accounted for through the z-vector showing up in the project evaluation rules. We will come back to this issue in the next section.

6.5 National accounts and sustainable development

The introduction of natural resources raises the question of what is meant by a sustainable development. There are many possible definitions, as shown by Pearce et al. (1990) and Pearce and Turner (1989), but two vague ones will be stated here.

(i) No degradation of resources is permitted. This means that the use of exhaustible resources is prohibited and that the harvest from renewable ones must not exceed their growth.

(ii) The economy should be run in such a way that the welfare of future generations can be sustained indefinitely at or above some minimum level.

The first of these definitions is hardly compatible with conventional views on the optimal economic use of natural resources. As was shown in the previous section, it may or may not be optimal to deplete a natural resource, whether renewable or not. Also, in the case of a renewable resource, there is not necessarily anything optimal about the present size of its stock, say R^1 in terms of Figure 6.2. It is possible, however, that mankind ceases to exist if R falls below some critical level $\bar{R}$ (for all strictly positive prices, incomes etc.). Thus, if $\bar{R}$ is interpreted as a measure of necessary current resource stocks, any depletion of these stocks is also obviously welfare-decreasing to the present generation, and it would resist all measures which cause a reduction of resource stocks. The second definition of sustainable development may seem more plausible to an economist than the first one, but is so vague that it is difficult to interpret.

In this section optimal growth theory is used to shed some further light on these issues. In particular, concepts such as sustainable income and sustainable development need an explicit dynamic model in order to be defined in a stringent way. However, the model in this section can also be interpreted in terms of project evaluations. As a consequence, we will be able to relate results on sustainable development as well as on conventional national income accounts to our sets of cost-benefit rules. The reader is also referred to sections 7.5–7.7, where we discuss the choice of social discount rate and the treatment of bequests in project evaluations when several generations are affected by a project.

One can find a variety of models in the literature on optimal growth theory. The one used here is built so as to resemble as far as possible the basic model of this book. The economy's single or representative household consumes a produced commodity and supplies labour. It also attributes a positive value to the stock of the economy's single natural resource and is hurt by some pollutant generated by the industrial sector of the economy. The present value of utility is written as:

$$\int_0^\infty e^{-rt} U(x^d,L,R,z)dt \tag{6.10}$$

where $U(\cdot)$ is the instantaneous (and well-behaved) utility function, r is the discount rate, x^d is demand for a produced commodity, L is supply of labour, z is interpreted as the rate of emissions implying that the partial derivative of U with respect to z is negative, while households derive a positive utility from natural resource stocks, e.g. through their value as a recreational source. The household (or succession of households) is assumed to live for ever and to discount future utility at the market rate of interest. Note that time variables are suppressed throughout this section.

Pollution is a by-product of production, but the rate of emissions is here viewed as fixed and determined by conditions outside the model. There is, however, a pollution abatement sector producing good environmental quality, i.e. neutralizing emissions, using produced goods and labour as variable inputs. Thus, net emissions are governed by the relationship:

$$z = \bar{z} - z^p(x^p,L^p) \tag{6.11}$$

where $\bar{z}$ is the fixed amount of emissions, $z^c = z^p(\cdot)$ is the amount of emission controlled (with $z^p(\cdot)$ interpreted as a usual (concave) production function),

x^p is inputs of a produced commodity, and L^p is inputs of labour (suppressing, for simplicity, any demand for real capital). Later on a stock pollutant will be introduced, but at present only the flow of emissions is considered.

There are only two firms in the model. One is harvesting the natural resource. Assume, for simplicity, that no resources are used up in the harvesting process, and that resource growth just depends on the stock. Then:

$$\dot{R} = f(R) - h \qquad (6.12)$$

This is simply a continuous time version of the harvesting constraint in (6.8), with a dot referring to a time derivative. Thus if natural growth exceeds the harvest, the stock will increase over time, and vice versa. If growth is zero, the resource can be considered as a non-renewable resource.

The economy's second firm or sector produces a commodity. The production function at any point in time is written as:

$$x = F(K, L^d, h, z) \qquad (6.13)$$

The sector thus uses capital, labour and the natural resource as inputs. The production process is assumed to be negatively affected by the flow of emissions. The accumulation of real capital is governed by a continuous-time version of (6.5).

The decision problem is to maximize the present value of utility, i.e. (6.10), subject to the pollution, accumulation and production constraints, and market-clearing conditions. The current-value Hamiltonian (see Seierstad and Sydsæter (1987)) for this optimization problem can be written as:

$$\left. \begin{aligned} &H(\cdot) = U(x^d, L, R, z) \\ &\text{A. } -p[x^d + x^p + I - F(K, L^d, h, z)] \\ &\text{B. } -w(L^d + L^p - L) \\ &\text{C. } +\mu_1(I - \delta K) \\ &\text{D. } +\mu_2[f(R) - h] \\ &\text{E. } -v[z - \bar{z} + z^p(x^p, L^p)] \end{aligned} \right\} \qquad (6.14)$$

Lines A and B simply say that in equilibrium demand must equal supply, with p and w being Lagrange multipliers. Lines C and D are differential equations covering the dynamics of real capital and natural resources, respectively, with I denoting investment in real capital. The multipliers μ_1 and μ_2 are co-state variables associated with the two state variables K and R of the model. Finally, line E is the accounting relationship for the flow of emissions, with v interpreted as a Lagrange multiplier.

Necessary conditions for an interior solution to the above maximization problem are stated in the appendix, but a few remarks are in order. With

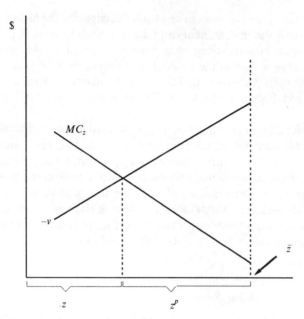

Figure 6.3. Optimal pollution abatement.

respect to net emissions z and the choice of pollution abatement inputs x^p, L^p, one has at optimum at each point in time:

$$\left. \begin{array}{l} U_z + pF_z = v \\ - vz_x^p = p \\ - vz_L^p = w \end{array} \right\} \quad (6.15)$$

where $U_z, F_z < 0$, $z_x^p = \partial z^p / \partial x^p > 0$, and $z_L^p = \partial z^p / \partial L^p > 0$. According to the first line in (6.15), the multiplier v expresses the sum of the household's marginal disutility from emissions, plus its impact on profits as measured by the value of the marginal product lost due to emissions. In evaluating pollution abatement measures, v shows up as a revenue, i.e. with a minus in front of it, as in Figure 6.3. At optimum, $-v$ is equal to the marginal control cost MC_z. Inputs used up in pollution control are valued at market prices. Moreover, if efficient, the pollution abatement sector employs a factor in such a quantity that the value of the factor's marginal product equals its price.

In the appendix, corresponding results for a *stock pollutant* are derived. Assuming that both households and firms are hurt not by the flow of emissions *per se*, but by the stock accumulated over time, v (equal to μ_3 in the appendix) is interpreted as the present value of all future losses to households and firms if the stock of pollutants increases by one unit. In principle, $U_z + pF_z$ in (6.15) is now multiplied by $1/(a + r)$ where the parameter a reflects the environment's assimilative capacity: the higher a is, the more emissions the environment can take care of on its own. It is also straightforward to add recycling of a harmful residual to the model. Recycling reduces the flow of the residual, and slows down the growth of the stock of the pollutant/residual. The reader is referred to Baumol and Oates (1988) and Forsund and Strom (1988), for example, for further discussion.

The reader should note that the dynamic model used here generates cost-benefit rules which are indeed very similar to those derived previously in this book. Along the optimal programme or trajectory the social profitability of the small projects considered previously would be zero, as can be seen from equations (6.15). There is also a close connection between these rules and a net welfare measure (NWM) which, following Hartwick (1990), can be obtained by making a linear approximation of the instantaneous utility function and using the current-value Hamiltonian (6.14):

$$NWM = px^d + px^p + p\dot{K}$$
$$- px^p + U_z z$$
$$+ U_R R + \mu_2 \dot{R} - wL$$

where the appropriate necessary conditions for an interior solution have been used; see the appendix for details. The first three terms on the right-hand side of this expression correspond to the conventionally measured closed economy net national product: private consumption plus public consumption plus net (of depreciation) investment.[3] The next two lines contain the corrections necessary in order to arrive at a net welfare measure. Public sector consumption is deducted since household valuation of public sector activities (pollution treatment in this simple model) is covered by the term $U_z z$. Similarly, household valuation of resource stocks and changes in these stocks must be included. This would also be true for stocks of pollutants if such were included in the model; see the appendix. Note, however, that changes in stocks, and not changes in values of stocks (capital gains or losses) are what matter. Note also that if R is a non-renewable resource, then $\dot{R}$ equals minus the harvest, highlighting the fact that losses of resources explicitly enter the augmented net welfare measure for the closed economy model used in this section.

The harvest of the natural resource does not enter the expression directly. The reason is that the flow service produced by the natural resource is used as an input in the production of finished goods, and hence shows up indirectly in the value of such goods. For a similar reason, firms' valuation of pollution abatement measures is implicitly included in the value of finished goods, and double counting would result if this valuation was included separately.

On the other hand, any direct defensive expenditures by households to improve their environment, and any direct consumption of flow services provided by the natural resource – if included in the model – would enter the measure directly.

Finally, wage income is deducted from the net welfare measure. One way to explain this is to note that the disutility of work effort is contained in the household utility function. We thus add commodities/services which contribute positively to household utility, and deduct services which contribute negatively to utility. Also, at the margin, the wage exactly matches the marginal disutility of work effort, showing that working time is valued at ruling market wages.

Turning now to an interpretation of the net welfare measure in terms of sustainable development, it can be shown (see Mäler (1991), Weitzman (1976) and the appendix) that:

$$dNWM/dt = r\dot{K}^{tot} = r(\mu_1\dot{K} + \mu_2\dot{R})$$ (6.16)

Economic development can thus be defined as *sustainable* if it is such that NWM never decreases, i.e. such that (6.16) has a non-negative sign. One can of course broaden the definition of the total stock of capital, K^{tot}, so as to include stocks of other resources, including stocks of pollutants; see, for example, Hartwick (1990), van der Ploeg and Withagen (1991), Tahvonen (1991), and also the appendix.

Equation (6.16) may give the impression that a society can freely reduce some stocks while increasing others and still have a sustainable development. This is a possibility, but definitely not a necessity. One can visualize cases where an environmental asset or an exhaustible resource is necessary in the sense that without it our resource consumption must eventually decline to zero. The reader interested in a detailed analysis of this issue is referred to Dasgupta and Heal (1979, ch.7).

An implication of a non-negative sign in equation (6.16) is that NWM yields the maximum consumption that can be allowed if decreasing future consumption is to be prevented (Mäler, 1991, p. 11). This is an ethical rule one may or may not hold to, depending on one's intergenerational welfare function. Maximizing a 'sum' of discounted utilities, as in (6.10), is a kind of utilitarian approach. This is elaborated upon in the next chapter. Moreover, as pointed out by Solow (1986), it is not self-evident that it is possible or even desirable to follow a constant per capita consumption path in a world characterized by technological progress and population growth.

Finally, let us try to interpret the net welfare measure in terms of cost-benefit rules. Indeed, the net welfare measure looks like a kind of cost-benefit rule. There is, however, a major difference. The net welfare measure aims at measuring society's total welfare, and has primarily been developed in order to improve conventional national accounts. A cost-benefit analysis, on the other hand, is usually used to evaluate a reasonably small change or project; we look at the difference between initial and final net welfare.

Appendix

The indirect utility function in equation (6.1) is obtained in the following way. The household maximizes a well-behaved function:

$$U = U(x_{11}, \ldots, x_{nT}, L_{11}, \ldots, L_{kT}, z_{11}, \ldots, z_{mT}) \qquad (6A.1)$$

subject to:

$$y + \sum_t \gamma^{t-1}(\tilde{w}_t L_t - \tilde{p}_t x_t) = 0 \qquad (6A.2)$$

where $\gamma = 1/(1+r)$, $\tilde{w}_t = [\tilde{w}_{1t}, \ldots, \tilde{w}_{kt}]$ with $w_{it} = \gamma^{t-1}\tilde{w}_{it}$, i.e. $\tilde{w}^t$ is a vector of current wages, L_t is a vector of period t labour supplies, $\tilde{p}_t = [\tilde{p}_{1t}, \ldots, \tilde{p}_{nt}]$ with $p_{it} = \gamma^{t-1}\tilde{p}_{it}$, x_t is a vector of period t demand, and $y = \sum_t \gamma^{t-1}\tilde{y}_t$. This maximization problem can in principle be solved so as to yield the indirect utility function in equation (6.1).

Note that in arriving at instantaneous consumer surplus measures, the utility function is assumed to be of the form:

$$U = \sum_t \gamma^{t-1} U(x_t, L_t, z_t) \qquad (6A.1')$$

where γ is the discount factor.

In order to examine the balance-of-trade issue discussed in section 6.1, let us consider a two-period variation of the model used in sections 6.1 and 6.2. The household budget constraints for periods 1 and 2, respectively, can be written as follows:

$$\left. \begin{array}{l} \Pi_1 + w_1 L_1 - \tau_1 - p_1 x_1^d - p_{1m} x_{1m}^d - s = 0 \\ \Pi_2 + w_2 L_2 - \tau_2 - p_2 x_2^d - p_{2m} x_{2m}^d + s = 0 \end{array} \right\} \quad (6A.3)$$

where $\Pi_t = p_t x_t^s + p_{te} x_{te} - w_t L_t^d$ for $t = 1, 2$, p_t is a vector of present-value prices, x_t^s is the corresponding vector of supplies to the domestic market, p_{te} is the domestic currency present-value price of an exported commodity, x_{te} is the quantity exported in period t, x_t^d is a vector of demands for domestic products, p_{tm} is the domestic currency present-value price of an imported commodity (x_{tm}^d), $\tau_t = p_t x_t^p - w_t L_t^p$, and s denotes (positive or negative) savings in period 1, earning interest of r per cent.

Adding the two lines in (6A.3) one finds that:

$$p(x^s - x^d - x^p) + w(L - L^d - L^p) + \sum_t (p_{te} x_{te} - p_{tm} x_{tm}^d) = 0 \qquad (6A.3')$$

where $p = [p_1, p_2]$ etc. If all 'domestic' markets clear, then the (two-period) balance of payments must also be in equilibrium. This shows in a simple way why no distinction is made in the main text between traded and non-traded goods.

The reader can use equations (6A.3) and (6A.3') to verify that a tariff on imports nets out from our cost-benefit rules. Suppose that the considered project uses an imported input. The tariff revenue is 'thrown back' to the household. The tariff thus appears both as a benefit and a cost, and nets out from the cost-benefit analysis. The relevant shadow price is therefore the domestic market price less the tariff. Note, however, that the exports needed to 'finance' the additional imports crowd out production for domestic consumption (assuming here fixed supplies of factors). If production for domestic uses is taxed at a rate θ, then the domestic price (less the tariff) of imports should be multiplied by $1/(1-\theta)$ in the cost-benefit analysis. This is parallel to the case considered in chapter 5; see in particular the appendix to that chapter.

First-order conditions for an interior solution to the maximization problem (6.8) are:

$$\left.\begin{array}{l} p_t^R - \mu_t = 0 \\ -\mu_t + \mu_{t+1}(f_R + 1) = 0 \end{array}\right\} \quad \forall t, t+1 \qquad (6A.4)$$

where $f_R = \partial f(R)/\partial R$. It can be shown (see, for example, Johansson and Löfgren (1985), that a steady-state optimum requires that $\mu_t = (1+r)\mu_{t+1}$, i.e. that the current resource price is constant over time. Using this condition in (6A.4) reveals that $f_R = r$ at a steady-state optimum. If the resource is a non-renewable one, $f_R = 0$ in (6A.4). An interior solution thus requires that the price increases at a rate $(1+r)$ from one period to another, i.e. that the present-value price is constant over time.

The canonical equations for an interior solution to the maximization problem (6.14) are:

$$\begin{array}{ll} \partial H/\partial x^d & = U_x - p = 0 \\ \partial H/\partial L^d & = pF_L - w = 0 \\ \partial H/\partial h & = pF_h - \mu_2 = 0 \\ \partial H/\partial I & = p - \mu_1 = 0 \\ \partial H/\partial x^p & = -p - vz_x^p = 0 \\ \partial H/\partial L^p & = -w - vz_L^p = 0 \\ \partial H/\partial z & = U_z + pF_z - v = 0 \\ -\partial H/\partial K = \dot{\mu}_1 - r\mu_1 = -pF_k + \delta\mu_1 \\ -\partial H/\partial R = \dot{\mu}_2 - r\mu_2 = -U_R - \mu_2 f_R \\ \partial H/\partial \mu_1 & = \dot{K} \\ \partial H/\partial \mu_2 & = \dot{R} \end{array} \qquad (6A.5)$$

To arrive at the net national welfare measure, we start by noting that along the optimal trajectory, the following must hold for the current-value Hamiltonian in equation (6.14):

$$H(\cdot) = U(\cdot) + \mu_1 \dot{K} + \mu_2 \dot{R} \approx U_x x^d + U_L L + U_R R + U_z z + \mu_1 \dot{K} + \mu_2 \dot{R} \qquad (6A.6)$$

where we have used the fact that all markets must be in equilibrium along the optimal trajectory. In performing the linear approximation of the instantaneous utility function it is assumed that $U(0, ..., 0) = 0$. Using appropriate conditions from (6A.5) one arrives at the net welfare measure in the main text.

Total differentiation of the Hamiltonian in (6.14) with respect to t, using (6A.5) and (6A.6), yields equation (6.16):

$$dH(\cdot)/dt = r(\mu_1 \dot{K} + \mu_2 \dot{R}) = r[H(\cdot) - U(\cdot)] \qquad (6A.6')$$

This is a first-order differential equation whose solution can be interpreted as the interest on the present value at time t of all future utilities. See, for example, Löfgren (1992) for a derivation of this result when there is also (anticipated) technological-progress. The reader is also referred to the seminal paper by Weitzmann (1976), and to Caputo (1990) and La France and Barney (1991).

The model specified by equations (6.14) can easily be adjusted so as to cover stock pollutants. Assume for example that the household is concerned about the stock z^s of a pollutant, whose change/accumulation over time is governed by:

$$\dot{z}^s = \bar{z} - z^p(\cdot) - az^s \tag{6A.7}$$

where a is a depreciation factor reflecting the environment's assimilative capacity. Thus, if we clean up what the environment cannot take care of, the stock of pollutants stays constant over time.

Replacing z by z^s in the household's utility function and the firm's production function, and using equation (6A.7) instead of equation (6.14E), one can solve the model in the same way as before to obtain:

$$\dot{\mu}_3 = -(U_z + pF_z) + (a+r)\mu_3 \tag{6A.8}$$

where μ_3 is the co-state variable associated with (6A.7). Thus, if $\dot{\mu}_3 = 0$ and the solution is 'well-behaved', μ_3 is the 'present value' of the value to households and firms of a once-and-for-all marginal reduction of the stock of pollutants using the environment's ability to assimilate emissions, as reflected by a, plus the market interest rate as discount factor.

In this case $U_z z^s$ and $\mu_3 \dot{z}^s$ would show up in the net welfare measure. Similarly, $\mu_3 \dot{z}^s$ would be included in the welfare change measure (6.16).

7 Valuation and aggregation: intragenerational and intergenerational issues

It is instructive to derive project evaluation rules for single-household economies using a general equilibrium approach. Many important valuation issues are best and most easily understood in such a context. This is why we have focused on single-household economies. Still, real-world economies are populated by many millions of households, some of which gain and some of which lose from any conceivable project. Similarly, some projects may have outcomes that affect those not yet born. Both of these problems have to be faced and somehow solved by anyone who wants to make statements about a project's desirability. This chapter takes a look at both the intragenerational and the intergenerational distribution issues without any pretension whatsoever to treat exhaustively all of the difficult problems involved. Hopefully, however, the chapter may provide some useful insights for applied cost-benefit analysis.

The chapter is structured as follows. Section 7.1 presents the concept of a *social welfare function*. In the subsequent section, the social welfare function is used to derive cost-benefit rules, and there is a focus on the possibility of summing monetary gains and losses across households. Section 7.3 discusses the possibility of interpreting the outcome of a social cost-benefit analysis in terms of the *compensation criteria* suggested by Hicks and Kaldor in the late thirties. The following section presents a couple of suggestions on how to deal with the aggregation issue in applied studies. Sections 7.5–7.7 are devoted to intergenerational aggregation issues. Since the aggregation across generations causes similar problems to aggregation within a generation, the presentation focuses on the choice of social discount rate when a project has long-term consequences. As a by-product these sections also shed some further light on the definitions of sustainable development discussed in the previous chapter. The chapter closes with a discussion on how to deal with altruism in cost-benefit analysis.

7.1 The social welfare function

Consider an economy consisting of H households, each demanding n goods and supplying k factors traded in markets, and demanding an unpriced environmental asset hereafter denoted 'environmental quality'. Each household is assumed to be equipped with a fixed lump-sum income. The indirect utility function of household h is written:

$$V^h = V^h(p,w,y^h,z) \qquad \forall h \qquad (7.1)$$

where V^h is the utility level attained, $p = [p_1, ..., p_n]$ is a vector of prices of private goods, $w = [w_1, ..., w_k]$ is a vector of wage rates, y^h is a lump-sum income including any profit income but less any taxes, and z denotes environmental quality. This function is assumed to have all the appropriate properties discussed in chapters 2 and 3. Since the aggregation problem can most easily be illustrated without introducing distortive taxes, such taxes will not be considered in this chapter. Similarly, the models considered in this and the next few sections are atemporal since the intragenerational problem can be illustrated within such a framework without loss of generality.

Let us now introduce a change or a project which moves the economy from one equilibrium, denoted by a superscript 0, to another equilibrium, denoted by a superscript 1. If the project makes everyone strictly better off, i.e. if:

$$V^h(p^1,w^1,y^{1h},z^1) > V^h(p^0,w^0,y^{0h},z^0) \qquad \forall h \qquad (7.2)$$

then the project is said to pass the (weak) Pareto test. On the other hand, if a project makes everyone worse off, it fails the Pareto test. Unfortunately, most real-world projects produce the following outcome:

$$\left. \begin{array}{ll} V^h(p^1,w^1,y^{1h},z^1) > V^h(p^0,w^0,y^{0h},z^0) & \exists h \in \eta \\ V^h(p^1,w^1,y^{1h},z^1) < V^h(p^0,w^0,y^{0h},z^0) & \exists h \in \eta \end{array} \right\} \qquad (7.3)$$

where η is the set of households. The Pareto criterion cannot handle such mixed outcomes where some gain while others lose from a project.

Thus whenever there is a utility conflict we need more than the Pareto principle in order to be able to rank social states. A complete and consistent ranking of social states is called a *social welfare ordering*, and is much like a household's preference ordering. If the social welfare ordering is continuous, it can be translated into a *social welfare function*. This is simply a function:

$$W = W(V^1, ..., V^H) = W[V^1(p,w,y^1,z), ..., V^H(p,w,y^H,z)] \qquad (7.4)$$

of the utility levels of all individuals such that a higher value is preferred to a lower one.

A priori and as explained in chapter 2, there is not much we can say about the form a social welfare function takes. The form depends on who is 'behind' the function: it may express the views of parliament or the reader's views, for example. In the literature, however, a social welfare function is generally assumed to have four convenient properties. Firstly, it is assumed to satisfy *welfarism*, which means that social welfare depends only on the utility levels of the households, just as in (7.4). Secondly, social welfare is assumed to be increasing with each household's utility level, *ceteris paribus*. The function is thus assumed to satisfy the (strong) *Pareto criterion*, since a *ceteris paribus* increase in the utility of any household increases social welfare. Moreover, if one household is made worse off, then another household must be made better off to maintain the same level of social welfare. Thirdly, the *intensity* of this trade-off is usually assumed to depend on the degree of inequality in society. Social indifference curves, just like the household's indifference curves, are therefore convex to the origin. Fourthly, it is often assumed that it does not matter who enjoys a high or low level of utility. This principle is known as *anonymity*.

In what follows we will assume that there is a well-behaved social welfare function having the properties outlined above. We also assume a sufficient degree of measurability and comparability of utilities, so as to have some freedom in the choice of social welfare function over and above the dictatorship from ordinal utility functions. See chapter 2 for a discussion and illustration of these issues. The next section uses the concept of a social welfare function to illustrate how money measures of utility changes should be aggregated across households.

7.2 Project evaluations

Let us now consider a project that moves the economy from one equilibrium to another equilibrium. We face two fundamental problems in evaluating the social profitability of this project. Firstly, the individual utility changes are unobservable. The way to overcome this problem is to calculate money measures of the individual utility changes. The second problem is to translate these monetary gains or losses into social welfare units, a procedure which requires an assumption about the properties of the social welfare function.

In order to further illustrate these steps, we define the project's impact on social welfare as:

$$\Delta W = W[V^1(p^1,w^1,y^{11},z^1), \ldots, V^H(p^1,w^1,y^{1H},z^1)] \\ - W[V^1(p^0,w^0,y^{01},z^0), \ldots, V^H(p^0,w^0,y^{0H},z^0)] \tag{7.5}$$

where a superscript 0(1) denotes initial (final) level values, implying that the project moves the economy from social state 0 to social state 1.

Next, let us define income-compensated or Hicksian money measures of individual utility changes. Such measures can be calculated for any reference level of utility, but as usual just two measures – the compensating and equivalent variations – will be considered here. These are defined as:

$$V^h(p^1,w^1,y^{1h} - CV^h,z^1) = V^h(p^0,w^0,y^{0h},z^0) \qquad \forall h \qquad (7.6)$$

$$V^h(p^1,w^1,y^{1h},z^1) = V^h(p^0,w^0,y^{0h} + EV^h,z^0) \qquad \forall h \qquad (7.7)$$

where CV^h denotes the compensating variation and EV^h the equivalent variation for household h. The compensating variation is thus an amount of money such that the household remains at its initial utility level following a change in prices, income and environmental quality. The equivalent variation is the amount of money that must be given to (taken from) the household in order to make it as well off as it could be at final prices, income and environmental quality.

Let us for the moment concentrate on the compensating variation measure. Substitution of (7.6) into (7.5) allows us to write the change in social welfare as:

$$\Delta W = W[V^1(p^1,w^1,y^{11},z^1), \ldots, V^H(p^1,w^1,y^{1H},z^1)]$$
$$- W[V^1(p^1,w^1,y^{11} - CV^1,z^1), \ldots, V^H(p^1,w^1,y^{1H} - CV^H,z^1)]$$
$$= \sum_{h=1}^{H} \int_0^{CV^h} W_h V_y^h dCV^h = \sum_{h=1}^{H} (\overline{W_h V_y^h}) CV^h \qquad (7.8)$$

where $W_h = \partial W / \partial V^h$, $V_y^h = \partial V^h / \partial y^h$, and a bar indicates that the intermediate value theorem has been used to find an 'average' value for $W_h V_y^h$ between its initial and final values[1] such that the final line equality in (7.8) is preserved. According to (7.8), for each household we must calculate the product of the average marginal social utility of income of the household, and its compensating variation. The project's impact on social welfare is obtained by summing the resulting amounts across all affected households.

We call the term $W_h V_y^h$ the *marginal social utility of income* of household h since it expresses how social welfare is affected by a marginal increase in the income of household h. It consists of two parts, W_h, which represents the change in social welfare if the utility of household h increases marginally, and V_y^h, which is the marginal utility of income of household h. In a utilitarian society, $W_h = 1$ for all households, so that changes in individual utility are added, while in a Rawlsian society, $W_h = 0$ for all households except the worst-off. It can also be shown that if social welfare is maximized, then the marginal social utility of income must be equal for all households; see equations (2.16). Alternatively, maximize (7.4) with respect to y^h for all h, subject to $\sum y^h = $ constant, i.e. redistribute a, for simplicity, fixed total wealth so as to maximize social welfare.

The problem in relying on money measures when assessing a project's social profitability is that $\sum CV^h > 0$ does not necessarily imply that $\Delta W > 0$. For example, if low income earners lose from the project while high income earners gain from it, social welfare may actually fall even though the aggregate compensating variation is positive. Therefore, unless the initial welfare distribution is optimal, so that the marginal social utility of income is equal across all households, and the project is (infinitesimally) small, the economist must make a value judgement – decide on the 'intermediate' marginal social utility of income to be attached to each affected household – in order to be able to assess the social profitability of a project. As hinted at above, in general this is true even for small projects, i.e. projects that leave all prices in the economy virtually unaffected. The assumption probably most commonly employed by project evaluators is that the marginal social utility of income is constant and equal across households so that the sign of the aggregate monetary measure always equates to the sign of the change in social welfare. However, many economists also seek to supply the decision-maker with a distributional analysis in order to give him an opportunity to impute his own 'welfare weights'.

Turning to the equivalent variation measure, we proceed by substituting (7.7) into (7.5) to obtain an expression for ΔW based on initial prices, incomes and environmental quality:

$$\Delta W = W[V^1(p^0,w^0,y^{01} + EV^1,z^0), \ldots, V^H(p^0,w^0,y^{0H} + EV^H,z^0)]$$
$$- W[V^1(p^0,w^0,y^{01},z^0), \ldots, V^H(p^0,w^0,y^{0H},z^0)]$$
$$= \sum_{h=1}^{H} \int_0^{EV^h} W_h V_y^h dEV^h = \sum_{h=1}^{H} (\overline{W_h V_y^h}) EV^h \tag{7.9}$$

Note that the marginal social utility of income attached to household h in (7.9) need not coincide with the one in (7.8) since utility levels, income, prices and environmental quality differ between the two measures of the change in social welfare. Nevertheless, we face the same problem in using $\sum EV^h$ to draw conclusions about the sign of ΔW as we did above, i.e. some value judgement is needed in transforming from monetary units to social welfare units. That is, to assess the project's impact on social welfare, the equivalent variation of household h must be weighted by $\overline{W_h V_y^h}$ and these weighted amounts must be summed across all households.

It should be emphasized that regardless of whether we base the project evaluation on the compensating variation measure or the equivalent variation one, we end up with the same number ΔW for the project's social profitability, i.e. (7.8) and (7.9) coincide. In general, however, $\sum CV^h \neq \sum EV^h$, which means that the aggregate compensating variation for a project could be positive while the aggregate equivalent variation is negative. In such a case, we need to know $\overline{W_h V_y^h}$ for all h to infer which money measure has the correct sign. However, even if both aggregate money measures have the same sign, say positive, this is no guarantee that the project increases social welfare. Depending on how gains and losses are distributed across households, social welfare could increase or decrease.

7.3 Compensation tests

In order to apply the Pareto criterion, we need only to know whether households are better or worse off following a policy change. Any project which makes everyone better off passes the Pareto test, while any project which makes everyone worse off is rejected by this test. Unfortunately, most real-world projects produce both gainers and losers, and, as noted above, the Pareto criterion cannot handle such mixed outcomes. In such cases, one may instead try to apply the *compensation principle* as a decision criterion. The compensation principle was suggested by Hicks (1939) and Kaldor (1939). Let us consider a project which moves the economy from state A to state B, and assume that some individuals gain from the move while others lose. We assume also that incomes can be costlessly redistributed across individuals. According to the *Kaldor criterion*, a project is desirable if, with the project, it is *hypothetically* possible to redistribute income so that everyone becomes better off than without the project. In other words, gainers should be able to compensate losers – although actual compensation is not required by the compensation criterion. (The *strong* compensation test limits the hypothetical redistribution to a reallocation of the aggregate commodity bundle produced in state A. The *weak* version of the test allows production to adjust in response to changes in prices.) To further illustrate the meaning of this criterion let us consider a proposed project from which one group of individuals gain $2 million and another group of individuals lose $1 million. Clearly then, gainers are hypothetically able to compensate losers, i.e. gainers could pay losers slightly more than $1 million so that all can be better off if the project is undertaken (at least if we ignore the fact that compensation may affect prices in a way that is shown below to complicate the argument). The *Hicks criterion* says that a project, i.e. what can be seen as a move from state A to state B, is desirable if, in state A, it is impossible to redistribute income so that everyone is made as well off as in state B. That is, the losers should not be able to hypothetically bribe the gainers not to make the move from A to B, i.e. to refrain from undertaking the considered project.

Unlike the Pareto principle, the compensation principle does not require the actual payment of compensation. The compensation principle is stated in terms of *potential* compensation rather than actual compensation. If compensation were required there would be no fundamental difference between the compensation principle and the Pareto principle. For example, if gainers from a policy change still remain gainers after having possibly more than compensated losers, the considered policy change clearly represents a Pareto improvement since no one is made worse off and at least one individual is made better off. By considering hypothetical compensation one focuses on the efficiency aspects of the policy change. That is, the policy change is considered desirable if its revenue exceeds its cost so that it is possible to undertake a potential Pareto-improving redistribution. Whether or not redistribution is actually carried out is considered to be an important but separate decision.

A positive aggregate compensating variation is sometimes interpreted as implying that those who gain from a project are able to compensate those who lose from it. If this interpretation is correct, interpersonal utility comparisons of the kind required by a social welfare function may seem avoidable in a cost-benefit analysis; we just check if gainers can compensate losers. In this section we will investigate if the Hicks and Kaldor compensation criteria can provide a solution to the aggregation problem in project evaluations. Scitovsky (1941) and Samuelson (1950) have suggested other compensation criteria, but these will not be considered here, because they seem to be extremely difficult to use in applied research.

The project considered in the previous section passes the Kaldor version of the compensation test if (hypothetically) there exists a redistribution of incomes such that:

$$V^h(p^2,w^2,y^{1h} - C^h,z^1) > V^h(p^0,w^0y^{0h},z^0) \qquad \forall h \qquad (7.10)$$

where (p^2,w^2) is the general equilibrium price vector with compensation, C^h is the positive (or negative) compensation paid by (to) household h, and $\sum C^h = 0$ (ignoring the fact that redistribution may alter aggregate income in society). According to (7.10), the project passes the compensation test if it is possible to redistribute incomes in such a way that everyone is better off with the project than without it. A redistribution of incomes/endowments will generally affect supply of and demand for commodities and hence change equilibrium prices. This is why the price vector (p^1,w^1) does not appear in (7.10); (p^1,w^1) is the equilibrium price vector before – and not after – compensation is undertaken.

Let us now consider the possibility of interpreting a positive sum of individual compensating variations as meaning that, hypothetically, gainers can more than compensate losers. The first problem we face is the fact that the price vector (p^1,w^1) is not a general equilibrium price vector when individuals are held at their initial utility levels as they are in (7.6). In other words, the allocation $(p^1,w^1,y^{11} - CV^1, ..., y^{1H} - CV^H,z^1)$ is not feasible, in general (although there may exist cases in which the allocation is feasible). Secondly, although a positive sum of compensating variations is a necessary condition for the Kaldor test to be passed, it is not in general a *sufficient* condition. Therefore $\sum CV^h > 0$ is no guarantee that compensation is possible. On the other hand, it can be shown that $\sum CV^h \leq 0$ is a sufficient but, in general, not a necesssary condition for the Kaldor test to be failed. If $\sum CV^h \leq 0$, the investigator can thus safely argue that compensation is impossible. These results are derived in Boadway and Bruce (1984). See also Blackorby and Donaldson (1990) for a critical assessment of the CV-measure.

Turning to the Hicks criterion, the project passes this test if those who lose from it hypothetically are unable to 'bribe' those who gain from it not to undertake the project. That is, it should *not* be possible to redistribute initial incomes in such a way that:

$$V^h(p^1,w^1,y^{1h},z^1) \leq V^h(p^i,w^i,y^{0h} + C^{ih},z^0) \qquad \forall h \qquad (7.11)$$

where a superscript i refers to any redistribution scheme and the corresponding equilibrium price vector. If (7.11) holds, the project fails the Hicks compensation test and should not be undertaken, provided one accepts this test as the decision criterion. Nevertheless, in interpreting the aggregate equivalent variation as a variation of the Hicks compensation test, we face the same problems as when using aggregate compensating variation as a proxy for the Kaldor compensation test. The price vector p^0,w^0 used in defining EV^h in (7.7) is not a general equilibrium price vector when individual incomes are $y^{0h} + EV^h$, in general. Thus the allocation $(p^0,w^0,y^{01} + EV^1, ..., y^{0H} + EV^H,z^0)$ is not feasible, in general. Moreover, a positive aggregate equivalent variation is sufficient, but not necessary, for the Hicks criterion to be passed, while a non-positive aggregate equivalent variation is necessary, but not sufficient, for the Hicks criterion to be failed.

We have thus a necessary condition ($\sum CV^h > 0$) for the Kaldor test to be passed and a sufficient condition ($\sum EV^h > 0$) for the Hicks test to be passed. Therefore, if both tests were passed whenever one of them was passed, one could obtain necessary and sufficient conditions for a Pareto improvement by calculating the aggregate compensating and equivalent variations. Unfortunately, it is well known that the two compensation tests may produce contradictory recommendations as well as fail to rank certain projects; see Boadway and Bruce (1984) for details. In addition, Boadway (1974) showed that for heavily distorted economies, $\sum CV^h > 0$ ($\sum EV^h > 0$) is neither necessary nor sufficient for the Kaldor (Hicks) compensation test to be passed.

In closing this section it should be emphasized that acceptance of compensation tests means that one accepts or at least uses a particular value judgement in one's project assessment. This is because compensation is only hypothetical, implying that some will actually lose from the project while others will actually gain. Thus even in the cases where compensation criteria function properly, they provide no escape from the distributional dilemma. This is also true for the approach used in deriving equation (5.10), where each household is held at a prespecified utility level. In this case, a profitable project can be said to pass the Pareto test since none is made worse off by the project and there remains a surplus to be distributed. The problem is just that in distributing this surplus, prices as well as income distribution will change, implying that there is no guarantee that everyone remains a winner from the project. In any case, this approach would simply be a variation of the compensation criteria presented above.

7.4 Pragmatic views on the aggregation problem

If the distribution of welfare in society is optimal, or society has at its disposal means for unlimited and costless redistributions, then monetary gains and losses can be summed across households. In all other cases a weighting procedure is required. Since the weights $(W_h V_y^h)$ are not directly observable, one faces a formidable problem in assessing the social profitability of a project such as a change in environmental quality. Unless one simply gives up, some indirect and approximate approach must be used to obtain information about the weights needed in the aggregation procedure. In what follows, a number of possible approaches are suggested.

In some cases it may be possible to estimate a social welfare function for a particular country. In fact, such attempts have been undertaken. Dantzig *et al.* (1989) and Yunker (1989), for example, have recently estimated social welfare functions for the US economy.

Alternatively, one may choose a particular social welfare function to show how different distributional considerations affect the outcome of a cost-benefit analysis. To illustrate, consider the social welfare function:

$$W = [\sum_h a_h (U^h)^{1-\rho}]/(1-\rho) \qquad (7.12)$$

If $\rho = 0$ and the weights $a_h = 1$ for all h, (7.12) reduces to the utilitarian social welfare function. As $\rho \to 1$ with $a_h = 1$, (7.12) reduces to the Bernoulli–Nash (Cobb–Douglas) social welfare function, while as $\rho \to \infty$ the limiting expression is the Rawlsian social welfare function; see Boadway and Bruce (1984). In this way, one can also use one's monetary measures to show the decision-maker how different distributional assumptions affect the sign of the cost-benefit analysis.

Mäler (1985) has suggested that the choice of compensated money measure should in some cases be influenced by distributional consider-ations. Suppose society initially, i.e. before a reasonably small project is undertaken, is indifferent to small changes in income distribution. Then the equivalent variation measure is the relevant measure. On the other hand, if we believe that the income distribution with the project is such that small changes in income distribution would not affect social welfare, then the cost-benefit analysis of the project should be based on the compensating variation measure. See Mäler (1985) for details.

Yet another possibility is simply to calculate the unweighted sum of gains and losses and complement this figure with a distributional analysis where gains and losses are allocated to different groups, e.g. high income earners, low income earners, people living in depressed areas, etc. See also the Lorenz curve in Figure 2.4.

The final approach suggested here is to discuss the outcome of a cost-benefit analysis in terms of compensation criteria, underlining both the lack of general equivalence between the two concepts, and the fact that compensation is only potential or hypothetical so that some will actually gain while others will actually lose from the project.

7.5 Discounting future generations: an infinite-horizon model

Thus far we have focused on the intragenerational distribution issue. However, sometimes a project or its consequences may also affect future generations. This raises the question of how to handle the intergenerational distribution issue. Unfortunately, there is not much one can say about how to treat future generations in project evaluations. A utilitarian, for example, would simply sum utilities across generations while a Rawlsian would look at the interests of the worst-off generation. The intergenerational distribution issue can thus be cast in much the same terms as the intragenerational distribution issue. For this reason, the analysis will not be repeated here. Instead, this and the next section briefly discuss the choice of social discount rate in projects which may affect several generations.

Let us consider an economy which produces a single composite commodity using homogeneous labour and capital as inputs. The instantaneous production function is assumed to be linearly homogeneous:

$$X = F(K,L) = Lf(k) \tag{7.13}$$

where $k = K/L$ (and $f'(\cdot) = \partial f(\cdot)/\partial k > 0$, $f''(\cdot) < 0$). Doubling the inputs of labour and capital doubles the output when the production function is homogeneous of degree one. One of the most widely used homogeneous production functions is the Cobb–Douglas function.

Next, assume that population (labour force) grows at some rate $l = \dot{L}/L$ over time, where a dot denotes a time derivative. Alternatively, this can be interpreted as labour-augmenting or Harrod-neutral technical progress.

Since output is either consumed or invested to augment future production possibilities, the instantaneous goods market equilibrium condition can be written as:

$$f(k) = x^d + \dot{k} + lk \tag{7.14}$$

where x^d is per capita household demand for goods, and $\dot{k} = (d/dt)(K/L)$ is investment per capita, assuming, for simplicity, that there is no capital depreciation. Multiplying both sides of the equation by L would yield a more familiar condition where supply and demand are expressed as absolute levels, not in per capita terms.

Suppose that society wants to maximize per capita consumption. This is one possible definition of sustainable development, as was discussed in the previous chapter. We would then look for a per capita capital stock in (7.14) such that:

$$dx^d/dk = f'(k) - l = 0 \tag{7.15}$$

where $\dot{k} = 0$ since we seek a steady-state or constant capital stock which sustains the highest possible per capita consumption over time. Equation (7.15) is the *golden rule*: the capital stock should be such that its marginal productivity equals the growth rate of population.

The first possibility for the choice of discount rate in projects affecting several generations is thus the rate of population growth l. One may also interpret l as a measure of labour-augmenting technical progress, but maximizing per capita consumption is a less self-evident goal of society when there is technical progress than in the case of a growing population. See, for example, Solow (1986) for a discussion of this issue.

In any case, society may aim to maximize (per capita) utility rather than (per capita) consumption. Suppose that the social welfare function takes the form:

$$W = \int_0^\infty e^{-\theta t} U(x^d) dt \tag{7.16}$$

where $\theta > 0$ is the marginal rate of time preference or subjective discount rate. Society thus maximizes the discounted sum of utilities: it has a kind of utilitarian welfare function although some utilitarians would surely find discounting future utilities morally objectionable; see, for example, Harrod (1948) and Ramsey (1928) for a discussion of this issue.

Maximizing (7.16) subject to (7.14) yields the following steady-state constraint on the capital stock:

$$f'(k) = \theta + l \tag{7.17}$$

This is the *modified golden rule*: the marginal product of capital should be equal to the sum of the marginal rate of time preference and the growth rate of population. The capital stock, and hence also per capita consumption, is reduced below the golden rule level (since $f'(k)$ is positive but decreasing in k, implying that k must be reduced to raise $f'(k)$ above l.) The impatience reflected in the rate of time preference means that it is not optimal to build up as large a capital stock as that corresponding to the golden rule.

This utility-maximizing society would thus use the sum of the marginal rate of time preference and the growth rate of population to discount new projects. Here we have considered the command optimum – there is a social planner whose aim is to maximize a social welfare function subject to some constraints. However, it can be shown that a decentralized market economy of the kind considered here, in equilibrium, would end up with a market rate of interest r such that $r = \theta + l$. The perfect market economy would thus also satisfy the modified golden rule.

7.6 Overlapping-generations models

In overlapping-generations (OLG) models, households have finite lives, several generations are alive simultaneously, and there are generations yet unborn whose preferences may not be registered in current market transactions. These properties make such models appealing for the analysis of projects which affect several generations. In this section, which draws on Blanchard and Fischer (1989), an OLG model is outlined and some of its implications discussed.

Let us consider a household born in period t and living for two periods. The household works in the first period of life, and saves part of its income to finance second-period retirement consumption. Parents care about their children's welfare by weighting their children's utility in their own utility function. We can therefore write the utility function of the (single-household) generation born at time t as follows:

$$U_t = U(x_{1t}^d) + \gamma U(x_{2t+1}^d) + \tilde{\gamma} U_{t+1} \tag{7.18}$$

where x_{1t}^d is the first-period consumption of the generation born at time t, x_{2t+1}^d is its second-period consumption, $\gamma = (1 + \theta)^{-1}$ is the subjective discount factor used to discount the generation's own utility, and $\tilde{\gamma} = (1 + \tilde{\theta})^{-1} \gtreqless \gamma$ is the discount factor applied to its heirs born at time $t + 1$ (and living for two periods). Solving (7.18) recursively forward reveals that there is an intergenerational link: although each generation only cares about the next generation, it will implicitly care about all future generations. There is a link between the present generation and all future generations, achieved in a more appealing way than in the infinite-horizon household model of the previous section.

The generation born at time t faces the following two budget constraints:

$$\left. \begin{array}{l} w_t + s_t^b - s_t - x_{1t}^d = 0 \\ (1 + r_{t+1})s_t - s_{t+1}^b(1 + l) - x_{2t+1}^d = 0 \end{array} \right\} \quad (7.19)$$

When young, i.e. in the first period, the generation is working, earning an income equal to w_t if working time is normalized to one unit. They also receive bequests s_t^b from their parents. Income is divided between consumption and saving. When retired, i.e. in the second period, the generation splits its savings, inclusive of interest income, between consumption and bequests s_{t+1}^b. We allow for population growth through the parameter l (so that each member of the smaller preceeding generation gave $s_t^b(1 + l)$). Population growth could also be interpreted as growth of renewable resources; see Löfgren (1991) for such an interpretation.

The saving of the young in period t generates the capital stock that is used to produce output in period $t + 1$. The firm's production function is still given by equation (7.13), and the economy is assumed to be competitive in the usual sense. It can be shown (Blanchard and Fischer, 1989) that the market economy will attain a steady-state such that:

$$1 + f'(k) = \tilde{\gamma}(1 + l) = (1 + \tilde{\theta})^{-1}(1 + l) = 1 + r \quad (7.20)$$

This is the modified golden rule. For small values of $\tilde{\theta}$ and l, it holds as an approximation that the optimal per capita capital stock is such that $f'(k) = \tilde{\theta} + l = r$. This solution assumes, however, that bequests are strictly positive. If they are zero in optimum, $f'(k) = r \leq \tilde{\theta} + l$, and the market economy would not necessarily be dynamically efficient. Two-sided altruism, i.e. gifts from parents to children and from children to parents, would not necessarily restore efficiency.

Suppose now that those living today do not care directly about the welfare of future generations, i.e. $\tilde{\gamma} = 0$ in (7.18). Instead, it is the job of a social planner to run the economy so as to maximize a social welfare function over T periods subject to various resource constraints. If this 'Super-Stalin' maximizes a social welfare function similar to the utility function (7.18) with $\tilde{\theta} > 0$, he or she would run the economy according to the modified golden rule. If the planner attributes the same weight to all generations, i.e. sets $\tilde{\theta}$ equal to zero, then the golden rule would apply even though each generation is allowed to discount its own future utility at the rate γ. The rate of population (resource) growth is the appropriate discount rate. If the planner wants to adjust the social welfare function for population growth he or she may want to set $\tilde{\theta} = -l$, ending up with a zero discount rate. Note that these results imply that we cannot generally conclude that the market rate of interest is equal to or smaller than the social discount rate. This only holds as a necessity if the planner respects household weighting $\tilde{\gamma}$ of future generations.

The overlapping-generations model of this section and the infinite-horizon model of the previous section may give the impression that $1/(\tilde{\theta}+l)$ is the appropriate social discount factor for social cost-benefit analysis of projects affecting several generations (with $\tilde{\theta} \gtrless 0$, but noting that it does not make sense to maximize an infinite-horizon model with $\tilde{\theta} \leq 0$ since the sum of utilities goes to infinity, with or without maximization). This is by no means a correct conclusion or impression. Other kinds of models may produce different results, the basic reason being that intergenerational aggregation, just as aggregation of households within a generation, is ultimately a normative issue. In undertaking cost-benefit analysis it is therefore important that the practitioner presents the model underlying his aggregation procedure. Both the decision-maker and others should be able to assess the ethical premises underlying the analysis.

7.7 Future generations, transfers in kind, and impure altruism

A measure undertaken today may have far-reaching consequences in the future, and may possibly mean the extinction of species, including mankind. In this section a very simple model is used to illustrate trade-offs between the interests of present and future generations. The model provides a useful complement to discussions of the meaning of sustainable development and its implications for project evaluations.

Let us assume that the present generation cares about the well-being of future generations, and that there are just two channels through which this can be accomplished. The individual household can transfer monetary wealth or conventional real capital, denoted s, to its heirs. At the aggregate level, society has the means to affect the amounts and quality of environmental assets passed on to future generations. Here this is denoted by resource stocks R. Let us assume that the representative household of the present generation is equipped with a function $u = g(s,R)$ which is increasing in both of its arguments. This function captures the value that is placed on the living standard of future generations. More is preferred to less, while recognizing that there is possibly a trade-off between different kinds of resources transferred to future generations. The indirect utility function of the representative household living today is written as:

$$V = V[p,w,y-s,z,g(s,R)] \tag{7.21}$$

Thus, $u = g(\cdot)$ appears as a separate argument in the indirect utility function of those living today. Suppose that the household is asked for its willingness to pay for a small project which increases future availability of environmental assets without producing any use or non-use benefits to those presently alive. We thus focus on intergenerational issues here. Differentiating (7.21) with respect to R, with the household paying so as to keep its utility constant, yields:

$$- V_y dCV - V_y ds + V_u g_s ds + V_u g_R dR = 0 \qquad (7.22)$$

where $V_u = \partial V/\partial u$, $g_s = \partial g/\partial s$, and $g_R = \partial g/\partial R$. In order to interpret (7.22), two cases will be considered.

A household may want to choose bequests, i.e. s, so as to maximize (7.21). One then finds that $V_y = V_u g_s$, since the household increases bequests s until the marginal utility of income spent today is equal to the marginal utility future generations are believed to derive from further incomes. Inspection of (7.22) immediately reveals that $dCV > 0$ in this case, provided that future generations are believed to place a value on improved environmental quality.

Consider next the case in which the present generation strives to achieve some minimum welfare level $\bar{u}$ for future generations. Given R, which is not controlled by the individual household, it selects a target for its bequests so as to achieve $\bar{u}$. It is easy to verify that $dCV = -ds$, since the two final terms in (7.22) sum to zero. That is, the household responds to the increase in R and a payment dCV by reducing its bequests by the same amount of money (or reports a zero net willingness to pay). This is a kind of Ricardian equivalence result. According to the Ricardian equivalence theorem introduced by Barro (1974), households adjust private saving in response to government budget deficits (negative public sector saving) so as to leave total saving, i.e. private plus public sector, constant. A stronger version of the theorem says that an increase in public sector spending induces households to reduce private consumption by the corresponding amount.

It is possible to interpret the above model in terms of *tied* transfers (or transfers in kind). If the transfer is given in cash, the donors may fear that future generations will consume too much and devote too little resources to the preservation of environmental resources. The present generation may therefore have an incentive to give the transfer in the form of environmental resources, i.e. tying the transfer. The reader is referred to Bruce and Waldman (1991) for a recent analysis of this so-called Samaritan's dilemma, which indicates that it may be both efficient and non-paternalistic to tie transfers.

Recently, there has been a growing interest in *impure altruism*; see Andreoni (1989, 1990), Kopp (1991), Quiggin (1989) and Rosenthal and Nelson (1991), for example. In terms of the model in equation (7.21), the concept of impure altruism can be explained as follows. First of all, let us now interpret s^h as (individual h's) voluntary contribution to the preservation of environmental resources for the benefit of future generations. Society's total contribution is denoted $R = R_\tau + \sum_h s^h$, where R_τ is the share contributed collectively through tax payments. Given the Nash assumption (see sections 11.2 and 11.3), individual h treats all other individuals' contributions as fixed when choosing s^h so as to maximize (the new version of) equation (7.21). A pure altruist derives satisfaction from the size of R, without deriving any satisfaction *per se* from his own contribution. A pure altruist is thus a person for whom g_R in equation (7.22) is strictly positive while g_s is equal to zero. An impure altruist, on the other hand, derives utility also from his own charity, i.e. both g_s and g_R are strictly positive for such a person. Finally, a pure egoist is defined as a person for whom g_s is strictly positive, while g_R is equal to zero. (We may take a super-egoist to be a person for whom both derivatives are equal to zero.) It is left to the reader to work through equation (7.22) for these different types of personalities.

A cost-benefit analysis of a project involving 'transfers' to future generations must try to take account of the distribution of people across different types of personalities. Otherwise, the outcome of the analysis will be misleading, as can easily be checked by working through equation (7.22). The idea of impure altruism also casts some doubt on the type of classification of values presented in section 3.4. At present there are some studies under way in which the concept of impure altruism is tested empirically, but to the best of my knowledge no results are yet available.

The model used in this section does not claim to come close to giving a realistic picture of real-world choice problems. Nevertheless, it produces a number of useful insights. Firstly, it illustrates the fact that the only way to recognize the interests of future generations is through the current generation. The real interests of future generations are unknown to us living today. The best we can do is to have some vague idea of, or possibly a function capturing, what resources and values contribute to the welfare of those coming after us. Secondly, depending on what we think is important to future generations, the function $g(\cdot)$ may take different forms. A number of examples were given above, but there are obviously other forms, as well as assumptions on the properties of the function(s), generating conclusions different from those drawn above. Thirdly, the model highlights the fact that there is a dependency between what is done today and what happens in the future, and that a particular policy or development chosen today need not be sustainable.

7.8 On the treatment of altruism in cost-benefit analysis

In the previous section we discussed some implications of altruism for cost-benefit analysis. In this section we will return to the social welfare maximization problem analysed in section 2.5, but now include altruism in the household indirect utility functions. There is an important reason for undertaking this exercise. It has recently been argued that the altruistic component should *not* be included in a social cost-benefit analysis; see Bergstrom (1982) and Milgrom (1992), for example. This casts doubt on the many empirical willingness-to-pay studies where altruistic motives, including existence values, amount to a considerable part of the total willingness to pay.

Let us assume that a household cares about the well-being of other households, and that society consists of only two households. This latter simplification means no loss of generality but will save us from notational clutter. The indirect utility function of household h is now written as follows:

$$V^h = V^h[p,w,y^h,z^h,V^j(p,w,y^j,z^j)] \tag{7.23}$$

where $h,j = 1,2$ and $h \neq j$. According to (7.23) household h cares about the overall well-being of the other household.

Next, let us define a social welfare function:

$$W = W[V^1(\cdot),V^2(\cdot)] \tag{7.24}$$

Using (7.23) in (7.24) provides us with the tool we need to analyse the role of altruism in cost-benefit analysis.

Maximizing social welfare subject to equations (2.12′) and (2.12″) yields first-order conditions for an interior solution, assuming such a solution exists, that are very similar to those stated in equations (2.16). For this reason we concentrate on the optimal provision of the public good. The optimal provision of z will satisfy:

$$\sum_h (a^h V_z^h / a^h V_y^h)dz = dC^p \tag{7.25}$$

where $a^h = [W_h + W_j(\partial V^j/\partial V^h)]$ for $h, j = 1, 2$ with $h \neq j$, W_h is the marginal welfare weight attributed to household h, a^h is interpreted as the marginal welfare society derives from a small increase in household h's utility when household j cares about the well-being of household h, V_z^h is the marginal utility derived from own consumption of the public good, here called use values, and V_y^h is the marginal utility of own income. Since a^h shows up in both the denominator and the numerator of (7.25), it nets out from the expression. Equation (7.25) therefore looks identical to the last line of equations (2.16). The perhaps surprising interpretation is that the inclusion of altruism in the utility function does not change the optimality condition as such: the same terms show up in (7.25) as in (2.16). Adding to (7.25) a separate estimate of the willingness to pay due to altruistic motives would therefore mean a kind of double-counting. The reader is invited to check that this conclusion holds also if there is one group of altruists (possibly interpreted as the present generation) and one group of egoists (possibly interpreted as representing future generations, who have no reason to care about our interests).

Several assumptions are needed in order to arrive at this conclusion. In particular, it is assumed that altruistic households are non-paternalistic in the sense that they respect the preferences of others. In other words, the utility function of household j is an argument in the utility function of household h. On the other hand, if household h only cares about the utility that household j derives from the public good, its indirect utility function will look as follows:

$$V^h = V^h(p,w,y^h,z^h,z^j) \qquad (7.23')$$

Using (7.23') in (7.24) and repeating the maximization procedure, equation (7.25) would look as follows:

$$\sum_h (1/W_h V^h_y)[W_h V^h_z + W_j(\partial V^j/\partial z^h)]dz = dC^p \qquad (7.25')$$

In this latter case, the marginal willingness to pay for the public good includes an egoistic part and an altruistic part. Note that the expression can be rearranged so that $\partial V^j/\partial z^h$ is replaced by household h's altruistic concerns, $\partial V^h/\partial z^j$, yielding the more appealing decomposition of (7.25') into household h's willingness to pay for use values and altruistic values, respectively. Equation (7.25') yields an upper bound for the project's social profitability in the sense that altruism is devoted exclusively to the project under investigation.

To further interpret these results, it is useful to consider a marginal or small project. Let us assume that both households are equipped with utility functions of the kind specified in equation (7.23). The change in social welfare caused by small *ceteris paribus* changes in τ and z can be summarized as follows:

$$dW = \sum_h W_h[V^h_z dz - V^h_y d\tau^h + (\partial V^h/\partial V^j)(V^j_z dz - V^j_y d\tau^j)] \qquad (7.26)$$

where the terms within parentheses reflect altruistic motives for household h's valuation of the project. If we are at a social welfare optimum and $\sum_h d\tau^h = dC^p$, equation (7.26) reduces to equation (7.25). From (7.26) it should be clear why altruistic values tend to vanish from the cost-benefit rule: a non-paternalistic household values both benefits *and* costs of other households. Basically, we just scale up benefits and costs by the factor $(1 + \partial V^h/\partial V^j)$. In any case, it can easily be verified that the expression within brackets in (7.26) is equal to household h's compensating variation, dCV^h, for the project multiplied by its marginal utility of own income, V^h_y. In other words, a willingness-to-pay question allowing households to pay for both use values and altruistic values will provide us with a correct dataset for the cost-benefit analysis: households correctly account for benefits and costs accruing to themselves and others. Alternatively, one can ignore altruistic components completely and estimate only use values, at least if one is prepared to assume that we are reasonably close to a social welfare optimum.

If the analysis is based on the utility functions (7.23'), then $(\partial V^h / \partial V^j)(V_z^j dz)$ is replaced by $(\partial V^h / \partial z^j) dz$ in (7.26). Equation (7.26) then reduces to (7.25') if we are at a social welfare optimum and the change in taxes just balances the marginal cost of producing the public good. In this case, we must ask respondents about their total willingness to pay, since use values underestimate the project's benefits.

We have thus identified two polar cases with respect to the treatment of altruistic motives when assessing small projects. Let us now discuss how to proceed when using the contingent valuation method to assess a non-marginal project. In general, we can proceed as usual and allow households to include an altruistic element in their answers to a WTP question. To illustrate, suppose a respondent equipped with the utility function (7.23) is asked to pay for a project changing y^h and z^h from y^{0h}, z^{0h} to y^{1h}, z^{1h}. The willingness to pay for this project, taking the compensating variation as our money measure, is defined as:

$$V^h[p,w,y^{1h} - CV^h, z^{1h}, V^j(p,w,y^{1j},z^{1j})] = V^h[p,w,y^{0h},z^{0h}, V^j(p,w,y^{0j},z^{0j})] \tag{7.27}$$

where CV^h denotes the compensating variation of household h, and any change in prices and wages is suppressed in order to avoid clutter. Next, using the social welfare function (7.24) to define the change in social welfare, and proceeding in the same way as in equations (7.5) to (7.8), one arrives at a social welfare change measure which contains the same terms as the expression for ΔW in equation (7.8). This holds also if we consider a move from one social welfare optimum to another, due to a change in the public sector's production function, for example. Alternatively, one may collect data on the willingness to pay for use values, assuming that one can factor out a^h as in (7.25) also for a large project.

Suppose next that the indirect utility function of household j is replaced by z^j in equation (7.27). It can easily be verified that the expression for ΔW once again will contain the same terms as (7.8). We have thus established the following result. Whether household h cares about the overall utility of household j or is paternalistic in the sense that it cares only about household j's consumption of the public good need not affect the design of a willingness-to-pay question which is used to undertake a cost-benefit analysis. That is, in both cases considered, we can ask households about their total willingness to pay for the project. In the aggregate, we will arrive at the correct benefits measure. Note, however, that the absolute magnitude of benefits may differ, depending on whether we use (7.23) or (7.23') as the basis for a cost-benefit analysis.

Still, there are cases in which it may be difficult to move from individual willingnesses to pay to aggregate money measures. The basic problem is that we can make many different assumptions about the way in which household h perceives how the project changes the utility of household j. To illustrate, what assumption does household h make about household j's contribution to the project? Is household j's utility kept at its initial level in (7.23) or does the household just contribute with a payment τ^j, as we assumed above? There is also the ethical question of what the social welfare function looks like. To illustrate, take a society consisting of a group of strongly altruistic persons and a group of egoists. A social welfare function adding utilities, for example, devotes a greater weight to the egoists than to the altruists. This is not a completely uncontroversial way of viewing social welfare.

These questions illustrate two important claims. Firstly, it is extremely important to derive a set of cost-benefit rules for the project that one wants to evaluate. Secondly, in a contingent valuation study, it is important to specify in detail the way a respondent should view other households, for example how much others are assumed to contribute to the project. It is also recommended that the investigator collects data on both the willingness to pay for use values and the total willingness to pay. The former data provide us with a kind of lower bound for the project's social profitability. We can then add an estimate of benefits (and possibly costs) due to altruistic concerns, and thereby motivate a consideration of why and how they should enter the analysis. This provides the decision-maker with an opportunity to judge the project's profitability with and without benefits (and costs) due to altruistic values. Moreover, it must be extremely difficult for a household to evaluate the complex changes implicit in (7.26) or (7.27), for example. Estimates of use values, which can be obtained using methods based on actual or hypothetical behaviour (see chapter 4), are probably more reliable. This provides another reason for collecting data on use values. An empirical study illustrating this discussion is presented in section 10.3.

8 Cost-benefit rules in a risky world

In general, cost-benefit rules are derived under the assumption that there is no uncertainty. In order to handle uncertainty, the cost-benefit practitioner usually performs a sensitivity analysis. To illustrate, suppose the analysis is based on an oil price of $20 per barrel, and that the investigator considers it extremely unlikely that the price will fall below $15 or rise above $30. Then the project is re-evaluated using these alternative oil prices. This is, however, a primitive way of handling risk and uncertainty. In particular, it implies that no distinction is made between evaluation uncertainty and project uncertainty. Evaluation uncertainty refers here to the fact that owing to poor data quality, missing data, etc., the investigator may be uncertain about the project's effects even if there is no underlying uncertainty. Project uncertainty or risk, on the other hand, refers to stochastic incomes, prices, environmental quality, etc. This chapter concentrates on project risk and derives cost-benefit rules that can be used to assess environmental changes of which the consequences are not known in advance. The chapter turns directly to project assessments but for convenient reference the appendix contains definitions of risk attitudes and similar concepts. An empirical study based on the money measures defined in this chapter is presented in section 10.3.

The chapter is structured as follows. The first section presents a simple atemporal framework for the analysis of risk. Households face an uncertain supply or quality of an environmental asset, but prices and incomes are known with certainty. A willingness-to-pay locus is introduced illustrating the fact that there is possibly an infinite number of money measures of utility change in a risky world. The question thus arises as to what money measure to use in a cost-benefit analysis of a project of which the consequences are uncertain. This question is addressed in section 8.1. Section 8.2 introduces the concept of option value, a concept which has received considerable attention in environmental economics, and is supposed sometimes to simplify cost-benefit analysis in a risky world. In section 8.3 time is introduced and a simple two-period model is presented. The model is used to derive cost-benefit rules in section 8.4. Finally, section 8.5 is devoted to a further discussion of some important issues in project evaluations in a risky world.

In this chapter we focus on the expected utility approach to the modelling of behaviour under uncertainty, or rather risk (since probabilities are assumed to be knowable). The reader interested in other approaches, as well as discussions of the choice of money measure in a risky world, is referred to Arrow (1971), Arrow and Kurz (1970), Arrow and Lind (1970), Dobbs (1991), Hammond (1981), Kahneman and Tversky (1979), Karni and Schmeidler (1991), Loomes et al. (1992), Lund and Oksendal (1991), Machina (1987), Milne and Shefrin (1987) and Ulph (1982), just to mention a few.

8.1 Uncertain supply or quality of an environmental asset

In this section, the analysis of the value of an environmental asset is extended to the case of a risky world. In the option-value literature, analyses are usually based on static models, as opposed to intertemporal models. In order to simplify the analysis, we will follow this tradition in this and the next section. The (Neumann–Morgenstern) household is assumed to consume an unpriced environmental asset z and a composite private priced good which serves as the numéraire. The smooth indirect utility function of the household is written as $V(y, z^i)$. In order to simplify the exposition, we will consider a finite probability space, i.e. assume that z takes on values in a finite set. There is a probability distribution assigning probabilities $\pi^1, \ldots, \pi^n$ to the points $z^1, \ldots, z^n$, with $\pi^i \geq 0$ for $i = 1, \ldots, n$, and $\sum_i \pi^i = 1$. The analysis is restricted to uncertainty with regard to z, but the model is easily extended to cover income uncertainty and/or state-dependent preferences, i.e. demand-side uncertainty. The reader interested in such analysis is referred to Freeman (1985), Graham (1981), and Schmalensee (1972). In what follows we thus consider the case where the supply or quality of the environmental asset is uncertain; the probability that supply/quality is z^i is π^i for $i = 1, \ldots, n$.

Expected utility of the household is defined as:

$$V^E = E[V(y, z^i)] = \sum_{i=1}^{n} \pi^i V(y, z^i) \tag{8.1}$$

where E is the expectation operator, and $\sum \pi^i = 1$. Expected utility is simply a weighted average of the utility levels attained in different states of the world, using the probabilities π^i as weights.

Let us now consider a stochastic change in environmental quality z from

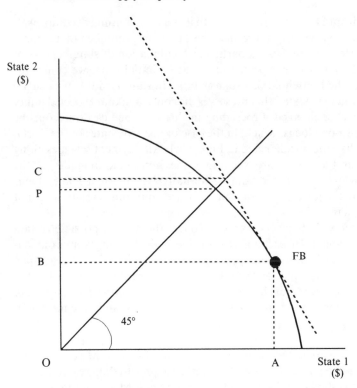

Figure 8.1. A willingness-to-pay locus.

$\tilde{z}^i$ to $z^i = \tilde{z}^i + \Delta z^i$, where Δz^i denotes the state i change ($i = 1,...,n$). The probability that state i occurs is denoted π^i. We can then, following Graham (1981), define a willingness-to-pay function associated with the stochastic change in environmental quality by the relationship:

$$E[V^h(y^h - S^{ih}, z^i)] = E[V^h(y^h, \tilde{z}^{ih})] \qquad \forall h \qquad (8.2)$$

where a superscript h refers to household h, S^{ih} is the payment collected from household h in state i, and the expectation is taken with respect to the distribution of environmental quality. According to (8.2), society collects state-dependent or independent amounts of money such that each household stays at its initial level of expected utility following the change in environmental quality. To illustrate, the maximal uniform or state-independent payment that can be collected from the household whose (two-states case) willingness-to-pay locus is depicted in Figure 8.1 is given by the intersection of the 45° line and the WTP locus. This 'contract' is often referred to as option price in environmental economics, but following

Finkelshtain and Kella (1991) we refer to it as a non-contingent compensating variation. Obviously there may be an infinite number of payment schemes since, starting from a particular combination of state-dependent payments S^i that leaves expected utility at its initial level, we could, for example, let the household pay slightly more in state 1 and then calculate the new payment in state 2 that preserves the constraint that expected utility should be left unchanged. Proceeding in this way, one can trace out the willingness-to-pay locus, which, in the case of just two states of the world, could look like the one depicted in Figure 8.1. All payment schemes along the locus in the figure are such that the household remains at the prespecified level of expected utility. Alternatively, one could define a locus based on the equivalent variation measure, but this variation is not performed here.

Suppose now that society wants to collect the highest possible certain aggregate payment S in exchange for a project which changes environmental quality.[1] Each household pays according to the willingness-to-pay function defined by equation (8.2). In order to proceed further, the kind of risk that society faces must be specified. If risk is fully *insurable*, the certain aggregate payment S is maximized subject to (8.2) for all households and:

$$S = \sum_h \{E[S^{ih}]\} = \sum_h \{\sum_i \pi^i S^{ih}\} \tag{8.3}$$

where $E[\cdot]$ is the expected payment by household h, and the sum of these expected payments across households must equal the aggregate certain payment. It is shown in the appendix that the first-order conditions of the aforementioned maximization problem imply that the marginal utility of income of a household is equalized across all states of the world. Note that the government acts as insurer here: there are no existing markets which households can use to insure themselves against the risk associated with the change in environmental quality. Moreover, according to (8.3), the government uses the probability that state i is experienced as the price of a monetary claim in state i, which, by the way, is true for an actuarially fair insurance system.

In order to illustrate this approach, it is useful to consider Figure 8.1. Suppose that households are alike, but that $\pi^1 H$ households experience state 1 and $(1 - \pi^1)H$ households experience state 2. Now let us consider alternative payment combinations with the same aggregate expected value. This is like looking at a budget line with slope equal to $-\pi^1/\pi^2$. Moreover, the further away from the origin the line is located, the higher the expected value ('income') it represents. The dotted line in Figure 8.1 is such a 'budget line'. By collecting $OA from each of those π^1 per cent of households which experience state 1, and $OB from each of those π^2 per cent who experience state 2, society can collect a certain payment corresponding to $H\cdot OC$ in the figure. In fact, this is the maximum certain aggregate payment the society can collect, since shifting the dotted line further outwards would mean that households are unable to remain at the initial level of expected utility. Shifting the line inwards would yield a smaller aggregate revenue than $H \cdot OC$. The optimum at FB in the figure is known as the 'fair bet' in the literature on insurance. At this point, the marginal utility of income of any household is equal in all (both) states of the world:

$$V_y^h(y^h - S^{*ih}, z^i) = V_y^h(y^h - S^{*jh}, z^j) \qquad \forall i,j,h \qquad (8.4)$$

where a subscript y refers to a partial derivative with respect to income, and i (j) refers to state i (j). The optimal payment scheme is thus such that the marginal utility of income is equalized across all states of the world. In terms of Figure 8.1, $S^{*1} = OA$, and $S^{*2} = OB$.

If markets for contingent monetary claims are available, the government could either collect money according to equation (8.4), or simply collect state-independent amounts from each household. In terms of Figure 8.1, if the government collects the state-independent amount \$OC, the household would reallocate its income across states so as to fulfil equation (8.4). If markets for contingent claims are not available to households, the maximum uniform payment the government can collect is \$OP in Figure 8.1. However, by allowing households to pay less in some states of the world and more in others, the government can obtain a higher certain aggregate payment than $H \cdot OP$ since $H \cdot OC > H \cdot OP$. The question arises, however, of what it would cost the government to design and collect payments so as to achieve equation (8.4) for all possible states of the world and all households. In any case, such costs should be a part of the cost-benefit analysis of the considered project. These transaction costs may or may not be so high that collecting state-independent amounts would yield a higher net revenue.

Turning to *collective* risk, the government maximizes the certain aggregate payment S subject to equations (8.2) and the constraint that the aggregate payment should be one and the same, regardless of what state of the world is actually realized:

$$S = \sum_h S^{ih} \qquad \forall i \qquad (8.5)$$

Recall that all households experience the same state when risk is collective. Obviously, collecting state-independent payments from each household would satisfy the constraint (8.5), since $S^{ih} = OP^h$ for all i. However, the government may do better than this. In the appendix it is shown that an 'interior' solution to the considered maximization problem requires that:

$$\pi^i V_y^h(y^h - \tilde{S}^{ih}, z^i) / \pi^j V_y^h(y^h - \tilde{S}^{jh}, z^j) = \mu^i / \mu^j \qquad \forall i,j,h \qquad (8.6)$$

where μ^i is the Lagrange multiplier associated with the state i version of equation (8.5), and $\tilde{S}^{jh}$ is the payment collected from household h if state j occurs. According to (8.6), payments should be such that the marginal rate

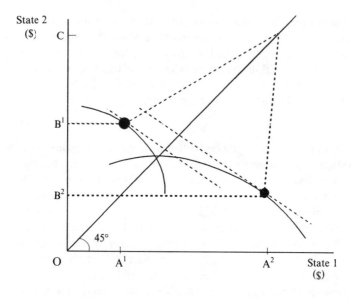

Figure 8.2. Willingness-to-pay loci for two households.

of substitution between any two states of the world is equalized across all households.[2] This is illustrated in Figure 8.2, where WTP loci for two households are drawn and the dotted tangents have slope $-\mu^1/\mu^2$. Collecting $OA^1 from household 1 and $OA^2 from household 2 if state 1 is experienced, and $OB^1 and $OB^2 respectively if state 2 is experienced, yields the highest possible certain aggregate payment ($OC in the figure). Using a ruler, the reader can easily verify that collecting state-independent payments from the households produces a smaller aggregate payment than $OC. However, if households are identical, the only way to satisfy both equations (8.5) and (8.6) is by setting $\tilde{S}^{ih} = \tilde{S}^{jh} = OP^h$ for all states i and j. The non-contingent compensating variation is thus the relevant money measure if risk is collective and individuals are identical. The reader should also note that designing complicated individual payment schemes or contracts according to equations (8.5) and (8.6) when individuals differ may be a difficult and expensive task. Therefore it is not self-evident that the sum of individual compensating variations is a second-best money measure in a world consisting of many different kinds of households.

The apparatus developed here can also be used to derive an aggregate willingness-to-pay locus. This can be achieved by maximizing:

$$\sum_h S^{ih} \tag{8.7}$$

subject to equations (8.2), and:

$$\bar{S}^j = \sum_h S^{jh} \qquad\qquad \forall j \neq i \qquad (8.7')$$

where $\bar{S}^j$ is a fixed sum of money collected if state j occurs. The first-order conditions for an interior solution to this maximization problem can be stated as follows:

$$\pi^i V_y^h(y^h - S^{ih}, z^i)/\pi^j V_y^h(y^h - S^{jh}, z^j) = p_i/p_j \qquad \forall i,j,h \qquad (8.8)$$

where p_j is the Lagrange multiplier associated with the state j version of equation (8.7'), and $p_i = 1$. This procedure identifies a point on the aggregate willingness-to-pay locus. Repeating the procedure for other S^j-values would identify other points on the locus. If project costs, whether certain or not, fall inside the aggregate locus, it is in principle possible to collect enough money to cover costs in each possible state of the world. The important point to make, however, is that individual non-contingent payments and the fair bets are just two special cases when one is trying to design money measures in a risky world.

8.2 Option value

In a seminal paper Weisbrod (1964) argued that an individual who was unsure of whether he would visit, say, a national park would be willing to pay a sum in excess of the *expected consumer surplus* to ensure that the park would be available:

To see why, the reader need recognize the existence of people who anticipate purchasing the commodity (visiting the park) at some time in the future, but who, in fact, never will purchase (visit) it. Nevertheless, if these consumers behave as 'economic men' they will be willing to pay something for the option to consume the commodity in the future. This 'option value' should influence the decision of whether or not to close the park and turn it to an alternative use. (Weisbrod, 1964, p. 472.)

One would thus expect the difference between the non-contingent willingness to pay (option price) and expected consumer surplus, called 'option value', to be positive. Furthermore, if the option value is positive, one would know that the expected consumer surplus was an underestimate of the gains from preserving a national park, for example. This would greatly simplify cost-benefit analysis in cases where an expected consumer surplus measure, but not the non-contingent money measure or option value, is available. This is so at least if the costs fall short of the expected benefits.

In what follows, we will concentrate on what Bishop (1982) calls supply-side option value. Bishop considered the case in which uncertainty pertains to the environment or to the supply side. The household will demand the good, such as a visit to a natural park, at its current price, but is uncertain about whether the park will be available. Generally speaking, the literature on supply-side option value compares a situation where the supply of the asset is stabilized at some level $\bar{z}$ to a situation where supply is $\bar{z}$ with probability π and zero with probability $1 - \pi$. Supply-side option value is defined as the difference between the non-contingent willingness to pay (option price) and expected consumer surplus. These concepts will be defined below.

In order for supply-side option value to be a useful concept, it seems reasonable to require at least that both the non-contingent willingness to pay and expected consumer surplus are sign-preserving measures of the underlying change in expected utility. Indeed, this requirement is fulfilled in the case considered by Bishop. In cases involving more general probability distributions, however, expected consumer surplus measures may fail to provide a correct ranking of choices. In many potentially important cases it may therefore simply not make sense to define and estimate the expected consumer surplus. Moreover, in such cases it is rather difficult to supply a meaningful interpretation of supply-side option value; recall that this value is defined as the difference between the non-contingent WTP and expected consumer surplus.

In order to prove the above claims, consider a household which consumes an environmental asset or public good z and a composite good which serves as the numéraire. Suppose there is an opportunity to stabilize the supply of the environmental asset at some level $\bar{z}$. This level is assumed to be no higher than the highest level attained in the stochastic case. For example, there is perhaps a positive probability that z, the population of waterfowl say, takes an extremely high value. A priori, there seems to be no reason to believe that 'supply' is always stabilized at this highest attainable level, although this is the case generally considered in the literature on supply-side option value.

The expected gain in moving from a stochastic z to $\bar{z}$ can be written as:

$$\Delta V^E = V(y,\bar{z}) - \mathrm{E}[V(y,z^i)] \tag{8.9}$$

where the expectation is taken with respect to the distribution of z.

We will consider two different money measures of the utility change in (8.9), namely a non-contingent payment and expected consumer surplus. Consider first the non-contingent payment. This is a state-independent payment, denoted CV, which makes the household indifferent between having z stabilized or not:

$$V(y - CV, \bar{z}) = \mathrm{E}[V(y,z^i)] \tag{8.10}$$

This expression defines the non-contingent compensating variation. Alternatively, one can base the definition on the equivalent variation measure. In any case, substitution of (8.10) into (8.9) yields:

$$\Delta V^E = V(y,\bar{z}) - V(y - CV,\bar{z}) \tag{8.11}$$

i.e. the sign of the change in expected utility is equal to the sign of the non-contingent compensating variation. CV is thus a sign-preserving money measure of utility change.

In order to arrive at the expected consumer surplus measure, one has to define the compensating variation in state i if the supply of the environmental asset is stabilized:

$$V(y - CV^i,\bar{z}) = V(y,\bar{z}) - V_y^i \cdot CV^i = V(y,z^i) \tag{8.12}$$

where the intermediate value theorem is applied to obtain the first equality, i.e. the derivative $V_y^i = \partial V(\bar{y}^i,\bar{z})/\partial y$ in the middle expression is evaluated at some intermediate point $\bar{y}^i, \bar{y}^i \in (y, y - CV^i)$. The compensating variation CV^i is the amount of income that must be taken from/given to the household in order to leave it as well off 'consuming' $\bar{z}$ units as consuming z^i units of the asset.

Substitution of (8.12) into (8.9), using the fact that the expected value of the product of two random variables is equal to the sum of the product of their expected values plus their covariance, yields:

$$\Delta V^E = E[V_y^i \cdot CV^i] = \{E[CV^i] + \text{cov}[V_y^i \cdot CV^i]/E[V_y^i]\}E[V_y^i] \tag{8.13}$$

where $E[CV^i]$ is the expected compensating variation. The reader is referred to Shiryayev (1984) for details on the kind of decomposition undertaken in (8.13).

From (8.13) it can be shown that there are two cases in which the expected compensating variation is necessarily a sign-preserving measure, i.e. $\text{sgn}E[CV^i] = \text{sgn}\Delta V^E$. First, if $\bar{z} \geq z^i$ for all i, obviously it must be the case that $\Delta V^E \geq 0$, $CV^i \geq 0$, and $E[CV^i] \geq 0$. This is the case generally considered in the literature on supply-side option value. The second case occurs when the covariance term in (8.13) is equal to zero. This arises if risk is insurable so that households are able to redistribute income y freely across states of nature so as to even out the marginal utility of income V_y^i. It is then simply a uniform or state-independent constant, implying that the covariance term in (8.13) vanishes. This is also true if the utility function is quasi-linear so that the marginal utility of income is independent of z and y.

In general, however, the expected consumer surplus measure is defined conditional on the initial distribution of income across states of the world, e.g. uniform across states as above. The expected compensating variation measure defined in equation (8.13) therefore need not have the same sign as the underlying change in expected utility. To prove this we need only consider the case in which z is stabilized at such a level that $\Delta V^E = 0$ in (8.13). $E[CV^i]$ cannot then be a sign-preserving measure unless the covariance term is equal to zero.

Thus, unless the supply of the resource is stabilized at the highest attainable level, one cannot know for sure that a project which produces a positive expected consumer surplus is worthwhile. Recall that the detailed properties of the underlying utility function are in general unknown. This property of $E[CV^i]$ also makes it rather difficult to apply simple economic intuition in the interpretation of option value, OV, since option value is defined as:

$$OV = CV - E[CV^i] \tag{8.14}$$

Option value is simply a residual, whose sign may be positive or negative regardless of household attitudes towards risk and the sign of the underlying change in expected utility. We must therefore conclude that the expected consumer surplus measure, i.e. expected compensating variation, expected equivalent variation, and expected measures based on ordinary or Marshallian demand concepts, as well as the concept of option value, must be used with great care in cost-benefit analysis.

8.3 A simple intertemporal extension

Thus far we have considered an atemporal model. This means that many of the problems one faces in real-world applications of cost-benefit analysis have been ignored. In this section we introduce an intertemporal extension of the model. Although simple in nature, it will enable us to shed some light on important issues such as the choice of money measure and discount rate in project evaluations.

In order to analyse the intertemporal utility maximization problem in a risky world, Bellman's (1957) technique of backwards induction is used. As this name suggests, the household works backwards. The household decides an optimal strategy in the final period, say T. In the light of this strategy, the household then selects the optimal strategy in period $T-1$, and so on. In what follows we will consider a simple two-period version of this technique, where period 1 is interpreted as 'today' and period 2 as the uncertain future. For a full and modern treatment of recursive methods, the reader is referred to Stokey and Lucas (1987).

Assume that the household has arrived at the final, i.e. second, period. The household's problem is to maximize:

$$U(x_2, z_2^i) \tag{8.15}$$

subject to the budget constraint:

$$\tilde{y}_2 + s(1+r) - \tilde{p}_2 x_2 = 0 \qquad (8.16)$$

where s is the amount of money saved in period 1 and carried over to period 2, r is the risk-free rate of interest, x_2 is a vector of private goods consumed in period 2, $p_2 = \tilde{p}_2/(1+r)$ is the corresponding transposed vector of present-value prices, and $y_2 = \tilde{y}_2/(1+r)$ is the present value of the income received in period 2. Since period 2 is the final period, it makes no sense to save for future periods, implying that current plus saved income is consumed in period 2. The formulation of the maximization problem (8.15) subject to (8.16) implies that decisions are assumed to be taken *after* uncertainty about the supply/quality of the environmental asset is resolved. Thus, when maximizing second-period utility, the household knows that the stochastic variable z_2 happened to take on value z_2^i.

However, as viewed from period 1, z_2 is a stochastic variable, and, as in section 8.1, we take the state space to be finite. The expected maximum value of future utility, as viewed from today, can thus be written as:

$$V_2(s) = E\{U[x_2(p_2, y_2 + s, z_2), z_2]\} \qquad (8.17)$$

where the expectation is taken with respect to the distribution of z_2, the maximization problem (8.15) and (8.16) has been solved to obtain the usual demand functions for private goods, and these functions are used in (8.17). As viewed from today, future demands for goods are stochastic. They depend, among other things, on the as yet unknown value of the supply/quality of the environmental asset. Thus, as shown in Figure 8.3, the position of a demand curve generally depends on the value of z_2.

The problem of the household in period 1 is to choose a bundle of goods and a level of saving so as to maximize expected utility over both periods:

$$V^E = U(x_1, z_1^i) + \beta V_2(s) \qquad (8.18)$$

subject to:

$$y_1 - p_1 x_1 - s = 0 \qquad (8.19)$$

where a subscript 1 refers to first-period levels, and β is the household's discount factor. The utility function is assumed to be separable to ensure that instantaneous preferences exist.

It can be shown (see the appendix) that the expected maximum utility as viewed from today can be written as:

$$V^E = U[x_1(p, y_1, y_2, z_1^i, \bar{z}, \phi), z_1^i] + \beta E\{U[x_2(p, y_1, y_2, z_1^i, \bar{z}, \phi, z), z]\} \quad (8.20)$$

where $p = [p_1, p_2]$, $z = z_2$, $\bar{z} = E[z_2]$, and ϕ contains moments about the mean characterizing the stochastic properties of z_2. The reader interested in

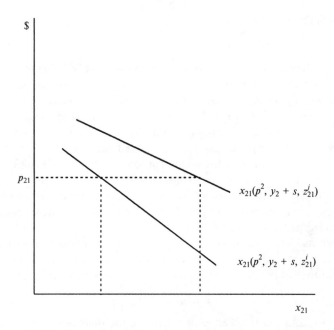

Figure 8.3. The future demand for a commodity depends on the stochastic variable z.

calculating the partial derivatives of V^E with respect to prices and income is referred to equations (8A.14). Note that first-period demands for private goods are non-stochastic, since they depend on the non-stochastic properties of the uncertain quality of the environmental asset, i.e. the mean $\bar{z}$ and moments ϕ about the mean. Future demands, on the other hand, are stochastic as viewed from today since they are functions of, among other things, the (currently) unknown value z will take on in period 2.

The model examined above does not allow for uncertainty in future income and prices. Let us outline such a generalization for the case of an infinite number of outcomes. Let the triple (Ω, B, μ) be a probability space, where B is a Borel algebra of subsets of the uncountable state space Ω, and μ is a probability measure defined on B; see Shiryayev (1984). The probability measure gives the probability assigned to each possible future state of the world. We assume that future income, environmental quality and prices are bounded away from zero and bounded from above.

The maximization problem (8.18)–(8.19) of the household can then be formulated in the following way:

$$\max_{\{x_1, s\}} \{ U(x_1, z_1^j) + \int_\Omega \beta V[p_2(\omega), y_2(\omega) + s, z(\omega)] d\mu(\omega) \} \qquad (8.18')$$

where $\omega \in \Omega$, and, as before, it is assumed that second-period consumption is chosen after uncertainty is revealed. We will not work through the model here, but Epstein (1975) provides a detailed analysis of a similar model, the main difference being that there is no environmental quality indicator in Epstein's model. In any case, the model outlined here illustrates the fact that we can easily generalize the model in equation (8.20) so as to cover 'demand' side uncertainty as well as an infinite number of outcomes or states of the world.

8.4 Assessing changes in future environmental quality

The expected intertemporal indirect utility function derived in the preceding section can be used to define a willingness-to-pay locus. Once again there may be an infinite number of contracts corresponding to a change in (future) environmental quality. The derivation of this locus is similar to the one in section 8.1 and is therefore not undertaken here; the reader is invited to use equation (8.20) to define payment schemes holding the household at its initial level of expected utility following a change in z_2. Instead we will concentrate here on the evaluation of a small project, and in addition proceed as if there is only one household in the economy under consideration. Let us consider an investment in period 1 that changes period 2 environmental quality and is possibly associated with operations costs in period 2. The project is assumed to be small, implying that z_2^i changes to $z_2^i + dz_2^i$ for all possible states i of the world. The project's outcome is stochastic as viewed from today, but uncertainty is revealed at the beginning of the second period. The question arises as to which of the money measures derived in section 8.1 we should employ. In this section we use the (marginal) non-contingent compensating variation, but the choice of money measure is discussed further in the next section.

Using equation (8.20) and the results derived in the appendix (see equations (8A.12) and (8A.13)), the cost-benefit rule for the considered project is simply:

$$dCV = - dI + \beta \{E[U_z \cdot dz]/V_y^E\} - dC_2 \qquad (8.21)$$

where dCV is the present value of a uniform or state-independent second-period payment (or compensation) such that expected utility remains constant following the change in costs and environmental quality, $dz = dz_2$, $dI = - dy_1$ is the first-period investment undertaken to improve environmental quality, dC_2 is the present value of any (certain) second-period operation costs, V_y^E is the present value of the expected second-period marginal utility of income, and U_z is the stochastic period 2 marginal utility of environmental quality.

The compensating variation in equation (8.21) is defined as the present value of the maximum future amount of money the household is willing to pay over and above the investment cost and any operations costs in exchange for a small but uncertain improvement in environmental quality. Alternatively, one could define a gross compensating variation by simply adding the present value of costs to dCV, as will be further illustrated below. If $dCV < 0$ in (8.21), the household needs compensation to be indifferent to the project. The non-contingent compensating variation can thus be viewed as the household's answer to the following question:

> Suppose the government undertakes a small project whose aim is to improve environmental quality in period 2. The project's outcome is uncertain. The outcome will be dz^i with probability π^i for $i = 1,...,n$. You will have to make a contribution to the project of $\$dI$ this period and $\$dC_2$ in period 2. What is the most you are willing to pay in period 2 (or the minimal compensation you need) over and above the costs of this project? The payment/compensation will be the same regardless of what value z happens to take on in period 2.

A few comments on equation (8.21) are in order. Firstly, the household is assumed to make the contribution dCV in period 2. However, equation (8.21) would look the same if the household paid in period 1. The present value of the expected second-period marginal utility of income in (8.21) is replaced by 'today's' marginal utility of income, but these two coincide at the optimum, as can be seen from equations (8A.14). The current value of the payment made 'today' and the present value of the future payment, i.e. dCV, must therefore also coincide for (8.21) to continue to hold. Secondly, the discount rate used in (8.21) to discount dCV and dC_2 is the market rate of interest. If there are several assets, one of which provides risk-free interest, it is this *risk-free* discount rate which should be used in (8.21). See Drèze and Modigliani (1972, pp. 318–19) for such a model. Including a risk premium in the discount factor would mean a double-counting of risk, since the money measure dCV reflects the household's attitude towards risk. See Starrett (1988) for a discussion of this issue.

Equation (8.21) can easily be extended to an arbitrary number of periods. To illustrate, let us consider a period 1 investment which changes environmental quality in a marginal but seemingly stochastic way in periods $2,...,T$. Because of the assumption that households can freely transfer incomes between periods, it does not matter whether they are requested to make once-and-for-all contributions to the project or annual payments. One way to present the cost-benefit rule for a single-household economy is as follows:

$$NPV = -I_1 + \sum_{t=2}^{T} \gamma^{t-1}(\tilde{B}_t - \tilde{C}_t) = dCV \qquad (8.22)$$

where NPV is the project's net present value, I_1 is the first-period investment, $\gamma = 1/(1+r)$ is the discount factor, $\tilde{B}_t$ is period t gross monetary current-value benefits, $\tilde{C}_t$, is period t current-value costs associated with the considered project, and dCV is the period 1 maximal once-and-for-all state-independent payment the household is willing to make to the project over and above the project's costs (minimal compensation needed to be indifferent to the project). Setting aside income-distributional issues, in a multi-household economy the project's social profitability is obtained by calculating equation (8.22) for each affected household and summing across all households. A positive aggregate net present value means that the project is socially profitable, while a negative aggregate NPV indicates that the project should not be undertaken. Equation (8.22) illustrates that the cost-benefit rule can be presented in different ways depending on what information is available. If households are asked to make once-and-for-all payments net of costs to the project, an estimate of dCV in (8.22) is appropriate; if they are asked to make annual contributions net of costs, $(\tilde{B}_t - \tilde{C}_t)$ is appropriate; while if they are asked for their period t gross willingness to pay, $\tilde{B}_t$ is appropriate: in terms of (8.21), $\tilde{B}$ is simply equal to $\beta E[U_z dz](1+r)/V_y^E$.

The way one presents the cost-benefit analysis is primarily a function of what information is available, and does not *per se* affect the project's social profitability, as the final equality in (8.22) illustrates. However, if households face borrowing constraints in the capital market, and are unable to freely transfer income between periods, the payment scheme will matter. In such cases, the maximal once-and-for-all payment a household is willing to make is smaller (or at least not larger) than the maximal present value obtained if the household is allowed to spread its contributions to the project across many periods; see section 6.1 for details.

8.5 Some further notes on cost-benefit rules in a risky world

In the previous section, cost-benefit rules for the evaluation of a small project were derived. In this section we will consider some important issues left out thus far. These issues include contingent versus non-contingent money measures in the evaluation of small projects, and the treatment of profit incomes and uncertain project costs. We will consider these in turn.

In section 8.4, the cost-benefit rule was based on a non-contingent payment. Let us now introduce the more general formula underlying equation (8.21). Expressed in units of utility a payment scheme can be written as follows:

$$E[V_y dS] = E[V_y]E[dS] + \text{cov}[V_y, dS] \tag{8.23}$$

where $dS = [dS^1, \dots, dS^n]$ is a contract specifying how much to pay in different states of the world, $E[V_y] = V_y^E$ and cov $[\cdot]$ denotes the covariance between the marginal utility of income and the payments made in different states. Equation (8.23) says that the expected value of the product of two stochastic variables is equal to the product of their expected values plus their covariance.

In a few cases the covariance term in (8.23) vanishes. If the contract is such that the household makes a state-independent payment, $dS = dS^1 = \dots = dS^n = dCV$, then cov$[\cdot] = 0$ since dS is a constant. This is the case considered in section 8.4. If the household is allowed to redistribute income across states of the world, it will do so until the marginal utility of income is equal across all states; this may also be achieved by the government as was shown in section 8.1. In this case too, cov$[\cdot] = 0$ in (8.23), since V_y is a constant, and the non-contingent payment dCV can once again be used to assess a small project. It is possible to design other forms of contract, though this seems unduly complicated and also opens up the possibility of moral hazard.

Equation (8.23) can be used to illustrate the danger in using the expected compensating variation (and option value) to assess even small projects. Suppose that the household pays dS^i if state i occurs, and that dS^i is such that the household remains at its initial level of expected utility following a change in z_2 from z_2^i to $z_2^i + dz_2^i$ for all i. We thus put $dS^i = dCV^i$ for all i in the first term on the right-hand side of equation (8.23). It can then be seen that there is no guarantee that the expected compensating variation $E[dS] = \sum_i \pi^i dCV^i$ has the same sign as $E[V_y dS]/E[V_y]$. The problem is that the covariance term may be of such a sign and magnitude that the sign of the change in expected utility, as reflected by $E[V_y dS]/E[V_y]$, is opposite to the sign of the expected compensating variation. The exception occurs when the marginal utility of income V_y for one reason or another is state-independent so that the covariance term vanishes. The expected consumer surplus measure, regardless of whether it is based on the compensating or the equivalent variation concept, must thus be used with great care also in evaluations of small projects.

It has thus far been assumed that firms are unaffected by the considered environmental project. Consider now a marginal but stochastic change in environmental quality and denote the resulting change in state i profits $d\Pi^i$. The corresponding change in expected profits is $E[d\Pi]$ as calculated from equation (5.4) with ∂z replaced by ∂z^i and any changes in prices suppressed (or netted out as in equation (5.7)). The question is whether we can simply add this change in expected profits to equation (8.21). The answer would be affirmative if there was no uncertainty, as a glance at equation (5.7) reveals. The problem under uncertainty is that the marginal utility of income of the household(s) owning the firm varies across states of the world, in general. This means that the kind of decomposition performed in equation (8.23) is relevant. In other words, we must add the following expression to the right-hand side of equation (8.21):

$$E[V_y d\Pi]/V_y^E = d\Pi^E + \text{cov}[V_y, d\Pi]/V_y^E \qquad (8.24)$$

where $d\Pi^E = E[d\Pi]$.

Equation (8.24) illustrates the fact that we cannot simply add changes in *expected* profits to our cost-benefit rule in (8.21). This result can be explained as follows. A risk-averse household is not indifferent to the distribution of income changes across states of the world. In fact, it prefers a certain income $d\Pi$ to an uncertain one with expected value $d\Pi$; see the appendix for details. The covariance term reflects this risk aversion (or risk loving in the case of a risk lover). For example, for a project which yields high incomes in states where the marginal utility of income is high and vice versa, $\text{cov}[\cdot]$ is positive. This means that the project works like an insurance in the sense that it evens out income (the marginal utility of income) across states of the world. This property is valued positively by a risk-averse household. For a risk-neutral household, on the other hand, V_y is a constant, implying that the covariance term in equation (8.24) vanishes so that (8.24) reduces to the result stated in the Arrow–Lind (1970) theorem. Note, however, that if information is collected on dCV for a profits-augmented version of equation (8.21), we do not have to worry about how to calculate changes in profits. These are covered by dCV. The problems appear if we have to estimate changes in profits separately. Then we must calculate equation (8.24), and add the complete left-hand side or right-hand side of (8.24) to our cost-benefit rule in (8.21).

Similar problems are present if project costs and/or taxes are state-dependent. In principle, we must estimate equations similar to (8.24), i.e. it is not sufficient in general to look at expected costs (taxes). Alternatively, one may ask households to evaluate the complete set of consequences of the project. That is, ask a willingness-to-pay question similar to the one stated below equation (8.21). A third approach would be to check if the net willingness to pay, i.e. after costs are covered, is positive for all possible states of the world. The project is recommended if this is the case; see also section 8.1. Finally, the reader should note that there are no irreversibilities in the models analysed in this chapter. In section 9.7 we will modify the set of cost-benefit rules so as to cover irreversibilities as well as learning behaviour.

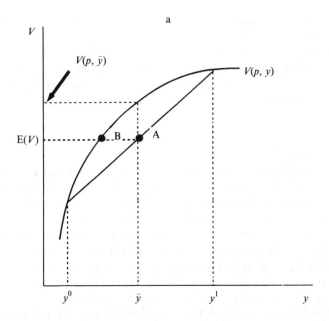

Figure 8A.1. Attitudes to risk: (a) risk-averse; (b) risk-loving; (c) risk-neutral.

Appendix A

In order to illustrate the meaning of risk attitudes, it is useful to consider a household which faces an uncertain income. Taking partial derivatives with respect to income of a well-behaved indirect utility function $V(p,y)$ of the form considered in previous chapters (suppressing here z) yields:

$$\left.\begin{aligned} \frac{\partial V}{\partial y} &= V_y(p,y) \\ \frac{\partial^2 V}{\partial y^2} &= \frac{\partial V_y}{\partial y} = V_{yy} \end{aligned}\right\} \tag{8A.1}$$

A household is said to be risk-averse with respect to income risk if $V_{yy} < 0$. Conversely, the household is a risk lover if $V_{yy} > 0$, and risk-neutral if the expression is equal to zero. Let us consider a Friedman–Savage (1948) diagram such as Figure 8A.1, in which utility is depicted as an increasing function of income while all prices are held constant.

Figure 8A.1a is drawn on the assumption that $V_{yy} < 0$. Assume that the household receives income y^0 with a probability of one-half, and income y^1 with a probability of one-half. Since the actual outcome is either y^0 or y^1, the expected utility is:

$$E[V] = 0.5 \ V(p,y^0) + 0.5 \ V(p,y^1) \tag{8A.2}$$

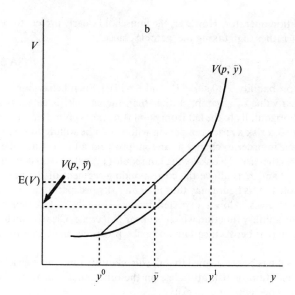

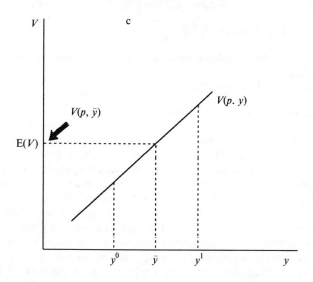

where E is the expectation operator. However, the household clearly prefers to get the expected income $\bar{y}$ rather than taking the 'gamble', since:

$$V(p,\bar{y}) > E[V] = \sum_i \pi^i V(p,y^i)$$ (8A.3)

where y^i occurs with probability π^i $(0 < \pi^i < 1)$, and $\bar{y} = E[y^i]$. Such behaviour, i.e. preferring the expected value of a gamble rather than the gamble, is called risk aversion. By moving horizontally to the left from point A towards point B in Figure 8A.1a it can be seen that a risk averter is a person who would be willing to forego some part of his income in order to change a random prospect into a certain one.

Figure 8A.1b pictures the case of a risk-loving household ($V_{yy} > 0$). In this case the straight line between y^0 and y^1 is above the corresponding segment of the utility function. The household in this figure may thus prefer a risky prospect to a certain one even if the former gives a lower expected income. Finally, a risk-neutral household ($V_{yy} = 0$) has a utility function which is linear in income. Clearly, such a household will be indifferent between certain and risky prospects, as is seen from Figure 8A.1c.

In previous chapters it has been assumed that the direct utility function is strictly quasi-concave. The definition of risk attitudes, on the other hand, turns on the stronger assumption of concavity or convexity.

A function is quasi-concave for all commodity bundles x^0, x^1 over a region if:

$$U[\pi x^0 + (1-\pi)x^1] \geq \min \{U(x^0), U(x^1)\}$$ (8A.4)

for all $0 \leq \pi \leq 1$. The function is strictly quasi-concave if the strict inequality holds for $0 < \pi < 1$.

A function is concave over a region if:

$$U[\pi x^0 + (1-\pi)x^1] \geq \pi U(x^0) + (1-\pi)U(x^1)$$ (8A.5)

for all $0 \leq \pi \leq 1$, and strictly concave if the strict inequality holds for all $0 < \pi < 1$. By reversing the sign of the inequalities in (8A.4) and (8A.5) we obtain definitions of quasi-convexity and convexity respectively. Referring back to Figure 8A.1, it should be obvious that the measures of risk attitudes are founded on the concept of concavity/convexity, i.e. $V[p,E(y)] \gtrless E[V(p,y)]$ when the indirect utility function is strictly concave (convex) in income, a theorem often referred to as Jensen's inequality. Moreover, Hanoch (1977) has shown that risk aversion with respect to income implies, and is implied by, risk aversion with regard to quantity bundles. Hence, $V_{yy} < 0$ means that the direct utility function is strictly concave.

Measures of risk aversion are defined cardinally, whereas conventional demand theory assumes an ordinal utility function. Ordinal measurability means that if a function $U(x)$ is a suitable representation of the household's preference orderings, any other increasing function or monotonic transformation of $U(x)$, say $F(x) = f[U(x)]$ with $\partial f/\partial U > 0$, will serve equally well. The signs of the first derivatives of an ordinal function are unchanged by a monotonic transformation, but signs of higher-order derivatives (the sign of V_{yy}, for example) can change since no restriction can be placed upon $\partial^2 f/\partial U^2$.

If the utility function is weakly cardinal, any positive affine transformation of the function, say $G(x) = a + bU(x)$ with $b > 0$, will serve equally well. Preferences are strongly cardinal if, in addition to being weakly cardinal, the ratio of two magnitudes of preference differences is also a meaningful magnitude of preference. The assumption of strongly cardinal preferences means that it is meaningful to say that $[U(x^1) - U(x^0)]/[U(x^3) - U(x^2)] = r$ means that a move from x^0 to x^1 is r times preferable to the move from x^2 to x^3 (see Morey (1984) for details). Furthermore, note that the signs of the partial derivatives of any order, and hence the sign of V_{yy}, are unchanged by any positive affine transformation. In both the cardinal and ordinal cases, the transformations leave the indifference map unchanged.

The magnitude of the second-order derivative V_{yy}, which was used as the risk indicator above, is not invariant under a linear transformation. This is readily verified by multiplying the (cardinal) utility function by a constant and taking the second-order derivative with respect to income. For this reason V_{yy} is not normally used as a measure of risk aversion. The best-known measure, the Arrow–Pratt coefficient of *absolute* risk aversion, is obtained by normalizing by V_y, and reversing the sign:

$$R(y) = -\left(\frac{\partial^2 V}{\partial y^2}\right) \Big/ \left(\frac{\partial V}{\partial y}\right) = -V_{yy}/V_y \qquad (8A.6)$$

Multiplying by income y yields the so-called Arrow–Pratt index of *relative* risk aversion:

$$R^R(y) = -yV_{yy}/V_y \qquad (8A.6')$$

In a cardinal world, the signs of the partial derivatives of these measures with respect to income tell us whether risk aversion is increasing or decreasing when income is increased (see Arrow (1971), Hey (1979, 1981) and Pratt (1964)).

Similarly, one can define risk aversion with respect to environmental risks. Reintroducing the argument z in the indirect utility function, one obtains:

$$\left. \begin{array}{l} R(z) = -V_{zz}/V_z \\ R^R(z) = -zV_{zz}/V_z \end{array} \right\} \qquad (8A.6'')$$

where $V_{zz} = \partial^2 V(p,y,z)/\partial z^2$. Thus, for a household which has risk aversion with respect to environmental risk, the absolute and relative risk aversion measures (8A.6'') have positive signs. A household which is neutral with respect to environmental risks would report $R(z) = R^R(z) = 0$.

Appendix B

To obtain the maximum aggregate sure payment in section 8.1, one maximizes S subject to equations (8.2) and (8.3). This yields:

$$\left. \begin{array}{l} 1 = \mu \\ \lambda^h \pi^i V_y^h = \mu \pi^i \qquad \forall i,h \end{array} \right\} \qquad (8A.7)$$

where μ and λ^h are the Lagrange multipliers associated with equations (8.3) and (8.2) respectively. The second-line equality in (8A.7) is obtained by taking the partial derivative with respect to S^{ih} and setting the resulting expression equal to zero. Using (8A.7) one arrives at equation (8.4).

Maximizing S subject to (8.2) and (8.5), assuming an 'interior' solution is possible, yields:

$$\left.\begin{array}{l} 1 = \sum_{i=1}^{n} \mu^i \\[2mm] \lambda^h \pi^i V_y^h = \mu^i \qquad \forall i,h \end{array}\right\} \quad (8A.8)$$

where μ^i is the Lagrange multiplier associated with the state i version of equation (8.5). Equation (8.6) follows directly from equation (8A.8).

The household in section 8.3 maximizes (8.18) subject to (8.19). Substituting (8.17) into (8.18), first-order conditions for an interior solution are:

$$\left.\begin{array}{l} u_x - \lambda p_1 = 0 \\ -\lambda + \beta E[U_x \cdot x_y^2] = 0 \\ y_1 - s - p_1 x_1 = 0 \end{array}\right\} \quad (8A.9)$$

where $u_x = \partial U(x_1, z_1^i)/\partial x_1$, $U_x = \partial U[x_2(\cdot), z]/\partial x_2$, $x_y^2 = \partial x_2(\cdot)/\partial y_2$, and λ is a Lagrange multiplier associated with the period 1 budget constraint. Note that the second-period optimal demands x_2 depend on first-period saving, a fact which explains the final term in the middle-row expression.

Assume that equations (8A.9) can be solved to yield:

$$\begin{bmatrix} dx_1 \\ ds \\ d\lambda \end{bmatrix} = A^{-1} \begin{bmatrix} -u_{xz} dz_1^i + \lambda dp_1 \\ \beta E[\lambda_p^2 dp_2 + \lambda_y^2 dy_2 + \lambda_z^2 dz] \\ -dy_1 + x_1 dp_1 \end{bmatrix} \quad (8A.10)$$

where A ($\neq 0$) is the determinant, and $\lambda_2 = \lambda_2(p_2, y_2 + s, z_y^i) = U_x \cdot x_y^2$ from second-period utility maximization so that λ_2 is the Lagrange multiplier associated with the maximization problem in equations (8.15) and (8.16). The Lagrange multipliers λ and $E[\lambda_2]$ are interpreted as the marginal utility of first-period income, and the expected second-period marginal utility of income respectively.

The properties of the initial distribution affect behaviour. To see this, it is useful to undertake a Taylor expansion of λ_z^2 around $E[z_2] = \bar{z}$ to obtain:

$$\lambda_z^2(p_2, y_2 + s, z_2^i) = \lambda_z^2(p_2, y_2 + s, \bar{z}) + \lambda_{zz}^2(z_2^i - \bar{z}) + \tfrac{1}{2}\lambda_{zzz}^2(z_2^i - \bar{z})^2 + \tfrac{1}{6}\lambda_{zzzz}^2(z_2^i - \bar{z})^3 + R \quad (8A.11)$$

where R represents higher-order terms, whose sum is assumed to be finite, all the derivatives involved in (8A.11) are assumed to exist and be finite, and the fact that saving s may change as z changes has been suppressed. Taking expectations of (8A.11) it can be seen that:

$$\left.\begin{array}{l} E(z_2^i - \bar{z}) = 0 \\ E(z_2^i - \bar{z})^2 = \text{var}(z_2^i) = \phi_1 \\ E(z_2^i - \bar{z})^3 = \text{skewness}(z_2^i) = \phi_2 \end{array}\right\} \quad (8A.11')$$

Equations (8A.10)–(8A.11') explain that $x_1 = x_1(p, y_1, y_2, z_1^i, \bar{z}, \phi)$ (and $s = s(p, y_1, y_2, z_1^i, \bar{z}, \phi)$) in equation (8.11). The discount factor β has been suppressed in these equations so as to simplify notation.

To arrive at equation (8.21), one differentiates equation (8.20) to obtain:

$$dV^E = u_x \cdot x_y dy_1 + \beta E[U_x(x_y^2 dy_1 + x_y^2 dy_2 + x_z^2 dz) + U_z dz] = 0 \qquad (8A.12)$$

where $u_x \cdot x_y dy_1 = \lambda p_1 x_y dy_1 = \lambda(dy_1 - ds)$ from the first-period budget constraint, and dy_2 is chosen so as to maintain expected utility at its initial level. Proceeding in this way, but now using the second-period budget constraint, the terms within parentheses in (8A.12) times U_x can be shown to equal $\lambda_2(dy_2 + ds)$. Noting that $\beta E[U_x x_y^2] = \beta E[\lambda_2] = \lambda$, and setting $dy_1 = -dI$ and $dy_2 = -dCV - dC^2$, one obtains:

$$dV^E = -\lambda dI - \lambda ds + \beta E[\lambda_2]ds + \beta E[U_z dz] - \beta E[\lambda_2](dCV + dC_2) = 0 \qquad (8A.13)$$

Dividing by $\beta E[\lambda_2] = V_y^E$, one obtains equation (8.21).

Finally, the following properties of the function V^E defined by equation (8.20) can be verified by invoking the first-order conditions (8A.9):

$$\left. \begin{array}{l} dV^E/dp_i^1 = -\lambda x_{i1} \\ dV^E/dy_1 = -\lambda \\ dV^E/dp_i^2 = -E[\lambda_2 x_{i2}] \\ dV^E/dy_2 = E[\lambda_2] \end{array} \right\} \qquad (8A.14)$$

where a subscript i refers to commodity i. Note that both λ_2 and x_{i2} are stochastic as viewed from today owing to the influence of the stochastic variable z_2, while the corresponding first-period entities are functions of the expected future level of z (and higher moments about the mean) and hence non-stochastic. This can be seen from equation (8.21).

9 Valuing changes in access conditions, health risks and information

Thus far, the value of an environmental asset has been considered in the context of a stochastic availability or quality. Frequently, however, one would expect a policy to affect the probability of a particular event without necessarily ensuring a certain outcome. For example, there is no guarantee that a programme aiming at the preservation of an endangered species will be successful. Rather, it is expected to increase the probability of survival of the species in question. Similarly, pollution of the air and the water changes the probability that people are stricken with illness.

This chapter concentrates on a discussion of money measures that can be used to assess the value of changes in probability distributions (access conditions). Section 9.1 defines the concept of access value and money measures that can be used to capture access value in applied studies. Sections 9.2 and 9.3 are devoted to money measures of changes in human health, and ultimately the value of life, while section 9.4 presents an empirical study valuing health effects due to air pollution. The chapter then turns to a discussion of the value of information, when some consequences of a project may be irreversible. As noted by Pindyck (1991, p. 1110), the ability to delay an irreversible investment expenditure invalidates the net present value rule as it is usually taught to students in business school: invest in a project when the present value of its expected cash flows is at least as large as its cost. The concept of quasi-option value is defined. The chapter then turns to a discussion of the choice of policy in an intertemporal context, highlighting the fact that an optimal policy may be time-inconsistent, while switching policy over time, though it may be time-consistent, creates the problem of credibility. The final section of the chapter discusses the optimal size of a pollution treatment plant when there is an irreversible constraint on investment, and the willingness to pay for pollution control is not known with certainty. It turns out that there is a kind of risk premium despite the fact that society by assumption is risk-neutral.

156

9.1 Access value

In this section we consider projects which affect the probability of a particular event, rather than its magnitude. To use a term coined by Gallagher and Smith (1985), the project leads to a change in access conditions for an asset whose availability is uncertain. Although the discussion will be conducted in terms of an asset, the reader can just as well think in terms of, say, changes in pollution which affect the probabilities of various kinds of damage.

An access value can be defined using two different probability distributions for the asset. The change in expected utility associated with a shift in the probability distribution can be written as:

$$\Delta V^E = E[V(y,z)] - E_0[V(y,z_0)] = \sum_{i=1}^{n} \Delta \pi^i V(y,z^i) \qquad (9.1)$$

where a subscript 0 refers to the initial probability distribution, and z and z_0 are assumed to be independently distributed. In equation (9.1) it is the probability that the environmental asset will be of a particular size or quality which changes, i.e. $\Delta \pi^i = \pi^i - \pi_0^i$ is the change in the probability that z takes on value z^i. Performing second-order Taylor series expansions around (say) the expected values of the asset $\bar{z}$ and $\bar{z}_0$ gives an idea of what forces are involved. The expected values, as well as the variations around these values, affect the sign of ΔV^E in (9.1). Expected utility increases if the change increases the expected access to the asset, *ceteris paribus*, or reduces the variability of the supply/quality of the asset, *ceteris paribus*. The latter result assumes, however, that the household is risk-averse with respect to supply risk. See Johansson (1987, p. 171) for an illustration of a result of this kind.

As was the case in the previous chapter, there is an infinite possible number of money measures of the change in expected utility caused by a change in access conditions. A simple money measure is, however, provided by a non-contingent payment/compensation such that:

$$E[V(y - CV,z)] = E_0[V(y,z_0)] \qquad (9.2)$$

CV is thus a payment (compensation) such that the household attains the same level of expected utility with the new access conditions as with the initial access conditions. Alternatively, the household is held at the final expected utility level through a payment/compensation, given initial access conditions. This yields the non-contingent equivalent variation.

Substitution of equation (9.2) into equation (9.1) yields:

$$\Delta V^E = E[V(y,z)] - E[V(y - CV,z)] \qquad (9.3)$$

Whatever the sign of the change in expected utility, CV must have the same sign. It is left to the reader to verify that the non-contingent equivalent variation is also a sign-preserving money measure of changes in expected utility. These results illustrate the fact that the non-contingent money measure is also useful in cost-benefit analysis of changes in access conditions, i.e. probability distributions.

Turning to expected consumer surplus measures, we can see that such measures may fail to rank correctly two distributions, E and E_0, at least in the absence of markets for monetary claims. The intuition behind this ranking failure is the same as in the case of an environmental resource whose supply is stabilized at some intermediate level. In section 8.2 it was shown that expected consumer surplus measures may have negative signs although a stabilization increases expected utility, and vice versa. Unfortunately, as shown by Helms (1984), this result generalizes to the case of changes in access conditions. It is therefore quite meaningless to define (access) option values since these may be of either sign regardless of whether a change in access conditions contributes to expected utility or not. Option value is simply not a useful tool in applied cost-benefit analysis, except in a few cases. Freeman (1985), for example, is able to sign access option value by employing very restrictive assumptions regarding the properties of utility functions, and restricting the analysis to a change in the probability of access to a resource like a park, which is either preserved or closed.

In closing this section, it should be noted that the marginal cost-benefit rules derived in chapter 8 can easily be modified to cover changes in the probability of the occurrence of a particular event. To illustrate, let us consider the model developed in this section. The relevant cost-benefit rule, using a non-contingent payment/compensation as the money measure, is simply:

$$dV^E/V_y^E = [\sum_i d\pi^i V(y,z^i)/V_y^E] - dCV = 0 \qquad (9.3')$$

where $d\pi^i$ is the change in the probability that the household will experience state i, V_y^E is the expected marginal utility of income, and $\sum_i d\pi^i = 0$ since probabilities must sum to unity both before and after the considered project. dCV thus equals the positive or negative monetary value the household places on a marginal change in the probability distribution, i.e. of probabilities across different states. This illustrates the fact that the cost-benefit rules derived in the previous chapter can be modified so as to cover changes in environmental assets other than those considered.

9.2 Valuing changes in health risks

The access-value model presented in section 9.1 was interpreted in terms of access conditions for an asset whose availability is uncertain. Alternatively, one may interpret z as a health quality index. For example, if there are n different health states, one may order these so that z^1 refers to full health, z^2 to some well-defined minor health deficiency, z^i to the more serious health deficiency i, and z^n to death.[1] A project can then be defined as any treatment that changes the probability that the household will experience a certain health state. Alternatively, the project is some activity in which the household engages which changes the probability distribution across health states. This ultimately raises the question of how one can meaningfully value a life.

Let us start, however, by considering a project or activity that affects morbidity while leaving the chance of dying (mortality) constant. The maximum non-contingent willingness-to-pay for a medical treatment, for example, that changes the probabilities of achieving different health states can be written as:

$$E[V(y - CV,z)] = E_0[V(y,z_0)] \tag{9.4}$$

This expression defines the non-contingent compensating variation, i.e. the maximum uniform or state-independent amount the household is willing to pay in order to ensure that a treatment which changes the probabilities of experiencing different health states is provided. As shown in the preceding section, this money measure is sign-preserving, i.e. if the treatment increases expected utility then CV will have a positive sign, while CV will be negative if the treatment lowers expected utility. Alternatively, one can base the definition on the equivalent variation measure. The household then gets a uniform compensation instead of the treatment such that expected utility without the treatment but with compensation is equal to the expected utility with the treatment.

We can therefore conclude that one can use the apparatus developed in this chapter to assess projects and activities that change the chance of experiencing different health states. Money measures of changes in morbidity can be meaningfully defined and used in cost-benefit analysis of such changes.

Turning now to the case where loss of life is involved, let us start by introducing a few assumptions. Initially, it is assumed that:

$$\left.\begin{array}{l} V(0,z^{\neq n}) > 0 \\ V(y,z^n) = 0 \qquad\qquad \forall y > 0 \end{array}\right\} \tag{9.5}$$

The household thus prefers to stay alive (avoid health state n) even if this means a zero income, and no income, however high (and transferred to one's heirs), can compensate for the loss of one's life. In other words, (9.5) says that inf $V(y,z^{\neq n}) >$ sup $V(y,z^n)$, where 'inf' means *infimum* and 'sup' means *supremum*.

Given these assumptions, monetary compensation is not possible for a 'project' which causes the certain and immediate death of a household. A cost-benefit analysis would reject any project which causes the immediate and certain loss of a life. This does not necessarily mean that the attempt to value life in terms of money is more or less doomed to failure (Broome, 1978). To see why, let us consider a project which increases the probability of death, π^n, but leaves it in the open interval $(0,1)$. Using (9.4) and the second line in (9.5) one finds that:

$$\sum_{i=1}^{n-1} \pi^i V(y - CV, z^i) = \sum_{i=1}^{n-1} \pi_0^i V(y, z^i) \tag{9.6}$$

In order to interpret this expression, it is useful to consider the two-states case. π_0^1 is then the initial probability of staying alive and π^1 is the corresponding probability with the considered 'project'. We assume that the project reduces the probability of survival.[2] Apparently, however, there is a finite compensation $CV < 0$ such that the household is willing to trade the resulting increase in wealth for a reduced probability of staying alive. This result generalizes to the more general case in which probabilities of experiencing various health states change in more complicated ways, as equation (9.6) illustrates. Money measures of projects/activities affecting human health, including the probability of death, are thus meaningful and useful tools in applied cost-benefit analysis, at least if the analysis is restricted to changes that do not cause the certain and immediate death of individuals.

9.3 Some further notes on the value of health changes

The loss of expected income is sometimes used as a lower bound of the value of life. If a household's lifetime income is y if alive, and a project reduces the probability of survival from π_0^1 to zero, the expected income loss is $\pi_0^1 y$. However, given the assumptions introduced in equations (9.5), it is not possible to relate the value of life to income losses. Therefore, following Jones-Lee (1976), we shall change the assumptions slightly to:

$$\left.\begin{array}{l} V(y^1, z^1) \leq A \\ V(y^n, z^n) \leq B \\ \pi_0^1 V(y^1, z^1) + (1 - \pi_0^1) V(y^n, z^n) \gtreqless B \end{array}\right\} \tag{9.5'}$$

where for simplicity only two states are assumed to be possible, with a superscript 1 (n) referring to being alive (dead); and the positive and finite constants A and B are such that $A > B$. If the least upper bound of utility in state n, i.e. B, falls short of expected utility as defined by the final line in (9.5'), no finite sum will be sufficient to compensate the household for the certainty of death. In fact, Jones-Lee shows that there is a range of probabilities of death (≤ 1) for which it will be impossible to compensate the household. The intuition behind this result is simply that compensation cannot raise utility above B, which in turn falls short of initial expected utility. Reversing the final line inequality makes compensation possible. Restricting the analysis to this case, one can meaningfully address the question of whether expected income losses constitute lower bounds on the value of life.

Let us now consider a project that changes the probability of survival from a strictly positive level to zero. Given that compensation is possible in the above sense, the change in expected utility in moving from $\pi_0^n < 1$ to $\pi^n = 1$ can be written as:

$$\Delta V^E = V(y^n, z^n) - [\pi_0^1 V(y, z^1) + (1 - \pi_0^1) V(y^n, z^n)]$$
$$= \pi_0^1 [V(y^n, z^n) - V(y, z^1)]$$
$$= V(y^n, z^n) - V(y^n - CV, z^n) \tag{9.7}$$

where the final line is obtained by noting that the compensation CV should be such that $V(y^n - CV, z^n)$ is equal to the expression within brackets in the first line of (9.7), initial expected utility. A linear approximation of (9.7) around (y^n, z^n) yields, after straightforward calculations:

$$\Delta V^E / V_y = CV = -(\pi_0^1 \Delta y - \pi_0^1 V_z / V_y) \tag{9.8}$$

where $V_y = \partial V(y^n, z^n) / \partial y > 0$, $V_z = \partial V(y^n, z^n) / \partial z < 0$ is interpreted as a left derivative, assumed to exist and be finite, $\Delta y = y^1 - y^n$, while Δz is set equal to minus unity. The expected loss of income is $\pi_0^1 \Delta y$ when the probability of survival falls from π_0^1 to zero. This expected loss must be lower than the compensation CV since the value of life $V_z \Delta z$ is positive. Thus, in the simple case under consideration, the expected loss of income can be used as the lower bound for the 'true' monetary value, CV, of the change in expected utility.

This conclusion does not, however, generalize to more complicated changes in the probability distribution in the n health-states case ($n \geq 3$). This is similar to the futile attempts to use expected consumer surplus as the lower bound for the true benefits of an environmental asset whose future availability is uncertain. Unless the analysis is restricted to special cases, option value, which is defined as the difference between CV and the expected consumer surplus, may be of either sign. Expected consumer surplus measures cannot generally be taken as lower bounds for the true benefits, as shown in the previous chapter. We claim here (without proof) that this also holds for expected income changes caused by health care programmes, for example.

The reader should also note that CV is a lower bound for the maximum willingness to pay for a treatment which improves health. Moreover, if markets for monetary claims are available, expected-value payments are of interest. The analysis performed in section 8.1 is therefore applicable in the case of health changes too. This is noted because health is a private and insurable good, although it may have collective elements, e.g. individuals may be concerned about the well-being of their relatives and friends. It should be stressed that in a cost-benefit analysis of a project involving certain or uncertain health effects, altruistic components should be treated in the way specified in section 7.8. That is, non-paternalistic altruism can be ignored, at least if the project is small and we are at a social welfare optimum, while a concern for others' health augments the benefits of a project that reduces health risks. The reader is referred to Jones-Lee (1992) for a detailed analysis of the treatment of altruism in health economics.

The reader may find the fact that the model used in this section is static, or atemporal, rather unsatisfactory, though this is a quite common approach used by, for example, Viscusi *et al.* (1991). After all, time is an essential ingredient in any analysis of decisions affecting probabilities of life and death. In closing this section, let us therefore hint at two possible extensions. One obvious possibility is to use the intertemporal discrete-time model developed in sections 8.3 and 8.4. The model was used to analyse an asset whose future availability is stochastic. Interpreting the model's z^2 as representing future health states, the model can also be used to analyse trade-offs between increases in wealth and reductions in future health, for example. In principle, all money measures generated by the model can be used for the analysis of projects affecting human health.

Alternatively, the household can be viewed as producing health. In principle, the production function approach presented in section 3.3 can be applied to health, and incorporated into the two-period model of chapter 8, for example. Environmental quality or pollution is then viewed as having a stochastic influence on the future health production function. In a more general multi-period model, the household can also be viewed as building up or investing in its health capital. See Cropper and Freeman (1991) for a review of different approaches to the modelling of health in environmental economics.

Another possibility is to generalize the model used in this section so as to be able to handle intertemporal trade-offs. This can be accomplished in various ways, but as in Jones-Lee (1976) a simple method is presented here. Suppose the household's utility function is increasing in initial wealth y, which is taken to be fixed, and the number of years of life. The maximum state-independent payment the household is willing to contribute towards (minimum compensation needed in order for it to accept) a change in the survival probability is implicitly defined by:

$$\int_0^T V[y - CV, z^1(t)]\pi^1(t)dt = \int_0^T V[y, z^1(t)]\pi_0^1(t)dt \tag{9.9}$$

where T is the latest date at which anybody can be alive, utility is increasing in the number of years being alive, $z^1(t)$, $\pi^1(t)$ is the continuous subjective probability density function for the time of the household's death if the considered 'project' is undertaken, and $\pi_0^1(t)$ is the corresponding function without the 'project'. Comparing equations (9.6) and (9.9), the reader can check that the technically more complicated expression (9.9) lends itself to much the same interpretation as the simpler expression (9.6), the main difference being that CV is now a uniform sum over time. In any case, whether or not health changes are considered in an intertemporal context, money measures useful in applied cost-benefit analysis can be defined. The reader interested in further discussion is referred to Cropper and Freeman (1991), and Jones-Lee (1976, 1989, 1992).

9.4 Valuing health benefits from air pollution abatement

In a recent study, Shechter (1991) values air quality in terms of its human health effects. The study was carried out in the city of Haifa in northern Israel. Evidence accumulated over some time has indicated a noticeably higher occurrence of respiratory illnesses in the polluted sections of the Haifa region, especially in relation to respiratory symptoms and diseases. Morbidity issues have therefore constituted the overwhelming determinant in shaping attitudes towards air pollution in the region. The purpose of Shechter's study is to apply alternative approaches to the valuation of health benefits from pollution abatement in the Haifa area.

The Shechter study is an extremely ambitious and well-done one, using three indirect valuation methods (via market goods) and three contingent valuation elicitation formats: open-ended, modified iterative bidding game, and referendum-style binary choice. Here we will concentrate on the contingent valuation studies. The household survey consisted of a stratified, cluster area probability sample of about 3,500 households in the metropolitan area of Haifa, and was carried out from May 1986 to April 1987. The overall response rate was 81 per cent; 9 per cent refused to be interviewed and 10 per cent could not be reached. Heads of household (either spouse) were interviewed, each interview lasting around 35–40 minutes. We focus here on the willingness-to-pay questions. The two central questions (Shechter, 1991, pp. 149–51) were as follows:

CV: I'd like to show you photographs taken in the Haifa area on two situations. Here you can see some where the air was relatively 'clean', and here we can see a few taken on relatively polluted days.

Now, pollution abatement devices could reduce the number of polluted days by about one-half. Abatement and control are expensive, however. The facts show that the costs of these activities are ultimately borne by consumers – either through additional taxes (to defray the cost of direct investments by government or of subsidies given by it to industry), or through higher prices of goods and services produced by the polluting plants. Consider the possibility that the local government is charged with the task of pollution abatement. Since its budget is already committed to other uses, it would have to raise the local municipal tax to this end.

Now, do you know the amount of your annual municipal tax you presently pay? (Interviewer: if yes, write amount. If not, calculate the amount of tax using the tax rate table and dwelling size. Next, flash the payment card.)

My next question then is: please indicate on the card the maximum percentage category you are willing to pay, in addition to your annual tax payment, in order to finance the stated reduction in pollution. (Interviewer: translate into money units.) It comes out to ___ NIS. Is this the sum you had in mind? If not, please correct it.

(A question on reasons for refusing to pay follows.)

EV: I asked you before about the possibility of improving air quality from present levels. I will now ask you a similar question, but regarding the possibility that pollution would worsen if no action is taken. Look again at the photos. Assume that the number of polluted days will rise by one-half if no action is taken. Now, look at the card and tell me the maximum percentage category you would be willing to pay in local taxes in addition to what you now pay to prevent this from happening. Please indicate (etc.).

(Question on reasons for refusing to pay follows.)

Suppose that the respondent interprets these questions as follows. Each photograph is associated with a probability distribution across health states. Through information provided by the media and the interviewer, the respondent has an idea of how a particular air quality level could affect his health: he has a subjective perception of the probability that this particular air quality will cause him a type z^i symptom or disease ($i = 1, \ldots, n$). Comparing photographs where the air is relatively 'clean' and relatively 'polluted', the respondent is able to assess how the probability of getting a type z^i symptom changes when air quality changes from 'clean' to 'polluted' or vice versa. In terms of the simple model in section 9.2, the answers to the two willingness-to-pay questions will then be such that:

$$\left.\begin{array}{l} E_1[V(y - CV, z_1)] = E_0[V(y, z_0)] \\ E_0[V(y - EV, z_0)] = E_2[V(y, z_2)] \end{array}\right\} \quad (9.10)$$

where $z_1^i = z_0^i = z_2^i$ denotes health state or symptom i, a subscript 1 (e.g. E_1) refers to a reduction in the number of polluted days by about one half, a subscript 0 refers to the current air pollution situation, and a subscript 2 to a

Table 9.1. *CVM experiments (NIS converted to US$)*

	CV	EV
Open-ended	17 (1855)	32 (1348)
Modified iterative bidding	30 (195)	40 (199)
Closed-ended	29 (360)	31 (360)

Note: Numbers of respondents are shown within parentheses. In the case of the bidding game, 343 and 369 respondents reported a first bid; the figures within parentheses refer to the numbers changing their bids.

situation where the number of polluted days has risen by one-half. According to the first line in (9.10), the household pays for a favourable change in the probability distribution for health states from E_0 to E_1. This yields the non-contingent compensating variation. According to the second line in (9.10), the household pays to avoid an unfavourable shift in the probability distribution from E_0 to E_2. This yields the non-contingent equivalent variation. Note that a property tax, which served as the payment vehicle, can be considered as a proxy for a lump-sum payment, since, at least in the short run, it is independent of agents' behaviour (it cannot be escaped).

Of course, there is no way of finding out how a respondent actually interprets a willingness-to-pay question and arrives at a monetary sum. Still, by applying economic theory as above, one is able to generate and test various hypotheses. This approach will hopefully increase our knowledge about human behaviour and produce (even) better empirical studies in the future. Schechter's study is in the same spirit: using different valuation techniques, Schechter wants to increase our understanding of the relative merits of these techniques.

Some results of the contingent valuation experiments are presented in Table 9.1. The average annual willingness to pay according to the open-ended questions cited above is $17 and $32, respectively. The average respondent is thus willing to pay more in order to prevent a worsening of air quality than for an improvement of this quality. This seems intuitively reasonable but is not self-evident from a purely theoretical point of view, as Shechter also points out. Figure 9.1 illustrates the non-stochastic case. Whether the willingness to pay for an improvement in the unpriced commodity, i.e. a move to the right in the figure, exceeds the willingness to pay to prevent a reduction in the commodity's quality, a move to the left, depends on the shape of the indifference curves. Under uncertainty, the

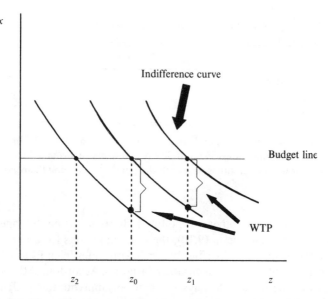

Figure 9.1. The willingness to pay for changes in the provision of z.

further complication of translating different air quality changes to changes in probabilities of experiencing different symptoms is added.

Table 9.1 also presents the outcome of the modified bidding game. According to this approach, respondents were asked whether they would increase – and then by how much – their initial payment, had they been informed that the original aggregated sum would not have been sufficient to accomplish the posited change in air quality. This yielded a significant increase in mean willingness to pay. Shechter interprets this as evidence of the efficacy of this approach in 'gleaning' consumer surplus.

According to the closed-ended willingness-to-pay question, respondents were asked to state whether they would be willing to pay a stated percentage increase in municipal tax for the postulated change in air quality. The percentage categories were identical to those used in the payment card for the open-ended question, and were randomly assigned to households. A logit model was estimated, producing the values in the final row of Table 9.1.

At least in the case of the EV measure, all three willingness-to-pay questions produce similar results. This is not true for the CV measure, but the difference between the open-ended measure and the two other measures is not unexpectedly large.

Finally, Shechter raises an important question for applied cost-benefit analysis. The willingness-to-pay measures reported here probably do not cover the direct costs of air pollution. Households are covered by subsidized medical insurance, and almost universal paid sick-leave. Such components therefore do not enter (directly) into the household's maximization process. In terms of equation (9.10), the household does not include any change in disposable income y caused by air pollution. If so, the aggregated sums of the amounts in Table 9.1 primarily reflect the direct disutility associated with morbidity, plus any aesthetic disutility due to reduced visibility. Adding direct monetary cost savings due to reduced morbidity and physical damage (on buildings, crops, etc.) to these amounts yields an estimate of the gross willingness to pay for a reduction of air pollution.[3] If this gross WTP exceeds the abatement costs, the improvement can be considered socially profitable, setting aside here the income distribution issue. In any case, Shechter makes the important point that in formulating willingness-to-pay questions, one must be careful to specify what individuals are supposed to pay for. Otherwise, it may be difficult to avoid double-counting of some benefits and/or costs in a cost-benefit analysis. For a further discussion of this issue, the reader is referred back to section 5.4.

9.5 The value of information and quasi-option values

Information plays a key role in all decision-making, including decisions involving environmental issues. There is often a trade-off between the extra benefits it is possible to obtain by postponing a project in order to learn more about its consequences, and the extra costs incurred, in terms of incomes foregone, for example.

A simple way to illustrate the value of perfect information is to consider a (risk-neutral) firm under two different scenarios. In the first, the firm must take a decision on its scale of operation before uncertainty is revealed. Suppose that uncertainty pertains only to the output price. A profit-maximizing risk-neutral firm will then equate expected price and marginal cost, i.e. produce $\bar{x}$ units if the expected output price is $\bar{p}$ in Figure 9.2. The actual price, however, will be p^0 (with a probability of one-half), or p^1 (with a probability of one-half). If the firm could postpone its output decision until uncertainty is revealed, it would therefore either produce x^0 units *or* x^1 units, depending on whether price turns out to be low or high. As a result, the firm would earn an extra profit equal to either area A or area B in Figure 9.2, as compared with the case where $x = \bar{x}$ units. In other words, in the simple case under discussion, the value of perfect information is equal to the extra profits the firm can earn by postponing a decision on its production level until the price is known. The expected value of perfect information is

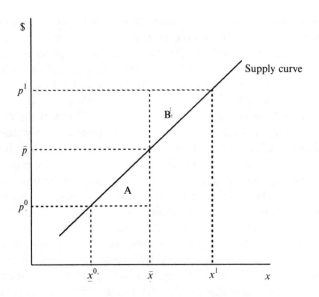

Figure 9.2. The value of information to a firm.

simply $\pi^0 A + \pi^1 B$, where $\pi^i = 0.5$ for $i = 0,1$ in Figure 9.2. This simple example illustrates the fact that postponing decisions until further information becomes available generally yields extra benefits. These extra benefits must, however, be compared to the costs of delaying a decision. For example, for the aforementioned firm, adjustment costs may be so high that it prefers to take production decisions before uncertainty about price is revealed. For good illustrations of the value of information in the case of irreversible investment expenditure, the reader is referred to Dixit (1992) and Pindyck (1991). They also show how optimal investment rules can be obtained from methods of option pricing.

In environmental economics, a special case of the value of perfect information, often referred to as 'quasi-option value', has received considerable attention. The two-period household model in section 8.3 can be used to illustrate this concept. The model was derived conditional on the assumption that the future, i.e. second-period, supply/quality of an environmental asset z is uncertain as viewed from today. Uncertainty, however, is revealed at the beginning of period 2. Therefore, first-period decisions are taken before the value of z is known, while second-period decisions are taken when z is known.

Suppose now that the government plans to undertake a project, which, as viewed from today, will change environmental quality in an unpredictable

Table 9.2. *Decision tree*

NU = project not undertaken; U = project undertaken

Period 1	Period 2
NU	NU
NU	U
U	No choice

way. For example, there is perhaps a strictly positive probability that the project causes the extinction of an endangered species. In order to simplify the interpretation, assume, without loss of generality, that the second-period value of z is known to equal $\bar{z}$ with certainty if the project is not undertaken, while $z^i \gtreqless \bar{z}$ for all states of nature i if the project is undertaken. Thus, the environmental impact of the project is stochastic as viewed from today; we do not even rule out the possibility that the project in fact will turn out to improve environmental quality. However, for some reason, e.g. research undertaken independently of the considered project, at the beginning of the second period it is known how this kind of project affects the environment.

Using a slightly modified version of equation (8.17), the second-period decision problem can be viewed as:

$$E\{\max_{D} U[x_2(p_2, y_2 + s + Y(D), z(D)), z(D)]\} \qquad (9.11)$$

where D is a binary variable, with $D = 1$ if the project is undertaken in the second period and $D = 0$ otherwise,[4] $Y(1)$ is an income generated by the project, if undertaken, $z(0) = \bar{z}$, and $z(1) = [z^1, \ldots, z^n]$ is stochastic as viewed from today. According to equation (9.11), the decision-maker compares utility attained for $D = 1$ and $D = 0$ *after* the project's effects on the environment have become known, i.e. the actual value of $z(1)$ is known to him. The decision-maker then picks the alternative, $D(1)$ or $D(0)$, which produces the highest utility level. Equation (9.11) yields the expected utility for the chosen alternative. Moving back to period 1, the decision-maker, which might be the household itself, asked for its opinion on the project, maximizes two-period expected utility as illustrated in section 8.3.

As shown in Table 9.2, there are three alternatives the household or the decision-maker must consider. If the project is not undertaken in period 1, two opportunities remain for period 2, while if the project is undertaken in period 1, no freedom will remain at period 2. We assume that the project, or rather its consequences, are *irreversible*.

Apparently, in this scenario, postponing a decision to undertake the project yields benefits (but also costs in terms of loss of income), the reason being that uncertainty is resolved at the beginning of the second period. Let us now assume that there is nothing to be learned. At the beginning of the first period, it is realized that the project's impact on the environment will not be revealed unless the project is undertaken. We will then have to live with its consequences whatever they turn out to be, the loss of some species, perhaps. In this scenario, the decision whether to undertake the project may as well be taken at the beginning of the first period. There is nothing to be gained by postponing a decision until the second period.

Comparing the two scenarios developed above is therefore essentially equivalent to comparing the following two maximization problems:

$$\bar{V}(D_1) = U(D_1) + \beta E\{\max_D U(\tilde{D},D,z)\}$$
$$\bar{\bar{V}}(D_1) = U(D_1) + \max_D\{\beta E[U(\tilde{D},D,z)]\}$$
$$\left.\right\} \quad (9.12)$$

where a subscript 1 refers to the first-period decision, $\tilde{D} = D_1 + D \leq 1$ with $D_1, D \geq 0$, and utility is written as a function only of the decision under consideration so as to simplify notation. According to the decision problem represented by the first line of (9.12), the decision *can* be taken after uncertainty is resolved, while, in the second-line problem, a decision *must* be taken before uncertainty is resolved. Note the irreversible nature of the problem as specified in (9.12): setting $D_1 = 1$ means that no choice is available in the second period, since $\tilde{D} = 1$: we have to live with the project's consequences whatever they might turn out to be.

The difference between the two lines in (9.12) represents the expected value of perfect information. In the literature on environmental economics, this value is usually defined conditional on $D_1 = 0$ (for reasons which should be obvious from what has been said above) and is termed quasi-option value. Quasi-option value thus shows the increase in expected utility/ benefits of not undertaking a project in the first period, when it is possible to take a decision after uncertainty is resolved instead of before. It has been shown (see Fisher and Hanemann (1990), for example) that quasi-option value, i.e. $\bar{V}(0) - \bar{\bar{V}}(0)$, is positive. In general, quasi-option value is strictly positive. The result can be obtained by invoking a theorem originally developed by Marschac. See Hey (1981, pp. 87–9) for details.

A simple example may help to clarify this result. Suppose that the monetary second-period value of the project, including its impact on the environment (as valued through the contingent valuation method, for example) is A with probability π, and $-B$ with probability $1 - \pi$. If $D_1 = 0$, one finds that $\bar{V}(0) = \pi \cdot A$, while $\bar{\bar{V}}(0) = \pi \cdot A - (1 - \pi)B$. The $-B$ does not show up in the first expression simply because the project is not undertaken if the decision-maker recognizes that its impact on the environment is so severe that its net benefits are negative. Recall that, in this scenario, the project's impact on the environment is learned before the decision on the project is taken. This is not the case in the other scenario, which is why B shows up in the expression for $\bar{\bar{V}}(0)$, i.e. we simply calculate the project's expected net value. In the first scenario we can therefore always do at least as well as in the second scenario, and, in general, even better. A policy rule such as that captured by the first line in (9.12) is called a *closed-loop policy*, since, at each decision-point, current as well as future anticipated information is exploited. The second line in (9.12) is an example of an *open-loop policy*, according to which a decision is taken conditional on the information initially available; see Fisher and Hanemann (1990) for further discussion.

9.6 Policy choices, time inconsistency and credibility

In the two-period model considered above, binary choices involving irreversible consequences tend to be more conservationist in the first period in the learning scenario than in the no-learning scenario. By waiting, the decision-maker keeps his options open. This makes it possible to change the decision should future information reveal that not undertaking the project is preferable. Hanemann (1982) has shown, however, that if a project, say development of a tract of wild land, i.e. D in equations (9.12), can take on any value in the closed interval $[0,1]$, then closed-loop policies need not be more conservationist than open-loop ones. The value of information is nevertheless still there, of course. In addition, development may itself provide information, i.e. the problem may allow for active learning, in the sense that the amount and types of information gained depend upon the action taken in the first period, as stressed by Miller and Lad (1984). Moreover, as in the Viscusi and Zeckhauser (1976) analysis, some developments can provide information regarding whether development is in fact irreversible. These results suggest that decisions involving a quasi-option are not necessarily more conservationist than decisions without the quasi-option.

Two-period models tend to produce strong results. Once the possibility of a third or fourth period is opened up, results usually become much more ambiguous. This is also true for models involving a quasi-option value. In a recent study, Fisher and Hanemann (1990) consider a multi-period decision problem where the decision-maker accumulates more and more information over time. The results are much more vague than in the two-period model. In some cases a project effectively eliminates future flexibility so that there is a positive flexibility premium. In other cases, however, the issue is less clear-cut. The prospect of future learning thus has an ambiguous effect – it may strengthen or weaken the case for a project affecting the environment.

To illustrate why, we return to the simple example presented above. Second-period net benefits are A with probability π, and B with probability $1 - \pi$. Suppose that new information becomes available at the beginning of period 3. It turns out that third-period benefits will be A with probability $\pi^1 \neq \pi$. Obviously, there is now a much richer choice-set than before. The decision-maker may choose an open-loop policy without feedback. At the beginning of period 1 he chooses the best three-period policy conditional on the information available at that point of time, i.e. π for periods 2 and 3. Or he could choose an open-loop policy with feedback, i.e. update the probability distribution as more information becomes available, but still take decisions conditional on the assumption that no further information will be available in the future. For example, at the beginning of the second period he maximizes expected future net benefits assuming that π does not change from period 2 to period 3. Once we arrive at the third period, however, the decision-maker realizes that the probability of a successful project has changed from π to π^1, and uses this new information to maximize expected third-period net benefits. Finally, a decision-maker adopting a closed-loop policy considers both current information and all future anticipated information. Such a decision-maker would expect third-period net benefits equal to $\pi^1 \cdot A$, because he would avoid undertaking the project if its net benefits turned out to be negative. Following an open-loop feedback rule, on the other hand, one would expect net benefits equal to $\pi^1 \cdot A - (1 - \pi^1)B$. This simplified example, hiding many assumptions and some of the richness of the Fisher–Hanemann model, gives an idea of the policy choice dilemma in a multi-period context. The reader interested in the details is referred to Fisher and Hanemann (1990).

One aspect of the policy choice problem usually overlooked in environmental economics is the *time-inconsistency* problem. A future policy that is optimal as viewed from today may not be optimal as viewed from 'tomorrow'. To illustrate the nature of this problem, let us consider a simple example. Suppose that the government collects taxes so as to finance an environmental project in periods 1 and 2. Suppose further that the government taxes labour and/or capital, i.e. lump-sum taxation is ruled out by assumption. The theory of optimal taxation says that both capital and labour should be taxed, in general, so as to minimize the excess burden of taxation. If the supply of labour and savings is elastic, as in Figures 9.3a and

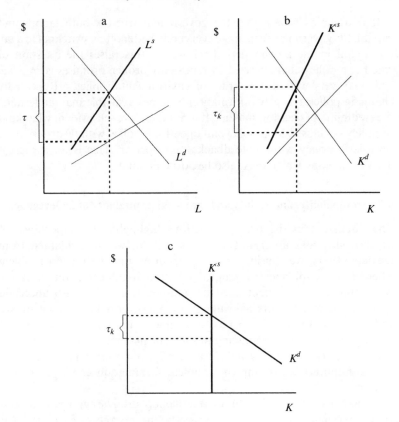

Figure 9.3. The time-inconsistency problem.

9.3b respectively, the optimal tax policy is to announce that *both* labour and capital will be taxed in both periods. However, once we arrive at the second period, the capital stock is fixed. We assume that it equals what was inherited from the past, plus the total savings from the first period: supply is completely inelastic, as illustrated in Figure 9.3c. Taxing a factor that is supplied inelastically is like imposing a lump-sum tax and causes no distortions. Thus, viewed from the second period, switching from a tax on both factors to a tax on capital is optimal.

The initially optimal policy – announcing a second-period tax on both labour and capital – is optimal but not time-consistent. Announcing that only capital will be taxed in the second period, on the other hand, is time-consistent but not optimal. The latter result follows from the fact that announcing a future tax on capital would adversely affect savings, and thus reduce the second-period stock of capital *and* welfare.

If households *believe* that the government will tax both labour and capital, the government can make everybody better off by switching to a tax on capital in the second period. However, this raises the question of whether a policy characterized by repeatedly broken promises is *credible*. This may very well also be true for environmental policies. Repeatedly changing policies as new information becomes available may undermine the credibility of decision-makers. It is not therefore self-evident what kind of policy – a closed-loop policy, an open-loop policy with feedback or an open-loop policy without feedback – is superior. This is an aspect of decision-making which must also be borne in mind.

9.7 Irreversibility, uncertainty and the social profitability of an investment

The discussion in the previous sections highlights the importance of irreversibility and uncertainty. In this section, which is adapted from Demers (1991), we consider in more detail an infinite-horizon problem where a social planner running a pollution treatment plant faces the constraint that investment must be non-negative and is also uncertain about the aggregate marginal willingness to pay for pollution control. We will formulate the problem so as to be able to use standard methods of stochastic dynamic programming to solve the maximization problem. The reader is referred to Stokey and Lucas (1987) for a detailed presentation of the assumptions underlying the problem formulation employed in this section.

Let us consider a small pollution treatment plant. The aggregate current-value marginal willingness to pay for pollution control in period t is denoted p_t, and the amount of emissions treated by the plant is denoted z_t. The plant uses capital K_t and labour L_t as inputs. In the short run, the stock of capital is fixed. The plant should therefore select its labour force so as to maximize social net benefits:

$$NB_t = p_t F(K_t, L_t) - wL_t \tag{9.13}$$

where $z_t = F(\cdot)$, $F(\cdot)$ is a strictly concave and twice continuously differentiable production function (satisfying the Inada conditions for both factors), w is the (for simplicity) constant wage rate, and p_t is known at the time when the short-run production decision is made. Note that all prices in this section are expressed as current-value prices in order to highlight some important results.

In the short run, we should select the scale of operations, i.e. the labour force, so as to equate the aggregate marginal willingness to pay for pollution control and the marginal cost of pollution control. This is the usual Samuelsonian condition for the optimal provision of a public good, derived in chapters 2, 5 and 6, for example.

In the long run, we must also choose the stock of capital. Let us assume that the law of motion of the capital stock is:

$$K_{t+1} = (1 - \delta)K_t + I_t \tag{9.14}$$

Thus, the plant's capital depreciates at a constant rate δ. Investing more (less) than δK_t adds to (detracts from) the future stock of capital. We assume that gross investment I_t is non-negative for all t. This is the irreversibility constraint.

Suppose that we use the contingent valuation method to collect information on the aggregate marginal willingness to pay p_t. Let us postulate that $p_t = p + \epsilon_t$, where the non-negative term ϵ_t is independently and identically distributed (i.i.d.) for all t, and p can take on n different values. In each period, the decision-maker can 'observe' p_t, which is a noisy signal about p. The CVM study also provides him with some further information about p such as changes in income and attitudes to environmental pollution. Let G denote the set of all possible signals g_t about the true value of p, and let us assume that the decision-maker revises his prior probability distribution for p, $\psi(g)$, by applying Bayes' law. Moreover, the evolution of the information state $\psi_t(g_t)$ is assumed to be time-invariant, $\psi_t(g_t) = h(\psi_{t-1}, g_t)$, i.e. has the Markov property. See Demers (1991) for details. A more sophisticated approach would be to allow the decision-maker to have a probability distribution function for each possible value of p, which is updated as more information arrives over time. This would mean that the decision-maker faces *uncertainty* rather than *risk*. See Dobbs (1991) for such a model, and note that in this book we use the two terms interchangeably, although we are always considering various forms of *risk*.

The decision-maker is assumed to be risk-neutral. His goal is to maximize the expected present value of the social net surplus $NB_t - \hat{q}I_t$, where $\hat{q}$ is the price of capital goods, over an infinite number of periods. Because of the recursive structure of the problem, dynamic programming methods are appropriate. Let $v(K_t, \psi_t)$ be the optimal-value function yielding the maximal expected present value of the future social net surplus when an optimal investment policy is chosen. For this maximization problem, Bellman's functional equation becomes:

$$v(K_t, \psi_t) = \max_{I_t} \{p_t F(K_t, L_t^*) - wL_t^* - \hat{q}I_t$$
$$+ \gamma \int_G v[K_{t+1}, \psi_{t+1}(g_{t+1})]\pi(g_{t+1} | \psi_t)dg_{t+1}\} \tag{9.15}$$

subject to (9.14), the irreversibility constraint, the information structure, and K_1, ψ_1 given. In (9.15) an asterisk denotes an optimal value, $\gamma = (1 + r)^{-1}$ is the discount factor, $\pi(\cdot)$ is the predictive density of the message g_t, and $\int_G \pi(\cdot) dg_t = 1$ for all t.

The first-order condition for the above optimization problem can be stated as follows:

$$-\hat{q} + \gamma \int_G [\partial v(\cdot)/\partial K_{t+1}] \pi(\cdot) dg_{t+1} \leq 0 \qquad (9.16)$$

where the equality holds if $I_t^* > 0$, and the weak inequality holds if $I_t^* = 0$. If the expected future marginal value of capital falls short of the price of capital goods, the decision-maker refrains from investing. If the reverse holds, he will invest until an equality is obtained.

Taking the partial derivative of (9.16) with respect to K_t and shifting the expression one period forward we find that:

$$
\left.
\begin{aligned}
E_t[p_{t+1}F_k(K_{t+1}, L_{t+1}^*)] &= (r+\delta)\hat{q} \quad \text{if } I_{t+1}^* > 0 \\
E_t[p_{t+1}F_k(K_{t+1}, L_{t+1}^*)] &= (r+\delta)\hat{q} + (1-\delta)E_t\{\hat{q} - E_{t+1}\gamma[\partial v(\cdot)/\partial K_{t+2}]\} \\
&\qquad\qquad\qquad\qquad\qquad\qquad\qquad \text{if } I_{t+1}^* = 0
\end{aligned}
\right\} \quad (9.17)
$$

where I_t^* is assumed to be strictly positive, and E_t denotes the expectation operator when $\pi = \pi(g_{t+1} \mid \psi_t)$.

If our plant could disinvest, i.e. put $I_{t+1}^* < 0$, then the two expressions in (9.17) would coincide, because we would choose $I_{t+1}^* \gtrless 0$ so as to equate the expected future marginal value of capital and the price of capital goods. Moreover, if there was no uncertainty, (9.17) would reduce to equation (6.5) Irreversibility, uncertainty about the marginal willingness to pay, and the anticipation of receiving more information give rise to an endogenous time-varying *risk premium*, which, using (9.17), can be defined as:

$$(1-\delta)\{\hat{q} - E_t \min[\hat{q}, \gamma E_{t+1}(\partial v(\cdot)/\partial K_{t+2})]\} \qquad (9.18)$$

Demers (1991) shows that this risk premium increases with I, $\hat{q}$ and r, and decreases with δ. Moreover, a plant facing irreversibility accumulates less capital than it would in the absence of such a constraint.

By assumption, our decision-maker is risk-neutral. Still, there is a risk premium due to irreversibility and learning. This confirms Pindyck's (1991) claim, mentioned in the introduction to this chapter, that the traditional net present value criterion must be used with great care. The cost-benefit rules in sections 8.4 and 8.5 reduce to the (expected) net present value criterion if agents are risk-neutral since V_y in equation (8.23) is a constant for risk-neutral agents. This is so because there are no irreversibility constraints in chapter 8. If such constraints were introduced, a risk premium, similar to the one in (9.18), would have to be added to the cost-benefit rules. In other words, if a project is associated with some irreversible phenomenon, using the set of cost-benefit rules in chapter 8 to evaluate the project would mean that one *overestimates* the social profitability of the project. Unfortunately, however, there seem to be no empirical studies available in which a risk premium for environmental projects is estimated. An important task for environmental economists is therefore to develop methods which can be used to estimate risk premiums.

10   Empirical applications

Unfortunately, there seem to be few, if any, cost-benefit analyses of environmental changes that strictly follow the project evaluation rules derived in previous chapters. Others are presented so sketchily that it is impossible to infer what rules have been used. Nevertheless, in this chapter a few empirical studies are summarized. The first two studies are both based on the contingent valuation method, one using continuous responses, the other using both continuous and binary responses. A study explicitly introducing risk is then presented. The possibility of using computable general equilibrium models is highlighted by summarizing a CGE-based evaluation of environmental regulations. A study by Hammack and Brown (1974) illustrates how optimal control theory and simulation models can be employed in evaluations. Finally an attempt to account for natural resource depletion in national accounts is discussed.

10.1   A cost-benefit analysis of land reclamation

Michael and Pearce (1989) assessed the benefits and costs of land reclamation at Higher Folds in the UK.[1] Prior to reclamation, which began in 1977, this 191 hectare site included a prominent plateau of colliery spoil heaps up to 25 metres high, some of which loomed over houses on the Higher Folds housing estate and collapsed into back gardens. The spoil heaps frequently caught fire, causing problems of nuisance from smoke and unpleasant sulphurous smells, and dust blew from the site in dry weather. The site also contained fourteen mine shafts, dangerous subsidence flashes and lagoons, derelict buildings, disused railway lines, a station and sidings and a former sewage works. Owing to the high acidity of the colliery spoil, vegetation was slow to colonize the site.

The complete removal of the enormous spoil heaps could not be justified on economic grounds, and so they were regraded to form gentle slopes for 122 hectares of agriculture, 67 hectares of tree planting and 2 hectares of football pitches.

The Higher Folds reclamation scheme was designed to produce aesthetic, environmental, health and safety benefits. It was a 'soft' after-use scheme, primarily undertaken to improve the environment, rather than a 'hard' after-use scheme, designed to provide land for development. The present-value cost of reclamation was estimated at about $5 million at 1987/8 prices.

To value the benefits of the reclamation scheme, Michael and Pearce (1989) conducted interviews in May and June 1988 among a random sample of 100 residents living in the immediate vicinity of the reclamation scheme (of whom 70 were reached). At the beginning of the questionnaire, each interviewee was shown a map to clarify the location and extent of the site. They were then shown sets of photographs of the site before and after reclamation.

The detailed wording of the willingness-to-pay questions is not reported, but bidding games with three different payment vehicles were used. Respondents were first asked if they would be willing to pay a $1.75 family entrance charge to visit the site. The amount was increased in steps of 18 cents until a negative response was obtained and then decreased in steps of 4 cents until a positive response was obtained. Respondents were then asked, supposing that the site was still unreclaimed, how large a single, once-and-for-all payment in rent or rates they would be willing to make towards the cost of reclaiming and maintaining the site in its present state. It was stressed that no rebates would be available from the local council and that this form of payment would be the only way of financing reclamation of the site. The starting point bid was $17.50 and the bidding steps used were the same as those for the entrance charge question. The final payment vehicle was willingness to pay for reclamation via electricity bills. The use of this alternative vehicle was justified by explaining that if the Coal Board did the reclamation work, it could increase the price of coal used to generate electricity, and therefore consumers' electricity bills. Respondents were asked, supposing that the site was still unreclaimed, how large an increase in their quarterly electricity bill they would be willing to bear as a single, one-off payment towards reclaiming and maintaining the site in its present condition. It was again emphasized that no rebates would be available for this payment from the local council and the starting-point bid and steps used in the bidding process were the same as those for the rent or rates vehicle.

Costs and benefits are reported in Table 10.1. In calculating the benefits, Michael and Pearce (1989) assume that 2,000 households are affected by the reclamation scheme. Apparently costs far exceed benefits, implying that the social profitability of the project is negative. Michael and Pearce point out, however, that benefits of reclamation other than user benefits may change the outcome of the analysis. These benefits include the increased attractive-

Table 10.1. *Costs and benefits ($)*
of Higher Folds reclamation
scheme (present values, 20-year
time horizon, and 5 per cent
discount rate)

Cost	5,600,000
Benefits:	
User charge	847,000
Rent/rates	30,000
Electricity bills	32,000

ness of the area to business and potential developers, and enhanced civic pride. They also note that social costs may have been overestimated since unemployment in the area is high. The cost figure reported in Table 10.1 refers to private costs, but the authors report no details of how they arrived at the cost of reclamation. The reader interested in the relationship between private and social costs in the presence of unemployment is referred to section 5.6.

Finally, a few remarks regarding the benefits estimate are in order. The estimate based on user charges seems to be the most relevant one (as Michael and Pearce also note). Asking a respondent to pay a higher price for some marketed commodity (housing or electricity) in exchange for an improved environmental quality is troublesome. Even a user charge is complicated to translate to an annual sum of money since the slope of the compensated demand curve is not known. One must therefore apply some quite arbitrary procedure when calculating the relevant area to the left of the compensated demand curve. It should also be noted that respondents may consider the payment vehicle as a part of the offered 'package', so that the stated willingness to pay in part reflects distributional considerations. For example, a user charge may be considered more 'fair' to low-income earners than a tax on housing or electricity consumption. This in turn means that the payment vehicle probably affects the stated willingness to pay.

10.2 Preservation of fragile forests

In a recent study Kriström (1990) attempts to shed light on the benefits and costs of preserving a specific set of forests in Sweden that have high recreational values and unique environmental qualities. The contingent valuation method was employed to estimate the benefits of preservation.

The opportunity cost, i.e. the value of the timber to domestic sawmills and pulp and paper mills, was estimated from market prices for timber.

Let us start by considering the benefits side. A random sample of 1,100 Swedes from all parts of the country were shown a map depicting eleven fragile and virgin forests, and were informed that these areas are important for recreation (for present and future generations) as well as for many endangered species. The respondents were then asked for their willingness to make once-and-for-all contributions to ensure preservation of the areas. Both continuous or open-ended valuation questions, and binary or closed-ended valuation questions were asked. The sample was split into two parts, sample A (for short) made up of 900, and sample B 200. Sample A was asked both types of questions, sample B only the continuous question. The questionnaires were identical in all other respects. The response rates for the two samples were almost exactly the same at 67 per cent.

In Figure 10.1 we plot the proportion of yes-answers at each given bid, invoking a smoothing procedure drawn from Ayer et al. (1955) to ensure that the probability of obtaining a yes-answer does not increase with the bid. The curves can be interpreted as follows. Less than 20 per cent of those asked their maximum willingness to pay 'paid' over $167 (1,000 SEK). On the other hand, when asked if they were willing to pay $167, almost 60 per cent answered 'yes'. In fact, as can be seen from the figure, the distribution for the binary response data appears to be outside the distribution for the continuous data. A simple chi-square test suggests that the distributions generating the data are different. This study thus confirms the impression drawn from previous studies that people think of and respond to the two types of valuation questions differently.

According to the open-ended valuation question, the average (once-and-for-all) willingness to pay is $167 per household. In order to compute a money measure from binary responses, a distributional assumption is required. The Ayer assumption used in constructing the outer curve in Figure 10.1 produces a mean willingness to pay of $417; the mean corresponds to the area below the Ayer-curve in the figure. It is a well-known fact, however, that the distributional assumption has a large impact on the mean. For example, the so-called extreme-value model produces a mean of just $33. The intuitive explanation of the large difference between the results is that one model, but not the other, rules out negative willingnesses to pay. Kriström's study highlights the fact that the assumption about the distribution's tails has a tremendous impact on the mean willingness to pay. In this context, the reader should note that one cannot rule out the possibility of a negative willingness to pay. This should be clear after having read sections 3.4 and 4.2. See also the discussion at the end of the next section.

Turning to the cost side, Kriström considers two forestry alternatives.

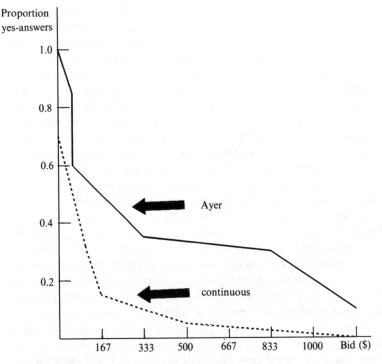

Figure 10.1. Empirical survival functions for the binary ('Ayer') and continuous bid questions.

The first is a pure timber mining alternative, where he simply calculates the value of a grand final felling. In the second alternative, Kriström views forestry as an investment and takes into account the value generated by future forest generations as well as the costs of regeneration.

Basically, Kriström estimates the social costs using the small project evaluation rules derived in chapter 5. As far as data permit, individual cost estimates are presented for each of the eleven areas used in the contingent valuation study. For example, unemployment among foresters in depressed parts of the country is accounted for, and market prices for different timber assortments are used to estimate the value of the areas to private forestry.

The results of the cost-benefit analysis are summed up in Table 10.2. In order to obtain the aggregate benefits of preservation, the household mean willingness to pay has been multiplied by the number of households (3.7 million) in Sweden. Timber mining is more attractive to the forestry industry than continuing forest harvesting. In other words, regeneration costs exceed the present value of timber sales (which accrue around 100

Table 10.2. *Benefits and costs of*
preserving eleven fragile forests in
Sweden ($ million in 1987 prices)

Aggregate benefits	
Continuous	633
'Ayer'	1,533
'Extreme value'	116
Aggregate costs	
Timber mining	850–1,000
Investment, $r = 0.01$	367–567
Investment, $r = 0.05$	100–250

Note:
r is the discount rate.

years from the time of planting). Mining is therefore more profitable to forestry, though it is of course more devastating to the environment. In fact, timber mining is prohibited by Swedish legislation.

According to Kriström's analysis, preservation is not unarguably profitable to society. It should be noted, however, that forestry, owing to the long rotation periods, is a very risky business. A glance at the risky-world project evaluation rules in chapter 8 reveals that there is a cost of risk-bearing, at least in the presence of risk aversion. Kriström may thus have overestimated the opportunity cost of preservation, i.e. the profitability of forestry. This is, however, just a possibility, although it illustrates the urgent need for explicit treatment of risk in cost-benefit analysis.

10.3 Preservation of endangered species

This section summarizes a study by Johansson (1989) that attempts to shed some light on the possibility of estimating money measures in a risky world. The study is based on a questionnaire completed by 122 Swedes,[2] who were told that about 300 endangered species – animals, birds and flowers – are living in Swedish forests. If no measures are taken, for example a ban on forestry in some areas and the introduction of soft cutting technologies in other areas, all the species may become extinct. Each respondent was therefore asked to make (once-and-for-all) contributions towards programmes that would save some or all of the species. Four different programmes that would achieve this were suggested. Firstly, the respondent was asked about his willingness to pay for a programme – denoted C –

which would save 50 per cent of the species. The respondent was then asked to contribute to programmes – B and A – which would save 75 per cent and 100 per cent of the species respectively. Finally, the respondent was asked to pay for a programme D designed so that there is a 0.5 chance that the programme saves all species, and 0.5 that it saves 50 per cent of the species.

In the case of programmes A to C, the willingness-to-pay measure follows from:

$$V(y - CV_j, z^j) = E_0[V(y, z_0^i)] = \sum_{i=1}^{n} \pi_0^i V(y, z_0^i) = V_0 \qquad (10.1)$$

where z^j is the number of species surviving with programme j, CV_j is the compensating variation, i.e. the maximum (once-and-for-all) payment the respondent is willing to make to secure the change, $j =$ A, B, C, a subscript 0 refers to the initial or no-programme case, E_0 is the expectation operator in the no-programme case, π_0^i is the probability that z_0^i species survive in the no-programme case, and V_0 is the expected level of utility attained in the no-programme case. The reason for taking expectations in the no-programme case is that the respondents were told that all species may (but need not) become extinct. The respondent is therefore assumed to use his own subjective probability distribution in order to calculate the expected utility of the no-programme case. We assume that no such uncertainty surrounds the final, with-programme, situation. Note that, for reasons of exposition, it is assumed that respondents consider the number of species as a collective good. In addition, people may indirectly attribute a use value to the suggested programmes since they would require a shift to soft cutting technologies in forestry. It is widely believed that today's forestry is performed in such a way that outdoor recreation is adversely affected. See also the discussion in section 3.4.

If utility is strictly increasing in z and the household is not satiated, it is trivially true that:

Proposition 1 $CV_A > CV_B > CV_C$.

Recall that programme A saves all species, programme B saves 75 per cent and programme C saves 50 per cent of the species. The set of strict inequalities in Proposition 1 constitutes the first hypothesis to be tested.

Turning next to programme D, the respondent faces uncertainty in both the initial and final situations. This is because the respondents were asked to contribute to a programme which saves all the species with a probability of one-half and saves every second species with a probability of one-half. The resulting money measure is called the non-contingent compensating variation:

$$E[V(y - CV, z^i)] = E_0[V(y, z_0^i)] = V_0 \tag{10.2}$$

where E is the expectation operator associated with the final (programme) situation, $z^i = 300$ with a probability of one-half and $z^i = 150$ with a probability of one-half. CV is thus a uniform (once-and-for-all) payment such that the expected utility with the programme is equal to the expected utility without the programme.

One purpose of the study was to examine whether respondents actually calculate the CV measure or, alternatively, misinterpret the valuation question and report some other money measure. Fortunately, theory suggests certain relationships between the measures which will give us a clue to this issue as well as to the question of whether or not pople have risk aversion. These relationships are summed up in Proposition 2.

Proposition 2 If the utility function is increasing and strictly concave in z, then $CV_A > CV_B > CV > CV_C$.

In order to prove these claims, we use the fact that, for a strictly concave utility function, Jensen's inequality asserts that:

$$V(y, \bar{z}) > E[V(y, z^i)] \tag{10.3}$$

where $\bar{z} = E(z^i)$, i.e. $\bar{z}$ is the expected value of z. In other words, if the consumer is risk-averse with respect to risk in z, he gains from having z stabilized at its mean value.

For programme D, the expected value of z is 0.75. Recall that the respondent was also asked to pay for a programme (programme B) which would save 75 per cent of the endangered species. Using the fact that all money measures refer to one and the same level of initial utility, (10.1)–(10.3) can be used to show that:

$$V(y - CV, \bar{z}) > E[V(y - CV, z^i)] = V_0 = V(y - CV_B, \bar{z}) \tag{10.4}$$

Since the left-hand side exceeds the right-hand side, it must be true that $CV_B > CV$. Thus, if the household is risk-averse, the willingness to pay for a programme which stabilizes z at $\bar{z}$ exceeds the willingness to pay for a 'stochastic' programme with $\bar{z}$ as the expected outcome.

Obviously, it also holds that $CV_A > CV_B > CV > CV_C$, provided utility is increasing and strictly concave in z. This set of strict inequalities constitutes the second hypothesis to be tested. It enables us to provide a simple test of whether consumers have risk aversion with respect to z. Moreover, it provides an indication of whether the respondent really calculated a CV measure.

However, it is possible that respondents actually calculated an expected consumer surplus measure. In the present context this measure is defined as:

Table 10.3. *Average willingness-to-pay measures ($)*

Subscripts A, B and C refer to programmes which save 100 per cent, 75 per cent and 50 per cent of the species respectively.

	Average	Female	Male
CV_A	213	130	305
CV_B	129	111	149
CV_C	93	84	102
CV	109	93	203
$E(CV)$	153	108	203

$$E(CV) = 0.5CV_A + 0.5CV_C \tag{10.5}$$

i.e. $E(CV)$ is a weighted average of the willingness to pay for the preservation of all species and the willingness to pay for the preservation of 50 per cent of the species. Proposition 3 relates the expected consumer surplus measure to CV, and the willingness to pay CV_B for having z stabilized at $z = 0.75$.

Proposition 3   If the household is risk-averse with respect to risk in z, then $CV \gtreqless E(CV)$. Moreover, if the expenditure function is strictly convex in z, then $CV_B > E(CV)$.

These claims will not be proved here; see Johansson (1989) for a proof. The first part of the claim, however, was discussed in section 8.2.

Turning to the empirical study, some results based on 120 observations are reported in Table 10.3. A glance at the table shows that most of the results are consistent with the hypotheses generated above. Not surprisingly, the more species saved, the higher the willingness to pay: $CV_A > CV_B > CV_C$. The non-contingent payment CV, associated with a programme that saves all species with a probability of one-half and every second species with a probability of one-half, falls short of the willingness to pay CV_B for a programme which saves 75 per cent of the species. This result is consistent with a utility function which is strictly concave in the number of species saved, z; i.e. people have risk aversion with respect to changes in z. Also, CV is different from the expected compensating variation $E(CV)$, the suggested interpretation being that the average respondent did not calculate his expected compensating variation when he was asked for his non-contingent compensating variation.

All these results are consistent with the hypotheses generated above. However, according to Table 10.3, $E(CV)$ exceeds CV_B, indicating an

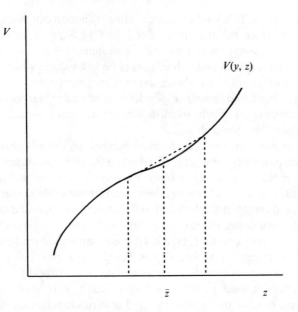

Figure 10.2. The relationship between utility and the number of species saved when the indirect utility function is concave in z for low z-levels and convex in z for sufficiently high z-levels. (The broken line shows that the consumer prefers a stochastic programme with expected outcome $\bar{z}$ to a non-stochastic programme with outcome $\bar{z}$. This indicates that the ranking of various programmes is sensitive to the curvature properties of the utility function as well as the z-level.)

expenditure function that is strictly concave in z, and not strictly convex as expected. Moreover, it can be seen that $E(CV) > CV_B > CV$. This set of inequalities is not easily explained. For example, an indirect utility function which is globally strictly concave or convex in z and income cannot produce $E(CV) > CV_B > CV$, as shown by Johansson (1989).

It seems reasonable to suspect that this unexpected result reflects a difference in risk attitudes between 'poor' and 'rich' people. However, the inequality $E(CV) > CV_B > CV$ is obtained for low-income earners as well as for high-income earners. The inequality is also robust with respect to the stated motives for 'paying' for the preservation of endangered species. On the other hand, there is a striking difference between men and women according to Table 10.3. For women one obtains the ranking $CV_B > E(CV) > CV$. This ranking suggests that women are risk-averse with respect to uncertainty in z; compare Propositions 2 and 3.

For male respondents, on the other hand, the Friedman–Savage (1948) type of diagram depicted in Figure 10.2 comes to mind. That is, the indirect utility function is concave in z for low z-levels and convex in z for sufficiently high z-levels. This kind of indirect utility function can, but need not necessarily, produce the inequality $E(CV) > CV_B > CV$ reported in Table 10.3. The interpretation is that male respondents are risk-averse when many species are threatened (when z takes on low values) while they are more inclined to accept risks when z exceeds some critical level. This difference between male and female respondents confirms earlier Swedish Gallup polls according to which Swedish women are more sensitive to environmental risks than Swedish men.

Besides these explanations of the observed behaviour, there is also the possibility that respondents are unable to calculate the non-contingent CV and therefore report some other money measure when the situation involves uncertain outcomes. However, there is no strong evidence for the suspicion that the respondents calculated and reported an expected compensating variation measure instead of a non-contingent willingness-to-pay measure. It is trivially true that, even if a dataset happens to confirm all of the hypotheses generated above, this is no ultimate proof that the respondents did calculate one or the other money measure. In addition, the sample of respondents used in the study reported here is very small, implying that some or all of the results may be due to random factors that a sufficiently large sample would net out.

In section 7.8, it was shown that use values provide a reasonable lower bound for the social benefits of a project even if individuals are altruistic. If altruism is non-paternalistic and we are at a social welfare optimum, the altruistic component nets out from a social cost-benefit analysis. In the study under discussion respondents were asked only for their total willingness to pay for different programmes. However, they were also asked about their motives for paying for programme A. It turns out that the small group that only paid for use values has an average willingness to pay of about $50, i.e. less than 25 per cent of the average total WTP for programme A in Table 10.3. This amounts to an annual payment of only $1–3 if the discount rate is 2–6 per cent; $50 = a/r$ if the time horizon is infinite, where a is the annual payment, and r is the discount rate.

If we accept that annual aggregate use values amount to around $4–11 million (since there are 3.7 million households), social benefits are probably much smaller than the as yet unknown costs of preserving the species in question. It has been estimated that as much as 10–15 per cent of the Swedish forests must be protected from forestry in order to save endangered species that live in the forests. The associated annual loss of value added is probably around $0.3–0.5 billion. As pointed out in the previous section, however, the value of Swedish standing forests lies in the fact that the investment cost is a sunk cost. If timber mining is ruled out, forestry is not a very profitable investment, in particular if risk premiums (see equation (9.18)) are included; a rotation period is 75–100 years in Sweden. A change to softer technologies in forestry that cause less damage than today's large-scale methods, and successively turning forests into natural parks, for example, need not be a very costly affair. The shift to less damaging cutting technologies is in any case already under way, in part as a response to criticism from environmentalists, in part due to new technologies becoming available.

Including altruistic values in the benefits measure increases the annual aggregate willingness to pay for protection to around $15–40 million. This illustrates the important role played by altruistic components in many contingent valuation studies. Even if altruistic benefits are accepted as part of a cost-benefit analysis, it is questionable whether the Swedish people are willing to bear the costs of protecting their endangered species.

Usually, a WTP question is supposed to provide us with a project's benefits, i.e. a money measure of use values plus any non-use values. The problem is that most projects, including the one considered here, create winners as well as losers. The latter group, here owners and employees in forestry and the forest industry, need to be compensated if they are to accept the project. The question is whether these people were able to value only the benefits of the project, or whether they valued both benefits and costs. The valuation question did not allow for negative bids, implying that losers had either to refuse to respond or to state a zero willingness to pay, unless they were able to value only the benefits of the project.

In fact, one cannot even completely rule out the possibility that the average respondent assessed something like CV in equation (5.9). The results in Table 10.3 then represent a cost-benefit analysis, given that society's welfare distribution is close to optimal and the project is considered to be small; compare equation (7.25'). This interpretation highlights the importance of specifying in detail what a respondent is supposed to value. In particular, it is important to tell those who derive both benefits and costs or just costs from the project what to value. Moreover, due to the uncertainty that prevails with respect to the treatment of altruistic motives in a cost-benefit analysis, it is recommended that the investigator should collect data on both use values and the total willingness to pay for a project (or its benefits).

10.4 Social cost of environmental quality regulations

By presidential executive order, US federal agencies are required to analyse new regulations, or changes in existing regulations, using cost-benefit analysis. According to Hazilla and Kopp (1990), a theoretically precise social cost measure is not used in practice, and current procedures, based on private costs, are subject to errors of unknown magnitude and without basis in modern applied welfare economics.[3] The objective of Hazilla and Kopp is to improve on these procedures by using the compensating variation welfare measure to evaluate the social cost of environmental quality regulations promulgated under the Clean Air and Clean Water Acts.

To estimate the dynamic social cost of environmental quality regulations, they construct an econometric general equilibrium model of the US economy. The model encompasses both static and intertemporal behavioural adjustments, and includes an explicit characterization of household utility that is used to assess welfare changes. Like the majority of computable general equilibrium models, the model employed by Hazilla and Kopp maintains the assumption of perfect competition in all markets. Production is modelled using a single form of malleable capital, and all inputs are assumed to be mobile. The capital stock is fixed in any given period and augmented at the end of the period by current-period net investment. The household is modelled using myopic expectations and assigned an initial wealth endowment. Transaction costs are assumed to be zero. Prices within the model are measured relative to a wage numéraire. Labour supply is endogenous while population growth is specified exogenously. Finally, as the major intertemporal link, household savings determine investment and the capital stock available in the next period. Through this intertemporal link, perturbations in the current-period labour market are transmitted to the capital market in the next period.

Production in the model is disaggregated into thirty-six producing sectors. With the exception of government services, each sector is algebraically formulated as a hierarchical system of translog cost functions exhibiting constant returns to scale. This system gives rise to competition-derived demand equations for capital and labour, four forms of energy, and thirty intermediate inputs. The translog system is estimated using data for the period 1958–74 subject to symmetry, linear homogeneity, monotonicity, and concavity constraints.

The consumption side of the model relies on the notion of a representative household and implies that households share common preferences. These common preferences, described by a set of hierarchical indirect translog utility functions, serve to model both intertemporal and intratemporal household decisions. The initial intertemporal decision faced by households concerns the choice between present and future consumption. A household must allocate a lifetime wealth endowment between present and future consumption of goods and leisure. Following this choice, the household focuses on two sequential intratemporal decisions. The first is to select the proportions of current-period consumption to take in the form of goods and leisure. This choice determines household labour supply and leisure. The second sequential decision is household allocation of current-period goods consumption among the following commodity groups: energy, durable goods, imported goods, agriculture and construction, manufacturing, commercial and transportation, and other services.

The social cost of environmental quality regulations can be computed from the econometrically estimated indirect utility function. Basically, Hazilla and Kopp define the social cost as:

$$V(p^1, y^1 - CV) = V(p^0, y^0) \qquad (10.6)$$

where a superscript 0 (1) refers to pre-regulation (post-regulation) general equilibrium values, and CV is the compensating variation measure of the social cost. There are no benefits of improved environmental quality included in the study by Hazilla and Kopp, which is why the z-variable does not appear in (10.6).

The Clean Air and Clean Water Acts' compliance expenditures may be separated into three categories. The first and largest is private firms' expenditures on air and water pollutant abatement equipment. The second category also includes pollution abatement expenditures, but pertains to those made by federal, state and local governments. The last group involves direct consumer expenditures such as the increased costs of unleaded petrol purchases and vehicle inspection fees.

Estimates of the social cost of environmental regulations are based on general equilibrium price and income vectors derived from two simulations. The first, termed the base-case simulation, pertains to the period 1970–90. The base-case simulation uses both historical values (1970–85) and forecasts (1986–90) for the exogenous variables. The second simulation, termed the regulatory scenario, uses the same exogenous variables but introduces regulation on the production technologies.

The estimates of social cost based on measures of compensating variation are displayed in Table 10.4. The general equilibrium model estimate of the social cost of federal air and water pollution control regulations in 1981 was approximately $28 billion. This may be directly compared to the EPA's $42.5 billion engineering cost estimate. These results imply that a 1981 cost-benefit analysis of the regulations based on the EPA estimates would understate the net benefits of the Clean Air and Clean Water Acts by $14.5 billion.

While the 1981 social cost estimate is significantly lower than the EPA estimate, one cannot conclude that social costs are always less than comparable estimates based on private expenditures. Economists have long recognized that governmental regulations have significant dynamic impacts. For example, the EPA estimates that federal air and water

Table 10.4. *Annual social cost and EPA compliance cost estimates of the Clean Air and Clean Water Acts ($ billion, current prices)*

Year	Social cost	EPA compliance cost
1975	6.8	14.1
1981	28.3	42.5
1985	70.6	56.0
1990	203.0	78.6
1981–90	977.0	648.0

pollution control costs total $525.8 billion (1981 dollars) between 1981 and 1990. If one distributes these expenditures uniformly over the 10-year interval and then converts them to nominal dollars (using the personal consumption expenditure price index in the model), the total nominal pollution control cost is approximately $648 billion. By contrast, the general equilibrium social cost estimate is $977 billion. Very few policy-makers have recognized that social costs can exceed private expenditures, but this is a direct result of household behaviour in which leisure is substituted for consumption. Hazilla and Kopp conclude by noting that their attention has focused on costs associated with environmental quality regulations. Any normative judgement about the desirability of the regulations depends on comparing appropriately measured costs with corresponding benefits. While benefits have generally been measured using an appropriate willingness-to-pay criterion, an intertemporal general equilibrium approach to benefit estimation might show similar divergences from reported results based on static partial equilibrium analysis.

10.5 The Brown–Hammack model for allocation of prairie wetlands

Brown and Hammack (1972) use a continuous-time infinite-horizon model to examine the optimal allocation of prairie wetlands in the north-central US and southern Canada. In their natural state, these wetlands are essential to migratory waterfowl, which are valued by hunters. On the other hand, the farmers who own the land would prefer to drain the marshes and ponds and convert them to cropland. The Brown–Hammack model and its empirical results are presented in this section.

The benefits of preserving the wetlands are the aggregate consumer's surplus, or the willingness to pay, of waterfowl hunters, while the costs are the opportunity costs or net value of the drained ponds to agricultural production. According to Brown and Hammack, the objective is to choose the bagged waterfowl kill and the number of ponds so as to maximize:

$$\int\limits_{0}^{\infty}[Hu(x_1(t),x_2(t)) - c(q(t))]e^{-rt}dt \tag{10.7}$$

where H is the number of hunters, $u(\cdot,\cdot)$ is the individual hunter valuation function, $x_1(t)$ is the bagged waterfowl kill at time t, $x_2(t)$ is consumption of other goods (net of goods used as inputs in hunting) at time t, $c(\cdot)$ is the pond cost function, $q(t)$ is the number of ponds at time t, and r is the discount rate.

Brown and Hammack employ a standard assumption in natural resource economics, namely that the utility function is additively separable (which is invariably the case with infinite-horizon models). It is important to note, however, that the valuation functions (like the cost functions) are expressed in monetary units and not in 'utils'. Given x_2, the valuation function gives the hunter's willingness to pay for bagged waterfowl. This function is assumed to be concave in the number of waterfowl killed and bagged. Moreover, the valuation function is constant over time, and relates to the 'representative' hunter. The latter explains that we multiply the valuation function by the (constant) number of hunters. The linear or convex cost function in (10.7) indicates the net value of agricultural output foregone as a function of the number of ponds not drained and converted.

The discount rate in (10.7) ought to reflect the individual's rate of time preference, i.e. the minimum premium the individual must receive before he will postpone a dollar's worth of consumption in one period. Assuming perfect capital markets, it is reasonable to set the rate of time preference equal to the market rate of interest r (see Dasgupta and Heal (1979, chs. 9–10)).

We must also describe the ecological system. The constraint on the waterfowl population is written as:

$$\dot{R}(t) = -R(t) + a[I(R(t),q(t)) + bR(t) - cHx_1(t)] \tag{10.8}$$

where a dot denotes a partial derivative with respect to time, R is the number of mature birds, $I = I(\cdot,\cdot)$ is the number of immature birds, a is the survival fraction of the autumn migration not killed by hunters from September to May, b is the survival fraction of adults from May to September, and c is an adjustment for unbagged kill.

Equation (10.8) describes the evolution of the waterfowl population over time. There is an outflow due to killing and other causes of death, and an inflow of immature birds. Note that if the constants a, b and c are all equal to one, the change in the population over time would simply equal the difference between the number of immature birds (the inflow), and the number killed and bagged by hunters (the outflow). In addition to (10.8), it must also hold that the initial population exceeds the threshold population and that, at any given moment in time, the resource stock and the harvest level cannot be negative.

In order to solve the problem raised by equations (10.7) and (10.8) we will use optimal control theory. The first step is to formulate the Hamiltonian function:

$$L = [Hu(x_1,x_2) - c(q) + \mu(-R + aI(R,q) + abR - acHx_1)]e^{-rt} \quad (10.9)$$

where time indices are suppressed so as to simplify the notation, and μ is a co-state variable. Among the necessary conditions for an 'interior' solution are:

$$\left.\begin{aligned}
\frac{\partial L}{\partial x_1} &= \frac{\partial u}{\partial x_1} - \mu ac = 0 \\
\frac{\partial L}{\partial q} &= \frac{\partial c}{\partial q} - \mu a\frac{\partial I}{\partial q} = 0 \\
\frac{\partial L}{\partial R} &= -\dot{\mu} + r\mu = \mu\left(-1 + a\frac{\partial I}{\partial R} + ab\right)
\end{aligned}\right\} \quad (10.10)$$

For purely expositional purposes, let us assume that the constants a, b and c all equal one. From the first line in (10.10), it can be seen that μ can be interpreted as the marginal value to hunters of waterfowl. A marginal increase in the number of ponds q creates not only a cost in the form of agricultural output foregone, but also a benefit in the form of an increased number of birds (immature) which are valued hunting objects. The second line of (10.10) tells us that the number of ponds should be increased to the point where the marginal cost is equal to the marginal revenue. In order to interpret the final line of (10.10), let us consider a steady state in which the marginal value of waterfowl is constant over time, i.e. $\dot{\mu} = 0$. It then follows that the optimal waterfowl stock is that at which the marginal growth rate $\partial I/\partial R$ is equal to the discount rate; it should be remembered that we have assumed that $a = b = c = 1$. This is exactly the result derived in section 6.4.

Brown and Hammack made an attempt to estimate the model described here, and some of their results are reported below. For a detailed presentation the reader should consult Brown and Hammack (1972) and Hammack and Brown (1974). A good summary of their work can be found in Krutilla and Fisher (1975, ch. 9).

In order to obtain information on the hunter valuation function Brown and Hammack used the interview technique. A sample of waterfowl hunters was questioned concerning the value each attached to hunting. The central question was as follows: 'About how much greater do you think your costs would have had to have been before you would have decided not to have gone hunting at all during that season?' (Hammack and Brown, 1974, p. 92). The resulting willingness-to-pay amounts were regressed on a number of independent variables to obtain:

Table 10.5. *Economic optimal values and historical values*

	Pond cost			
	$4.76	$12	$17	Historical values
Breeders, R (millions)	33	15	11	8
Ponds, q (millions)	22	6	4	1
Marginal value of waterfowl, μ (dollars)	2	3	4	
Total kill, x_1 (millions)	15	7	5	4

Assumptions: $a = 0.84$, $b = 0.95$, $c = 1.25$, $r = 0.08$ and numbers of hunters, $H = 0.279$ million.
Source: Krutilla and Fisher (1975, p. 229).

$$\ln u = 1.5 + 0.4\ln x_1 + 0.4\ln y + 0.2\ln A + 0.1\ln B \quad R^2 = 0.22 \quad (10.11)$$
$$ (12.9) \quad (8.4) \quad (4.4) \quad (5.6)$$

where numbers in parentheses are t values, y is income, A is the number of seasons of waterfowl hunting, B is hunter costs for the season, and the number of observations is 1,511. Taking the partial derivative with respect to x_1, and rearranging, yields:

$$\frac{\partial u}{\partial x_1} = 0.4\frac{u}{x_1} \tag{10.12}$$

This expression indicates the valuation of a marginal unit of bagged kill and can be used to construct a (downward-sloping) 'demand' curve for waterfowl kill. Note, however, that (10.12) is not defined for a zero hunting level; in fact, the underlying indifference surface does not intersect the $x_1 = 0$ hyperplane. Given the fact that the hunter is confronted with a sufficiently high (hypothetical) hunting cost to prevent him from hunting at all, it is not obvious why Hammack and Brown choose a functional form that is not consistent with such behaviour.

The growth function $I(s,q)$ was estimated using time series data running from 1955 to 1968. One of several different estimated relationships is:

$$\ln I = 1.4 + 0.3\ln R + 0.5\ln q \quad R^2 = 0.83 \tag{10.13}$$
$$ (1.6) \quad (6.7)$$

where I is the number of immature birds in September, R is the continental breeding population in the preceding May, and q is the number of Canadian prairie ponds in July of the same year.

A number of results are shown in Table 10.5. The cost function $c(q)$ was not estimated. As can be seen from the table, Brown and Hammack assumed that the cost of a marginal pond is constant. Assumptions about the parameters are set out below the table.

It is interesting to note that the economically optimal level of breeding stock far exceeds the one actually observed, at least for reasonable pond cost levels. This result is probably due to the fact that the wetlands are privately owned. There is a market for wetlands, while there is no market for hunting. In other words, ponds cause a positive external effect which is not reflected in the maximization problems of the landowners.

The results can also be used to calculate the maximum sustainable yield stock of breeders. Differentiating (10.8) with respect to t, with q and x_1 fixed, and setting the resulting expression equal to zero, yields:

$$-1 + a\frac{\partial I}{\partial R} + ab = 0 \qquad (10.14)$$

This expression can be solved to obtain the steady-state stock that gives the highest possible sustainable level of kill. This level corresponds to point R^S in Figure 6.2. Using the growth function given in (10.13), Brown and Hammack estimated the maximum sustainable yield stock to be 10 million for a pond value of 1.4 million. The corresponding figure for total kill is 6 million.

These maximum sustainable yield values are much lower than the economic optima given in Table 10.5, at least for reasonable pond cost values. The reason for this is that the maximum sustainable yield values are calculated from the actual number of ponds. The economic optimal solution requires a much larger number of ponds; although a sufficiently high pond cost will reverse the result. Krutilla and Fisher (1975, pp. 231–3) point out that these results illustrate the problems with the biological, or maximum sustainable yield, solution, i.e. how the decision-maker is to choose the number of ponds. The (bio-)economic approach used by Brown and Hammack, on the other hand, indicates the optimal number of ponds, although this figure, like the rest of the results, must be interpreted with great care. Nevertheless, their approach is an interesting and promising one.

A final comment relates to the fact that the demand derived from the amenity services of a natural area may vary over time. Clearly, such factors as the degree of availability of substitute areas, as measured by cross-price elasticities and travel costs, and the rate of increase in real income are of critical importance when forecasting demand. Hammack and Brown do not consider such reasons for fluctuations in demand. The reader interested in practical methods used to forecast demand for scarce amenity resources is referred to Krutilla and Fisher (1975), who consider the case of a unique natural area, and Cuddington *et al.* (1981), who deal with a case where the resource in question is not unique and has recognized substitutes. Basically, Cuddington *et al.* multiply the present value of the consumer's surplus in year *t* by $(1 + i)^t$ with *i* reflecting the rate of increase in real income. The size of the surplus depends on the presence of substitute areas, as measured by a cross-price elasticity. Obviously such modifications may have quite a strong influence on the size of the present value of natural amenities. More generally, variations over time in benefits and/or costs highlight the fact that the decision *when* to undertake a project is of the utmost importance.

10.6 Accounting for natural resource depletion

In section 6.5 measures of sustainable income were defined. To the best of my knowledge, however, no country has yet adopted such accounting measures. This section briefly summarizes Peskin's (1989) attempt to present a modified set of national accounts for Tanzania.

Two adjustments were made to the conventional accounts, and the modified accounts are reported in Table 10.6. Firstly, the employee compensation figure was modified to account for the imputed value of household labour used for the cutting, gathering and transport of fuelwood from natural forests. An estimate was obtained by multiplying an estimated 137 million person days per year spent in household fuelwood production by the Tanzanian minimum wage of 13 cents per day. This calculation yields an estimate of $18 million as opposed to the official estimate of $1.3 million.

The second modification was to depreciate the forests due to the fuelwood consumption. A rough estimate was obtained by setting depreciation equal to the imputed value of fuelwood cutting, minus the value of regeneration. This yields a net depreciation of $13 million.

These two modifications had the effect in 1980 of increasing the Tanzanian national income by 2 per cent and the gross domestic product by 6 per cent. It is important to note, however, that the modified measures reported in Table 10.6 do not correspond directly to the closed economy net welfare measure in chapter 6. There are two main differences. Firstly, owing to a lack of data, the Tanzanian accounts do not include any estimate of environmental benefits and environmental costs other than depreciation of forests. Secondly, they include wage income. According to the net welfare measure in chapter 6, employee compensation is deducted from a welfare measure. The reason for this is that, at the margin, people are indifferent between taking a job and spending the time on recreation or on their own work.

Another example of attempts to revise national accounts is provided by

Table 10.6. *Modified Tanzanian accounts, 1980 ($ millions)*

Input			Output		
Employee compensation	71.5		Government purchases		36.8
Plus value of household fuelwood production	17.0		Private consumption	210.2	
Modified employee compensation		88.5	*Plus* household fuelwood consumed	17.0	
Profits and proprietors' income	156.2		Modified private consumption		227.2
Less depreciation of natural forests	−12.8		Investment		58.6
Modified profits and proprietors' income		143.5	Exports		38.1
			Imports		−72.9
Modified national income		232.0			
Indirect taxes		34.7			
Subsidies		−2.7			
Modified net national product		263.9			
Capital consumption	11.2				
Plus depreciation of forests	12.8				
Modified capital consumption		23.9			
Modified gross domestic product		287.9	**Modified expenditure on GDP**		287.9

Source: Peskin (1989, p. 43).

Repetto *et al.* (1991). They revised the conventional national income measure for Costa Rica. By conventional measures, Costa Rica's economy grew by 4.6 per cent a year between 1970 and 1989. More than a quarter of this growth disappears when adjusted for the depreciation of forests, soils and fisheries. By far the largest losses came from deforestation, while the possibly severest ones were in fishing, where catches of some valuable fish collapsed in the mid-eighties.

11 Policy instruments and international environmental problems

Thus far the question of how to achieve a socially reasonable allocation of environmental resources has not been addressed. Nor has the evaluation of activities which harm other countries been considered. This final chapter takes a brief look at both these issues, but the reader interested in details is referred to Barrett (1990), Baumol and Oates (1988), Bohm (1990), Forsund and Strom (1988), Hoel (1992), Holmer and Howe (1991), Nordhaus (1991), Opschoor and Vos (1989), Siebert (1987), Tietenberg (1992) and Weitzman (1974), just to mention a few. In section 11.1 the most commonly used policy instruments (regulations, emission charges and tradeable emission permits) and their properties are discussed. Section 11.2 is devoted to the treatment of a unidirectional externality in a social cost-benefit analysis. The usual example of this kind of externality is an upstream country polluting a river and hence harming downstream countries. The chapter ends with a presentation of a study of sulphur emissions in Europe. The costs and benefits of different strategies for reducing such emissions are presented.

11.1 Policy instruments

There are several ways of inducing polluting firms to reduce their emissions. In this section, the three most common are briefly presented. These policy instruments are regulations, emission charges and tradeable emission permits.

Let us consider a profit-maximizing firm producing a single homogeneous good, and treating all prices as unaffected by its actions. The production of this good causes emissions of some pollutant. Profits can be defined as:

$$\Pi = px - c(x) - h(z) \tag{11.1}$$

where x is output, the cost of producing the good $c(x)$ is stated as a strictly convex function of the output level, and $h(z)$ denotes the costs of clean-up as

200

a strictly convex function of the quantity of emissions controlled (z). It is assumed that there is some technology making it possible for the firm to control any proportion of its emissions.

If there is no law regulating emissions, or if the law is ambiguous, the firm will clean up zero units of its emissions.[1] That is, a profit-maximizing firm will produce an amount of the good such that its price is equal to the marginal cost, i.e. $p = c'(x)$ with $c'(x)$ denoting the marginal cost of production. Let us now consider three often-proposed ways to reduce emissions: regulations, uniform emission charges and transferable emission permits.

The traditional legal approach is to impose a separate emission standard (*regulation*) on each polluting source. However, there is not much we can say about how a controlling authority actually works, i.e. what z-value it forces the firm to insert into its clean-up cost function in (11.1), and on what grounds. We therefore leave this approach for the moment.

As an alternative the authority could levy a *uniform emission charge* on each unit of pollutant. In this case, the problem of the firm is to maximize:

$$\Pi = px - c(x) - h(z) - \tau_e[e(x) - z] \tag{11.2}$$

where τ_e is the emission charge, $e(x)$ is gross emissions as a convex function of the firm's output level, and $e(x) - z \geq 0$ is net emissions, i.e. what the firm actually emits into the air or water.

First-order conditions for an interior solution are:

$$\left. \begin{array}{l} p = c'(x) + \tau_e e'(x) = C'(x) \\ h'(z) = \tau_e \end{array} \right\} \tag{11.3}$$

where a prime denotes a partial derivative. According to the first line in (11.3), the overall marginal cost now consists of two parts. First, there is the usual direct marginal cost $c'(x)$ of production. Second, a marginal change in production affects emissions and hence the emission charges the firm has to pay. The second line in (11.3) shows that the firm reduces/treats its emissions to an extent such that the marginal control cost $h'(z)$ is equal to the emission charge. The solution is illustrated in Figure 11.1, where an asterisk denotes a profit-maximizing level. The firm controls z^* units of its emissions and pays $\tau_e[e(x^*) - z^*]$ in emission charges. Note, however, that for sufficiently high (low) τ_e-levels, the firm is expected to treat all (none) of its emissions: corner solutions cannot be ruled out.

Under a *transferable emission permit system* each firm is required to have a permit to emit. The permit specifies how much the firm is allowed to emit, and the permits are freely transferable. The idea is thus to establish a well-defined market. Suppose that the market-clearing price of a permit to emit one unit is p^p. At this price, demand for permits is exactly matched by the fixed supply of permits.

a

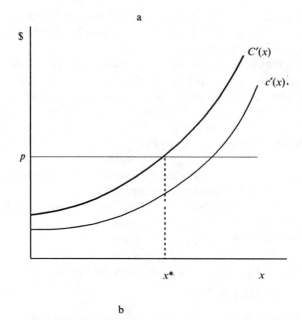

b

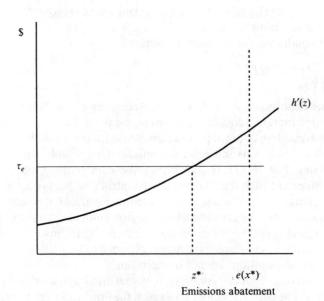

Emissions abatement

Figure 11.1. The optimal levels of (a) production (x^*) and (b) pollution abatement (z^*) when there is an emission charge τ_e.

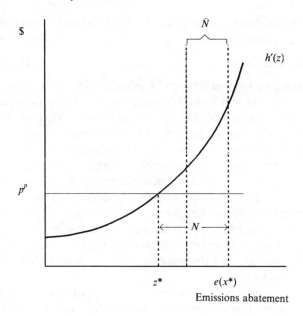

Figure 11.2. A firm buying emission permits.

In this case, the problem of the firm is to maximize:

$$\Pi = px - c(x) - h(z) - p^p N + p^p \bar{N} \qquad (11.4)$$

where $N = e(x) - z$ is the number of permits the firm must possess, and $\bar{N}$ is the number of permits initially assigned to the firm.

From a purely formal point of view, the necessary conditions for an interior solution to the maximization problem (11.4) parallel those in (11.3). The firm will reduce its emissions to an extent such that the marginal control cost is equal to the price of a permit. We denote this optimal control level z^*. The firm will buy $e(x^*) - z^* - \bar{N}$ permits at the ruling market price p^p. However, as can be seen from Figure 11.2, if the permit price is sufficiently high, the firm prefers to eliminate all of its emissions (and sell its $\bar{N}$ initial permits). Similarly, if the permit price falls below some critical level, the firm in Figure 11.2 will buy permits rather than control its emissions. Note also that the profit-maximizing output level x^* depends on, among other things, the market price of emission permits. This can be seen from a glance at equations (11.3). The quantity $e(x^*)$ in the figure is thus endogenous, and not a fixed constant.

In the aggregate, net demand for permits must be zero: in equilibrium, prices must be such that firms demand exactly the initial endowment of permits:

$$\bar{N}_A + N_A^d(p^p, p, \ldots, N_A) = N_A^S \qquad (11.5)$$

where $\bar{N}_A$ is the aggregate number of permits initially allocated to firms, which is equal to the number of permits N_A^S issued, and $N_A^d(\cdot)$ is net demand for permits, viewed here as a function of all equilibrium prices in the economy and the distribution across firms (N_A) of permits issued. In equilibrium, N_A^d must be equal to zero. At the individual firm level, however, net demand for permits may be positive or negative. Firms with relatively high marginal control costs will demand permits, while firms with relatively low marginal control costs will supply permits. Trade will continue until $p^p = h'(z)$ for all firms, and the price is such that aggregate net demand for permits is zero, assuming here an interior solution for all firms. This is illustrated in Figure 11.3 for the two-firms case, where firm 1 supplies and firm 2 demands permits and the price of a permit is such that net demand $(N_1^S + N_2^d)$ sums to zero.

By simply issuing the appropriate number of emission permits and letting the market do the rest, the control authority can therefore achieve a *cost-effective* allocation without having the slightest idea of the firms' control costs. A uniform emission charge system also has this cost-effective property, as can be seen from equations (11.3), assuming an interior solution for all firms, the difference being that the charge system seems to require more information. It may be difficult for the control authority to find the level of the charge which secures the emission reduction target. A permit system, on the other hand, simply requires the authority to issue an appropriate number of permits.

The revenues from issuing transferable permits or from introducing an emission charge system have not been accounted for in the preceding analysis. From the indirect utility functions defined in sections 5.2 and 5.5, for example, it can be seen that tax revenues collected from firms must either be passed on to households or used to expand the public sector. This means that the pollution control system causes some general equilibrium effects which are not covered by the analysis in this section. Moreover, income distribution is affected both by the choice of policy instrument(s), and the distribution of actual clean-up costs across firms and households, most obviously in the case of emission permits. Depending on how these endowments are distributed, one would expect different general equilibrium prices and incomes.

There are also many pollutants which are difficult to handle through uniform charges or emission permits systems. For example, some pollutants are local in the sense that the location of the emitting source is

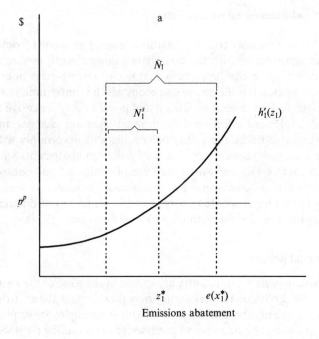

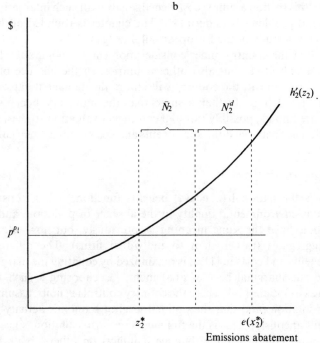

Figure 11.3. A two-firm market for transferable emission permits.

important. This is obviously true for health-damaging emissions from a car. It is not unimportant whether the car is driven along a hardly used road in the countryside or in the heart of a major city during rush hours. Similarly, in some cases, it is the mix of emissions which is important, not a single particulate. In such cases it is difficult and possibly very expensive to construct and implement effective differentiated emission charges and permit markets. In addition, there may be considerable uncertainty with respect to the (marginal) benefits and costs of pollution abatement. Such factors may in part explain the widespread use of command-and-control approaches (regulations) to environmental problems. The reader is referred to Tietenberg (1992) for a detailed analysis of the properties of different policy instruments. See also the seminal paper by Weitzman (1974).

11.2 International pollution

In many cases, emissions in one country are spread by the wind or the water to other countries. Pollution in one country may thus damage the environment and those living in other countries. Well-known examples are sulphur emissions contributing to acid rain and greenhouse gases causing (?) global warming. In this section a simple cost-benefit analysis of such international environmental problems is undertaken. The chapter is rounded off by a presentation of a study of the European sulphur 'game'.

Suppose that the country under consideration emits a pollutant which damages not only itself, but also other countries. In the absence of an international settlement, the country will ignore the damage it causes to other countries. Let us further assume that the monetary benefits of abatement are known, possibly through contingent valuation studies, and that the difference between domestic benefits and costs of abatement can be written as:

$$B[A - e(x) + z] - h(z) \qquad (11.6)$$

where $B(\cdot)$ is the national (concave) benefits function, A is a constant interpreted as environmental quality in the absence of pollution, and all other symbols have the same meaning as previously, but now refer to national aggregates (rather than to individual firms). The difference between benefits and costs in (11.6) is maximized by equating the marginal benefit and the marginal cost of abatement, i.e. choosing z such that $B'(\cdot) = h \cdot (\cdot)$ as in Figure 11.4, where the country controls z^d units, assuming an interior solution (and that the optimal level of economic activity x is chosen simultaneously). This is the full *non-cooperative* solution, since the country ignores completely the damage it inflicts on others. Note that marginal benefits $B'(\cdot)$ can be interpreted as the sum of households'

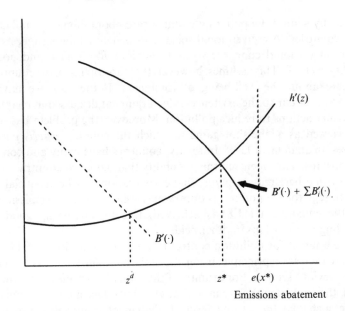

Figure 11.4. The non-cooperative (z^d) and co-operative (z^*) solutions to pollution abatement.

marginal willingness to pay for pollution control, plus any change in producer surplus from a small change in z, as in equation (5.7). As in the previous section, any public sector revenues from emission charges, for example, have been neglected.

The full *co-operative* solution is found by internalizing the externality. The country controls emissions so as to maximize the difference between *global* benefits and domestic costs of abatement:

$$B[A - e(x) + z] + \sum_i B_i[A_i - e(x) + z] - h(z) \qquad (11.7)$$

where $B_i(\cdot)$ is the monetary benefit function for country i as a function of abatement in the polluting country. The interpretation of (11.7) is that a single country is the source of the problem but all countries suffer from the problem. We will come back to other kinds of international environmental problems later on, but let us first consider the (interior) solution to the maximization problem (11.7):

$$B'(\cdot) + \sum_i B_i'(\cdot) = h'(\cdot) \qquad (11.8)$$

According to (11.8), the polluting country should choose a z-level such that the *global* marginal benefit of abatement is equal to the marginal cost of abatement. This is the full co-operative solution, denoted z^* in Figure 11.4.

But why should the polluting country care about damage it inflicts on other countries? A conventional social cost-benefit analysis suggests that the country should choose z so as to achieve $B'(\cdot) = h'(\cdot)$, and not the equality in (11.8). This assumes, however, that those living in the country do not care about the well-being of foreigners. If they do, we have an argument, similar to the existence-value argument discussed in chapter 3, for further actions to reduce pollution. Moreover, the problem has so far been viewed as a one-shot game in which the country, *ceteris paribus*, chooses an abatement level. In reality, countries have many and complex relationships. This opens up the possibility that damaged countries might retaliate in other areas, implying that co-operation may be beneficial. The best strategy for the polluting country may well be to reduce emissions so that the equality in (11.8) is achieved, thereby preserving good and rewarding relationships in other fields.

Once a target for pollution control has been chosen, this target can be achieved (at least in principle) using one of the policy instruments presented in the previous section. For example if the target is to achieve the equality (11.8), the control authority may choose to introduce a uniform emission charge such that the desired level of abatement is achieved. Equations (11.3) then will hold for each polluting firm, assuming, as usual, an interior solution. Similar conditions will hold if the authority instead uses emission permits.

These approaches are in accordance with the *polluter pays* principle. Alternatively, the *victim pays* principle may be applied. Hence, the victims of the country's emissions 'bribe' the polluter to reduce its emissions. Domestic and foreign victims could together pay polluting industries an aggregate amount such that, in terms of Figure 11.4, z^* units of emissions are controlled. Thus, independently of the distribution of property rights (i.e. who 'owns' the air and water), we may end up at the same Pareto-efficient allocation. This result is known as *Coase's theorem*. Unfortunately, the theorem has a quite limited validity. For example, redistributing property rights (endowments) may affect prices in other markets (not covered by our analysis above) and hence move the economy from one Pareto-efficient allocation to another. More generally, there is the question of what is a fair distribution; not everyone may be indifferent to which party must compensate and which party is being compensated. The theorem also assumes that all participants have access to perfect and costless information about each other's preferences, i.e. have access to all the information needed to locate the curves in Figure 11.4. Relaxing the assumption of full information opens up the possibility that bargaining will result in Pareto-inefficient allocations. The reader is referred to Inman (1987) for a discussion of such outcomes.

In an open economy context, the introduction of policy instruments to reduce domestic emissions may induce firms to shut down or move to other countries. If emission charges, for example, are higher in the home country, and firms are free to choose the location of their plants, one must account for the possibility that domestic firms relocate to other countries. Similarly, foreign firms may cancel their plans to invest in the country under consideration. In a sense this is nothing to be worried about. The reason for having higher emission charges than the rest of the world is reasonably that the marginal willingness to pay for reduced pollution is higher in the home country than elsewhere. The residents should be happy that polluting firms relocate to countries where people are less concerned about environmental quality or where marginal pollution control costs are lower. However, this does not always seem to be the case. There may be several reasons for negative reactions to announcements (or threats) that firms will move abroad if emission charges or other taxes are increased. For example, trade unions fear a loss of jobs and an adjustment of wages so as to sustain competitiveness in international markets. Others fear that firms will relocate to poor countries where they may cause long-run and possibly irreversible damage to the environment. In any case, in a cost-benefit analysis, the investigator must consider the possibility that firms relocate their investments as a consequence of policy instruments introduced as a part of the project under investigation.

11.3 The acid rain game

In order to illustrate some of the points made in the previous section, a study by Mäler (1990) is summarized here.[2] Mäler studied the use of the European atmosphere as a dump for sulphur oxides. It has been a well-known fact for at least twenty years that such emissions contribute to acid rain, with detrimental effects on ground and surface water and on forests. It is also known that nitrogen oxides contribute to acid rains. We will for simplicity leave nitrogen out of the discussion. The reader can easily imagine the qualitative changes that would be necessary to accommodate emissions of other substances.

Although it may seem that European problems of acid rain are rather special, Mäler's study has a much wider application. The problems of global warming and the emission of greenhouse gases have essentially the same economic nature, and the discussion on sulphur emissions will throw light on this larger issue.

Sulphur oxides are emitted when fossil fuels are burnt and in some industrial processes. In the atmosphere, the oxides are oxidized into sulphates, which can be transported by the wind over very long distances.

They are finally removed from the atmosphere by rain (wet deposition), and by contact with plants, surface water, etc. (dry deposition). In either case, deposition of sulphates increases the acidity of surface water, the topsoil, etc. and will have detrimental environmental effects.

Since wind direction varies, this is a case of a reciprocal externality, although because of the existence of prevailing winds, the situation is not completely symmetric. Some countries are more often upwind than others and some more often downwind. The extent to which a country is a net receiver of sulphates can be shown by a transport model. In this case the annual transport between countries can be described in terms of a matrix A with coeficients a_{ij} indicating the amount of sulphur deposited in country j from the emission of one ton of sulphur in country i. As most of the sulphur emitted in a country will be deposited in the same country, the diagonal elements of the transport matrix will in general be large compared with the non-diagonal elements.

Mäler assumes that for each country there is a well-defined cost function for reducing sulphur emissions, and a well-defined damage function from the deposition of sulphur (benefit function for pollution abatement). If a country is acting rationally, and if it is not bound by international agreements, it will emit sulphur to the point where the marginal abatement cost equals the marginal damage cost (marginal benefits from pollution control). The marginal damage cost from domestic emissions is equal to the marginal damage cost from sulphur depositions multiplied by the proportion of the deposition that originates from domestic sources. Country i thus emits sulphur until:

$$h_i'(e_i) = a_{ii}B_i'(Q_i) \qquad (11.9)$$

where e_i is the emission in country i, h_i' the marginal abatement cost, here taken as a function of domestic emissions (and not the level of pollution control), Q_i the deposition in country i, and B_i' the marginal damage cost in country i from further deposition of sulphur. Note that $Q_i = \sum_j a_{ji}e_j$ in (11.9).

Condition (11.9) describes the Nash non-cooperative equilibrium that would be the outcome from the interplay of rational countries who are not bound to take into account the effects of their emissions on other countries. However, this Nash non-cooperative equilibrium will not correspond to a collectively rational outcome. A collectively rational outcome would be a situation where the total net gain to all countries is maximized, and would correspond to the following necessary condition:

$$h_i'(e_i) = \sum_j a_{ij}B_j'(Q_j) \qquad \forall i \qquad (11.10)$$

This condition means that the marginal abatement cost in each country should be equal to the marginal damage to all countries that are affected by the emissions. This is a straightforward generalization of equation (11.8).

In order to use this model for illustrative purposes, the unknown cost and damage functions must be numerically specified and a relevant transport model must be found. Within the European Monitoring and Evaluation Programme (EMEP) a transport model has been estimated and used to produce 'sulphur budgets' for Europe. The matrix A above has been estimated on the basis of the sulphur budgets for 1980–85. Cost-of-abatement functions have been estimated by IIASA, and although these estimated abatement functions have some serious drawbacks, they were used for this application.[3] There are no consistent estimates of damage functions from acid rain available. In order to overcome this problem, the following procedure was followed.

Mäler assumes that 1984 was a year when the emissions of sulphur in Europe could be characterized as a Nash equilibrium. This assumption implies that if we know a_{ij} and the marginal damage cost h'_i we would be able to calculate the marginal damage cost B'_i. We thus have all the information needed for a calibration of B'_i in 1984. Finally, Mäler makes the assumption that the marginal damage costs are constant and independent of the amount of deposition, implying that the whole model can be calibrated numerically. It should be stressed that the damage function estimate thus obtained is quite different from the concept used previously. It may be interpreted as the revealed preferences of the governments for reductions in emissions of sulphur. Because of this procedure of calibrating the damage functions and the model, all numerical results should be interpreted with caution. The simulations do not purport to give numerical predictions but only qualitative insights into the problem of regional reciprocal externalities.

By using the calibrated model, different co-operative outcomes can be illustrated. One possible outcome is achieved if the sum of the net benefits over all European countries is maximized. This will be called the full co-operative solution. The consequences of this solution for some countries are summarized in Table 11.1.

One can first note that substantial gains of almost $3.8 billion can be made from co-operation. Moreover, in view of the calibration procedure, it is certain that the gains are understated in Table 11.1. The full co-operative solution requires an average reduction of sulphur emissions in Europe of almost 40 per cent, more than that given in the protocol to the convention on long-range pollutants reductions, the so-called Thirty Per Cent Club. More interestingly, the net benefits from co-operation are very unevenly distributed among the countries. Some countries will even experience losses from co-operation. This is mainly due to the geographic location of these countries, since some are more upwind than others and thus will not have as great net benefits as those countries that are more downwind. An extreme case is provided by the United Kingdom, which is very much upwind, and

Table 11.1. *Net benefits from the full co-operative solution*

Country	Emission reduction (per cent)	Net benefit ($ millions)
Czechoslovakia	75	91
Finland	14	−2
Germany (eastern)	80	7
Germany (western)	86	198
Poland	27	361
Sweden	4	364
Soviet Union	2	907
United Kingdom	81	−203
Europe	39	3,787

therefore would have to abate its emissions quite a lot, while not benefiting from the abatement in other countries. Sweden is an example of a downwind country, having to reduce emissions by only 4 per cent, and making substantial net benefits. The former Soviet Union is a special case because it is large and very little of its substantial emissions affect other European countries.

Why should the United Kingdom be willing to sign an agreement by which it would lose more than $200 million? We are obviously back to the earlier issue of the 'polluter pays' principle versus the 'victim pays' principle. The only reason the UK would be willing to accept this burden is because it would expect to gain something in some other arena. Let us maintain the assumption that it is possible to measure this other gain in dollars. In other words, we assume that the transferable utility can be measured in this currency. The UK would need a gain worth more than $200 million in order to sign the full co-operative agreement. In fact, in the full solution, four countries (Finland, Italy, Spain and the UK) would experience losses that must be compensated in order to induce these countries to sign the agreement. However, the net benefits in the rest of Europe would be more than sufficient to cover their losses.

The situation is rather more complicated than this suggests, however, because if the United Kingdom does not sign an agreement, while the other countries do, the UK will benefit from the reduction of emissions in the rest of Europe, while not bearing any burden. It may pay the UK to become a free-rider. Let us assume that all the four countries that would experience losses decide not to sign an agreement but that the rest of Europe decides to go ahead and maximize their total net benefit. The result is shown in Table 11.2.

Not only have the losses of the countries disappeared, but they have even

Table 11.2. *Net benefits from coalition formation*

Country	Emission reduction (per cent)	Net benefit ($ millions)
Co-operating countries		
Czechoslovakia	75	75
Germany (eastern)	80	−28
Germany (western)	86	47
Poland	27	327
Sweden	3	287
Soviet Union	—	826
Total for co-operating countries	37	2,970
Defecting countries		
Italy	—	91
United Kingdom	—	53
Total for defecting countries	—	149
Total for Europe	28	3,119

Note: — denotes value missing in Mäler's (1990) study.

turned into substantial gains. These are the gains from being a free-rider, enjoying the benefits from the co-operation among other countries without having to make any sacrifices. However, these free-rider gains could be achieved by all countries. By defecting, Sweden could achieve a gain, although only a very small one as Sweden would not have to abate much of its emissions in the full co-operative solution. Similarly for every other country: they could all gain by not signing the agreement and hoping that the rest of Europe would co-operate. The outcome would obviously be that there would be no agreement that included all European countries. The free-rider incentives in this model are so pervasive that we should not expect a full co-operative solution to emerge. Note that exactly the same mechanism will be working in the case of unidirectional externalities when there is more than one country receiving pollution from other countries, and the downwind countries have to compensate the upwind countries.

In conclusion, Mäler's (1990) study illustrates the use of cost-benefit analysis, as well as the policy-instrument choice problem, in dealing with international (and interregional) environmental problems. These are probably two of the most important fields for environmental economists during the remainder of this decade. They provide many fascinating and important challenges for theoreticians as well as those working in more applied fields.

Notes

2 Some basic concepts

1 We assume now that $Y^h = 0$ while $\tau^h \gtrless 0$, i.e. τ^h is interpreted as tax payments net of any transfers.
2 Usually a cost-benefit analysis is expressed in monetary units, i.e. we convert the change in welfare from units of social welfare to monetary units.

3 Consumer surplus measures

1 The sign convention used to define CV (and later EV) is arbitrary but means that the sign of CV (EV) is equal to the sign of ΔV. See equation (3.5).
2 Note that integrating for prices higher than the one for which x_i^c becomes zero does not add to the consumer surplus since $\int 0 \cdot dp = 0$. See also equations (3A.12)–(3A.14).
3 There are exceptions. The reader is invited to check this by using the quasi-linear and separable utility function $U = \ln x_1 + a x_2 + u(z)$ where a is a strictly positive constant, and z is the single public good referred to as existence value.

4 Valuing public goods

1 The study is summarized in Johansson (1987, pp. 95–103).
2 In some recent applications, the respondent is asked a second valuation question; if he accepts the first bid, the second bid is higher, while it is lower if he rejects the first bid. See, for example, Morey et al. (1991) for details.
3 Note, however, that Shechter, in terms of equation (4.4) adds a component γz. This means that his money measures do not cover this component since it cannot be derived from market data (compare (4.5)). See also equation (II–1) in Shechter's paper.
4 Similarly, wage differentials may be used to examine how workers react to health risks in their workplace.

5 General equilibrium cost-benefit rules

1 Note that $\partial \Pi(\cdot)/\partial p = x(p,w^0,z^0)$ for $p \geq 0$ (with $x = 0$ for $p \leq \bar{p}$), i.e. $\int(\partial \Pi/\partial p)dp = \int xdp$ in (5.2).

6 Cost-benefit rules, national income accounts and sustainable development

1 K_1 is assumed to be fixed. The presentation here draws heavily on Nickell (1978, pp. 7–11).

2 Note that if marginal growth equals zero, then an interior solution requires that $p_t^R = p_{t+1}^R$, i.e. that the price increases by r per cent from period t to period $t+1$ so that the present-value price remains constant. This is Hotelling's rule. See the appendix for details.

3 Strictly speaking, the NWM measure is expressed in units of utility. Dividing through by V_y would convert the measure to units of money.

7 Valuation and aggregation

1 Note that W_h is a function of household utility levels, while V_y^h is a function of prices, wages, utility and environmental quality. Line integrals are additive, and in (7.8) it is assumed that the compensating variations are changed in order from initial to final values. See the appendix to chapter 3 for necessary and sufficient conditions for a line integral to be path-independent.

8 Cost-benefit rules in a risky world

1 We ignore here and in what follows the problem that a surplus of revenues over costs must somehow be distributed. See sections 5.3 and 7.3.

2 The slope of a WTP locus is $ds^{2h}/ds^{th} = \pi^1 V_y^h(y^h - S^{th},z^1)/\pi^2 V_y^h(y^h - S^{2h},z^2)$, assuming just two states. The slope of the locus is interpreted as the marginal rate of substitution between states.

9 Valuing changes in access conditions, health risks and information

1 Thus, it is assumed that $V(y,z^1) > V(y,z^2) > \ldots > V(y,z^i) > \ldots > V(y,z^n)$ for all $y \geq 0$. Moreover, these functions are assumed to be bounded above and below.

2 Thus, $0 < \pi^1 < \pi_0^1 < 1$, $\pi^1 + \pi^n = 1$, and $\pi_0^1 + \pi_0^n = 1$.

3 In terms of the cost-benefit rule (8.21), $dC_2 < 0$ (suppressing any abatement costs here). Thus, the question is what part, if any, of this cost reduction the household includes in its stated willingness to pay.

4 Assuming here that the project was not undertaken in period 1, since then there would be no alternatives to choose among in period 2.

10 Empirical applications

1 This section draws heavily on Michael and Pearce (1989).
2 The questionnaire was mailed to a random sample of 200 Swedes, of whom 61 per cent completed it. Only one bid was recognized as a protest bid. This bid by a male respondent (on the CV_A-question to be defined below) has been deleted; of the remaining bids there is one bid of SEK 20,000 ($\approx$ $3,000) while the rest of the bids fall short of SEK 8,100. The reader should also note that the study was not primarily concerned with the absolute level of the willingness to pay for a commodity, but rather with the ranking of different measures. The ranking is the same whether or not the two extreme bids mentioned above are included or excluded.
3 This section follows very closely Hazilla and Kopp (1990).

11 Policy instruments and international environmental problems

1 One can, however, conceive of cases in which it is a profitable investment in goodwill for a firm to reduce emissions of pollutants into the air and water.
2 This section follows very closely Mäler (1990, pp. 89–92).
3 See Amann and Kornai (1987). IIASA is the International Institute for Applied Systems Analysis in Vienna.

References

Amann, M. and Kornai, G. (1987). 'Cost functions for controlling SO_2 emissions in Europe'. Working Paper 87-06-05, International Institute for Applied Systems Analysis, Vienna.

Andreoni, J. (1989). 'Giving with impure altruism: applications to charity and Ricardian equivalence', *Journal of Political Economy* **97**, 1447–58.

—— (1990). 'Impure altruism and donations to public goods: a theory of warm glow giving', *Economic Journal* **100**, 464–77.

Arrow, K.J. (1951). *Social Choice and Individual Values*. Wiley, New York.

—— (1971). *Essays in the Theory of Risk-Bearing*. North-Holland, Amsterdam.

Arrow, K.J. and Hahn, F.H. (1971). *General Competitive Analysis*. Holden-Day, San Francisco.

Arrow K.J. and Kurz, M. (1970). *Public Investment, the Rate of Return, and Optimal Fiscal Policy*. Johns Hopkins University Press, Baltimore.

Arrow, K.J. and Lind, R.C. (1970). 'Uncertainty and the evaluation of public investment decisions', *American Economic Review* **60**, 364–78.

Atkinson, A.B. (1970). 'On the measurement of inequality', *Journal of Economic Theory* **2**, 244–63.

Auerbach, A.J. (1985). 'The theory of excess burden and optimal taxation', in Auerbach, A.J. and Feldstein, M. (eds.), *Handbook of Public Economics*, vol. I North-Holland, Amsterdam.

Ayer, M., Brunk, H.D., Ewing, G.M. and Silverman, E. (1955). 'An empirical distribution function for sampling with incomplete information', *Annals of Mathematical Statistics* **26**, 641–7.

Barrett, S. (1990). 'The problem of global environmental protection', *Oxford Review of Economic Policy* **6**, 68–79.

Barro, R.J. (1974). 'Are government bonds net wealth?', *Journal of Political Economy* **82**, 1095–117.

Baumol, W.J. and Oates, W.E. (1988). *The Theory of Environmental Policy*, 2nd edition. Cambridge University Press.

Bellman, R. (1957). *Dynamic Programming*. Princeton University Press.

Bergman, L. (1991). 'General equilibrium effects of environmental policy: a CGE-modeling approach', *Environmental and Resource Economics* **1**, 43–61.

217

Bergson, A. (1938). 'A reformulation of certain aspects of welfare economics', *Quarterly Journal of Economics* **52**, 310–34.

Bergstrom, T.C. (1982). 'When is a man's life worth more than his human capital?', in Jones-Lee, M.W. (ed.), *The Value of Life and Safety*. North-Holland, Amsterdam.

Bishop, R.C. (1982). 'Option value: an exposition and extension', *Land Economics* **58**, 1–15.

Bishop, R.C. and Heberlein, T.A. (1979). 'Measuring values of extra-market goods: are indirect measures biased?', *American Journal of Agricultural Economics* **61**, 926–30.

(1984), 'Contingent valuation methods and ecosystem damages from acid rain', Staff Paper no. 217, Dept. of Agricultural Economics, University of Wisconsin–Madison.

Blackorby, C. and Donaldson, D. (1990). 'The case against the use of the sum of compensating variations in cost-benefit analysis', *Canadian Journal of Economics* **13**, 471–9.

Blackorby, C., Donaldson, D. and Moloney, D. (1984). 'Consumer's surplus and welfare change in a simple dynamic model', *Review of Economic Studies* **51**, 171–6.

Blackorby, C., Nissen, D., Primont, D. and Russell, R.R. (1973). 'Consistent intertemporal decision making', *Review of Economic Studies* **40**, 239–48.

Blanchard, O.J. and Fischer, S. (1989). *Lectures on Macroeconomics*. MIT Press, Cambridge, Mass.

Boadway, R.W. (1974). 'The welfare foundations of cost-benefit analysis', *Economic Journal* **84**, 926–39.

(1975). 'Cost-benefit rules in general equilibrium', *Review of Economic Studies* **42**, 361–73.

Boadway, R.W. and Bruce, N. (1984). *Welfare Economics*. Basil Blackwell, Oxford.

Bohm, P. (1990). 'Efficiency aspects of imperfect treaties on global public bads: lessons from the Montreal Protocol', mimeo, Stockholm University.

Boyle, K.J. and Bishop, R.C. (1985). 'The total value of wildlife resources: conceptual and empirical issues'. Invited paper, Association of Environmental and Resource Economists Workshop on Recreational Demand Modeling, Boulder, Colo., 17–18 May 1985.

Bradford, D. and Hildebrandt, G. (1977). 'Observable public good preferences', *Journal of Public Economics* **8**, 111–31.

Broome, J. (1978). 'Trying to value a life', *Journal of Public Economics* **9**, 91–100.

Brown, D.J. (1991). 'Equilibrium analysis with non-convex technologies', in Hildenbrand, W. and Sonnenschein, H. (eds.), *Handbook of Mathematical Economics*, vol. IV. North-Holland, Amsterdam.

Brown, G.H., Jr and Hammack, J. (1972). 'A preliminary investigation of the economics of migratory waterfowl', in Krutilla, J.V. (ed.), *Natural Environments: Studies in Theoretical and Applied Analysis*. Johns Hopkins University Press, Baltimore.

Bruce, N. and Waldman, M. (1991). 'Transfers in kind: why they can be efficient and nonpaternalistic', *American Economic Review* **81**, 1345–51.

Burt, O.R. and Brewer, D. (1971). 'Estimation of net social benefits from outdoor recreation', *Econometrica* **39**, 813–27.

Cameron, T.A. (1988). 'A new paradigm for valuing non-market goods using referendum data: maximum likelihood estimation by censored logistic regression', *Journal of Environmental Economics and Management* **15**, 355–79.

Caputo, M.R. (1990). 'How to do comparative dynamics on the back of an envelope in optimal control theory', *Journal of Economic Dynamics and Control* **14**, 655–83.

Chavas, J.-P. (1987). 'Constrained choices under risk', *Southern Economic Journal* **53**, 662–76.

Cicchetti, C.J., Fisher, A.C. and Smith, V.K. (1976). 'An econometric evaluation of a generalized consumer surplus measure: the Mineral King issue', *Econometrica* **44**, 1259–76.

Clark, C.W. (1976). *Mathematical Bioeconomics: The Optimal Management of* University Press.

Clawson, M. (1959). 'Methods of measuring demand for and value of outdoor recreation'. Reprint 10, Resources for the Future, Washington, D.C.

Coase, R. (1960). 'The problem of social cost', *Journal of Law and Economics* **3**, 1–44.

Courant, R. and John, F. (1974). *Introduction to Calculus and Analysis*, vol. II. Wiley, New York.

Cropper, M.L. and Freeman, A.M. (1991). 'Environmental health effects', in Braden, J.B. and Kolstad, C.D. (eds.), *Measuring the Demand for Environmental Quality*. North-Holland, Amsterdam.

Cuddington, J.T., Johansson, P.-O. and Löfgren, K.G. (1984). *Disequilibrium Macroeconomics in Open Economies*. Basil Blackwell, Oxford.

Cuddington, J.T., Johnson, F.R. and Knetsch, J.L. (1981). 'Valuing amenity resources in the presence of substitutes', *Land Economics* **57**, 526–35.

Dantzig, G.B., McAllister, P.H. and Stone, J.C. (1989). 'Deriving a utility function for the U.S. economy', *Journal of Policy Modeling* **11**, 391–424.

Dasgupta, P.S. and Heal, M. (1979). *Economic Theory and Exhaustible Resources*. James Nisbet/Cambridge University Press, Oxford.

Dasgupta, P.S., Sen, A. and Marglin, S.A. (1972). 'Guidelines for project evaluation'. United Nations Industrial Development Organization, Vienna.

Davis, R.K. (1964). 'The value of big game hunting in a private forest', in *Transactions of the Twenty-ninth North American Wildlife Conference*. Wildlife Management Institute, Washington, D.C.

Demers, M. (1991). 'Investment under uncertainty, irreversibility and the arrival of information over time', *Review of Economic Studies* **58**, 333–50.

Diewert, W.E. (1983). 'Cost-benefit analysis and project evaluation. A comparison of alternative approaches', *Journal of Public Economics* **22**, 265–302.

Dinwiddy, C. and Teal, F. (1990). 'Foreign exchange equivalence and project appraisal procedures', *Economic Journal* **100**, 567–76.

Dixit, A.K. (1992). 'Investment and hysteresis', *Journal of Economic Perspectives* **6**, 107–32.

Dixit, A.K. and Norman, V. (1980). *Theory of International Trade*. Cambridge

University Press.

Dobbs, I.M. (1991). 'A Bayesian approach to decision-making under ambiguity', *Economica* **58**, 417–40.

Drake, L. (1992). 'The non-market value of the Swedish agricultural landscape', *European Review of Agricultural Economics* **19**, 351–65.

Drèze, J.H. and Modigliani, F. (1972). 'Consumption decisions under uncertainty', *Journal of Economic Theory* **5**, 308–35.

Drèze, J. and Stern, N. (1987). 'The theory of cost-benefit analysis', in Auerbach, A.J. and Feldstein, M. (eds.), *Handbook of Public Economics*, vol. II. North-Holland, Amsterdam.

Dupuit, J. (1933). *De l'utilité et de la mesure* (reprints of works published in 1844 and the following years). La Riforma Sociale, Turin.

Eckstein, O. (1958). *Water Resource Development.* Harvard University Press, Cambridge, Mass.

Epstein, L. (1975). 'A disaggregate analysis of consumer choice under uncertainty', *Econometrica* **42**, 877–92.

Finkelshtain, I. and Kella, O. (1991). 'Obtaining contingent bounds for non-contingent equivalent variations', *Economics Letters* **36**, 257–61.

Fisher, A.C. and Hanemann, W.M. (1990). 'Information and the dynamics of environmental protection: the concept of the critical period', *Scandinavian Journal of Economics* **92**, 399–414.

Fletcher, J.J., Adamowics, W.L. and Graham-Tomasi, T. (1990). 'The travel cost model of recreation demand: theoretical and empirical issues', *Leisure Sciences* **12**, 119–47.

Forsund, F. and Strom, S. (1988). *Environmental Economics and Management: Pollution and Natural Resources.* Croom Helm, New York.

Freeman, M.A., III (1979). *The Benefits of Environmental Improvement: Theory and Practice.* Johns Hopkins University Press, Baltimore.

(1985). 'Supply uncertainty, option price, and option value', *Land Economics* **61**, 176–81.

(1990). 'Water pollution policy', in Portney, P.R. (ed.), *Public Policies for Environmental Protection.* Johns Hopkins University Press, Baltimore.

Friedman, M. and Savage, L.J. (1948). 'The utility analysis of choices involving risk', *Journal of Political Economy* **57**, 463–95.

Gallagher, D.R. and Smith, V.K. (1985). 'Measuring values for environmental resources under uncertainty', *Journal of Environmental Economics and Management* **12**, 132–43.

Graham, D.S. (1981). 'Cost-benefit analysis under uncertainty', *American Economic Review* **71**, 715–25.

Gramlich, E.M. (1990). *A Guide to Benefit-Cost Analysis.* Prentice Hall, Englewood Cliffs, N.J.

Green, C.H., Tunstall, S.M., N'Jai, A. and Rogers, A. (1990). 'Economic evaluation of environmental goods', *Project Appraisal* **5**, 70–82.

Gregory, R. (1986). 'Interpreting measures of economic loss: evidence from contingent valuation and experimental studies', *Journal of Environmental Economics and Management* **13**, 325–37.

Griliches, Z. (ed.) (1971). *Price Indexes and Quality Change.* Harvard University Press, Cambridge, Mass.

Hammack, J. and Brown, G.M., Jr (1974). *Waterfowl and Wetlands: Toward Bioeconomic Analysis.* Johns Hopkins University Press, Baltimore.

Hammond, P.J. (1981). 'Ex ante and ex post welfare optimality under uncertainty', *Economica* **48**, 235–50.

Hanemann, M.W. (1982). *Information and the Concept of Option Value.* Department of Agricultural and Resource Economics, University of California, Berkeley.

— (1984). 'Welfare evaluations in contingent valuation experiments with discrete responses', *American Journal of Agricultural Economics* **66**, 332–41.

— (1991). 'Willingness-to-pay and willingness-to-accept: how much can they differ?', *American Economic Review* **81**, 635–47.

Hanoch, G. (1977). 'Risk aversion and consumer preferences', *Econometrica* **45**, 413–26.

Harberger, A.C. (1969). 'The opportunity cost of public investment financed by borrowing', in Layard, R. (ed.), *Cost-Benefit Analysis.* Penguin Books, Baltimore.

— (1971). 'Three basic postulates for applied welfare economics: an interpretative essay', *Journal of Economic Literature* **9**, 785–97.

Harless, D.W. (1989). 'More laboratory evidence on the disparity between willingness to pay and compensation demanded', *Journal of Economic Behavior and Organization* **11**, 359–79.

Harrod, R.F. (1948). *Towards a Dynamic Economy.* Macmillan, London.

Hartwick, J.M. (1990). 'Natural resources, national accounting and economic depreciation', *Journal of Public Economics* **43**, 291–304.

Hazilla, M. and Kopp, R.J. (1990). 'Social cost of environmental quality regulations: a general equilibrium analysis', *Journal of Political Economy* **98**, 853–73.

Helms, J.L. (1984). 'Comparing stochastic price regimes: the limitations of expected surplus measures', *Economics Letters* **14**, 173–8.

Hey, J.D. (1979). *Uncertainty in Microeconomics.* Martin Robertson, Oxford.

— (1981). *Economics in Disequilibrium.* Martin Robertson, Oxford.

Hicks, J.R. (1939). 'The foundation of welfare economics', *Economic Journal* **49**, 696–712.

Hoel, M. (1992). 'Emission taxes in a dynamic international game of CO_2 emissions', in Pethig, R. (ed.), *Conflicts and Cooperation in Managing Environmental Resources.* Springer-Verlag, Berlin.

Hogg, R.V. and Craig, A.T. (1978). *Introduction to Mathematical Statistics*, 4th edition. Macmillan, New York.

Holmer, H. and Howe, C.W. (1991). 'Environmental problems and policy in the single European market', *Environmental and Resource Economics* **1**, 17–41.

Hotelling, H. (1931). 'The economics of exhaustible resources', *Journal of Political Economy* **39**, 137–75.

— (1938). 'The general welfare in relation to problems of taxation and of railway and utility rates', *Econometrica* **6**, 242–69.

— (1947). Unpublished letter to Director of National Park Service.

Ingersoll, J.E., Jr (1987). *Theory of Financial Decision Making*. Rowman & Littlefield Publishers, Savage, Md.

Inman, R. (1987). 'Markets, government, and the "new" political economy', in Auerbach, A.J. and Feldstein, M. (eds.), *Handbook of Public Economics*, vol. II. North-Holland, Amsterdam.

Johansson, P.-O. (1986). 'The macroeconomic effects of productive public expenditure: a review of the literature'. Working Paper, The World Bank, Washington, D.C.

(1987). *The Economic Theory and Measurement of Environmental Benefits*. Cambridge University Press.

(1988). 'Option value: comment', *Land Economics* **64**, 86–7.

(1989). 'Valuing public goods in a risky world: an experiment', in Holmer, H. and van Lerland, E. (eds.), *Valuation Methods and Policy Making in Environmental Economics*. Elsevier, Amsterdam.

(1991). *An Introduction to Modern Welfare Economics*. Cambridge University Press.

Johansson, P.-O., Kriström, B. and Mäler, K.G. (1989). 'Welfare evaluations in contingent valuation experiments with discrete response data: comment', *American Journal of Agricultural Economics* **71**, 1054–6.

Johansson, P.-O., Kriström, B. and Mattsson, L. (1988). 'How is the willingness to pay for moose hunting affected by the stock of moose?', *Journal of Environmental Management* **26**, 163–71.

Johansson, P.-O. and Löfgren, K.G. (1985). *The Economics of Forestry and Natural Resources*. Basil Blackwell, Oxford.

(1989). 'Disequilibrium cost-benefit rules: an exposition and extension', in Holmer, H. and van Lerland, E. (eds.), *Valuation Methods and Policy Making in Environmental Economics*. Elsevier, Amsterdam.

Johnson, F.R., Krutilla, J.V., Bowes, M.D. and Wilman, E.A. (1983). *Estimating the Impacts of Forest Management on Recreation Benefits; part I: Methodology; part II: Application with Reference to the White Mountain National Forest* (by Johnson and Krutilla). Multiple Use Forestry Project, Resources for the Future, Washington, D.C.

Jones-Lee, M.W. (1976). *The Value of Life*. Martin Robertson, Oxford.

(1989). *The Economics of Safety and Physical Risk*. Basil Blackwell, Oxford.

(1992). 'Paternalistic altruism and the value of a statistical life', *Economic Journal* **102**, 80–90.

Jorgenson, D.W. (1990). 'Intertemporal general equilibrium modeling of United States environmental regulation', *Journal of Policy Modeling* **12**, 715–44.

Just, R.E., Hueth, D.L. and Schmitz, A. (1982). *Applied Welfare Economics and Public Policy*. Prentice Hall, Englewood Cliffs, N.J.

Kahneman, D. and Tversky, A. (1979). 'Prospect theory: an analysis of decisions under risk', *Econometrica* **47**, 263–91.

Kaldor, N. (1939). 'Welfare propositions of economics and inter-personal comparisons of utility', *Economic Journal* **49**, 549–52.

Karni, E. and Schmeidler, D. (1991). 'Utility theory with uncertainty', in Hildenbrand, W. and Sonnenschein, H. (eds.), *Handbook of Mathematical Economics*, vol. IV. North-Holland, Amsterdam.

Kokoski, M.F. and Smith, V.K. (1987). 'A general equilibrium analysis of partial-equilibrium welfare measures: the case of climate change', *American Economic Review* **77**, 331–41.

Kopp, R.J. (1991). 'The proper role of existence value in public decision making', Discussion Paper QE91-17, Quality of the Environment Division, Resources for the Future, Washington, D.C.

Kreps, D.M. (1990). *A Course in Microeconomic Theory*. Princeton University Press.

Kriström, B. (1990). 'Valuing environmental benefits using the contingent valuation method: an econometric analysis'. Umeå Economic Studies no. 219. University of Umeå.

Krupnick, A.J. (1992). 'Using benefit-cost analysis to prioritize environmental problems', *Resources*, no.106, 34–7.

Krutilla, J.V. (1967). 'Conservation reconsidered', *American Economic Review* **57**, 777–86.

Krutilla, J.V. and Eckstein, O. (1958). *Multiple Purpose River Development*. Johns Hopkins University Press, Baltimore.

Krutilla, J.V. and Fisher, A.C. (1975). *The Economics of Natural Environments: Studies in the Valuation of Commodity and Amenity Resources*. Johns Hopkins University Press, Baltimore.

La France, J.T. and Barney, L.D. (1991). 'The envelope theorem in dynamic optimization', *Journal of Economic Dynamics and Control* **15**, 355–85.

Lesourne, J. (1975). *Cost-Benefit Analysis and Economic Theory*. North-Holland, Amsterdam.

Little, I.M.D. and Mirrlees, J.A. (1968). 'Manual of industrial project analysis in developing countries', vol. I, Organization for Economic Cooperation and Development, Paris.

Löfgren, K.-G. (1991). 'Another reconciliation between economists and forestry experts: OLG-arguments', *Environmental and Resource Economics* **1**, 83–95.

(1992). 'Comment on C.R. Hultén "Accounting for the wealth of nations: the net vs. gross output controversy and its ramifications"', *Scandinavian Journal of Economics* **94** (suppl.), 25–8.

Loomes, G., Starmer, C. and Sugden, R. (1992). 'Are preferences monotonic? Testing some predictions of regret theory', *Economica* **59**, 17–33.

Loomes, G. and Sugden, R. (1982). 'An alternative theory of rational choice under uncertainty', *Economic Journal* **92**, 805–24.

Lund, D. and Oksendal, B. (eds.) (1991). *Stochastic Models and Option Values*. North-Holland, Amsterdam.

Maass, A. (1966). 'Benefit-cost analysis: its relevance to public investment decisions', *Quarterly Journal of Economics* **80**, 208–26.

Machina, M.J. (1987). 'Choice under uncertainty: problems solved and unsolved', *Journal of Economic Perspectives* **1**, 121–54.

McKean, R.N. (1958). *Efficiency in Government Through Systems Analysis*, 6th edition. Wiley, New York.

McKenzie, G.W. (1983). *Measuring Economic Welfare: New Methods*. Cambridge University Press.

McMillan, M.L. (1979). 'Estimates of households' preferences for environmental quality and other housing characteristics from a system of demand equations', *Scandinavian Journal of Economics* **81**, 174–87.

Mäler, K.G. (1974). *Environmental Economics: A Theoretical Inquiry*. Johns Hopkins University Press, Baltimore.

(1985). 'Welfare economics and the environment', in Kneese, A.V. and Sveeney, J.L. (eds.). *Handbook of Natural Resource and Energy Economics*, vol. I. Elsevier, Amsterdam.

(1990). 'International environmental problems', *Oxford Review of Economic Policy* **6**, 80–108.

(1991). 'National accounts and environmental resources', *Environmental and Resource Economics* **1**, 1–15.

Marglin, S. (1967). *Public Investment Criteria: Benefit-Cost Analysis for Planned Economic Growth*. MIT Press, Cambridge, Mass.

Mayshar, J. (1991). 'On measuring the marginal cost of funds analytically', *American Economic Review* **81**, 1329–35.

Meade, J.E. (1955). *Trade and Welfare*. Oxford University Press.

Michael, N. and Pearce, D. (1989). 'Cost benefit analysis and land reclamation: a case study'. Paper 89–02, International Institute for Environment and Development, London.

Milgrom, P.R. (1992). 'Is sympathy an economic value? Philosophy, economics, and the contingent valuation method', in *Contingent Valuation: A Critical Assessment*. Cambridge Economics, Inc., Washington, D.C.

Miller, J.R. and Lad, F. (1984). 'Flexibility, learning, and irreversibility in environmental decisions: a Bayesian analysis', *Journal of Environmental Economics and Management* **11**, 161–72.

Milne, F. and Shefrin, H.M. (1987). 'Ex post efficiency and ex post welfare: some fundamental considerations', *Economica* **55**, 63–79.

Mitchell, R.C. and Carson, R.T. (1989). *Using Surveys to Value Public Goods: The Contingent Valuation Method*. Resources for the Future, Baltimore.

Morey, E.R., Rowe, R.D. and Watson, M. (1991). 'An extended discrete-choice model of Atlantic salmon fishing: with theoretical and empirical comparisons to standard travel-cost models'. Discussion Paper in Economics no. 91–7. University of Colorado, Boulder.

Mueller, D.C. (1989). *Public Choice II*. Cambridge University Press.

Musgrave, R. (1969). 'Cost-benefit analysis and the theory of public finance', *Journal of Economic Literature* **7**, 797–806.

Navrud, S. (ed.) (1992). *Pricing the European Environment*. Oxford University Press.

Ng, Y.-K. (1979). *Welfare Economics: Introduction and Development of Basic Concepts*. Macmillan, London.

Nickell, S.J. (1978). *The Investment Decisions of Firms*. Cambridge University Press.

Nordhaus, W.D. (1991). 'To slow or not to slow: the economics of the greenhouse effect', *Economic Journal* **101**, 920–37.

Opschoor, J.B. and Vos, M.B. (1989). *Economic Instruments for Environmental Protection*. OECD, Paris.

Pearce, D., Markandya, A. and Barbier, E.B. (1990). *Blueprint for a Green Economy*. Earthscan Publishers, London.

Pearce, D. and Turner, K. (1989). *Economics of Natural Resources and the Environment*. Simon & Schuster, London.

Peskin, H.M. (1989). 'Accounting for natural resource depletion and degradation in developing countries'. Working Paper no. 13, Environmental Dept., The World Bank.

Pindyck, R.S. (1991). 'Irreversibility, uncertainty, and investment', *Journal of Economic Literature* **29**, 1110–48.

Ploeg, F. van der and Withagen, C. (1991). 'Pollution control and the Ramsey problem', *Environmental and Resource Economics* **1**, 215–36.

Polinsky, A.M. and Rubinfeld, D.L. (1975). 'Property values and the benefits of environmental improvements: theory and measurement'. Discussion Paper no.404, Harvard Institute of Economic Research, Cambridge, Mass.

Porter, R.C. (1984). 'The optimal timing of an exhaustible, reversible wilderness development project', *Land Economics* **60**, 247–54.

Pratt, J. W. (1964). 'Risk aversion in the small and in the large', *Econometrica* **32**, 122–36.

Quiggin, J. (1989). 'Do existence values exist?'. Unpublished paper, Department of Agricultural and Resource Economics, University of Maryland, College Park, Md.

Ramsey, F. (1927). 'A contribution to the theory of taxation', *Economic Journal* **37**, 47–61.

——— (1928). 'A mathematical theory of saving', *Economic Journal* **38**, 543–59.

Randall, A. (1991). 'Nonuse benefits', in Braden, J.B. and Kolstad, C.D. (eds.), *Measuring the Demand for Environmental Quality*. North-Holland, Amsterdam.

Rawls, J. (1972). *A Theory of Justice*. Clarendon Press, Oxford.

Repetto, R. and others (1991). *Accounts Overdue: Natural Resource Depletion in Costa Rica*. World Resources Institute, Washington, D.C.

Rosen, S. (1974). 'Hedonic prices and implicit markets: product differentiation in pure competition', *Journal of Political Economy* **82**, 34–55.

Rosenthal, D.H. and Nelson, R.H. (1992). 'Why existence value should not be used in cost-benefit analysis', *Journal of Policy Analysis and Management* **11**, 116–22.

Samuelson, P.A. (1947). *Foundations of Economic Analysis*. Harvard University Press, Cambridge, Mass.

——— (1950) 'Evaluation of real national income', *Oxford Economic Papers* (NS) **2**, 1–29.

——— (1954). 'The pure theory of public expenditure', *Review of Economics and Statistics* **36**, 387–9.

——— (1972) 'Maximum principles in analytical economics', *American Economic Review* **57**, 249–62.

Schmalensee, R. (1972), 'Option demand and consumer's surplus: valuing price changes under uncertainty', *American Economic Review* **62**, 813–24.

Scitovsky, T. (1941) 'A note on welfare propositions in economics', *Review of*

Economic Studies **9**, 77–88.

Seierstad, A. and Sydsæter, K. (1987). *Optimal Control Theory with Economic Applications*. North-Holland, New York.

Shapiro, P. and Smith, T. (1981). 'Preferences for non-market goods revealed through market demands', in Smith, V.K. (ed.), *Advances in Applied Microeconomics*, vol. I. JAI Press, Greenwich, Conn.

Shechter, M. (1991). 'A comparative study of environmental amenity valuations', *Environmental and Resource Economics* **1**, 129–55.

Shiryayev, A.N. (1984). *Probability*. Springer-Verlag, New York.

Siebert, H. (1987). *Economics of the Environment*. Springer-Verlag, Berlin.

Smith, V.K. (1991). 'Household production functions and environmental benefit estimation', in Braden, J.B. and Kolstad, C.D. (eds.) *Measuring the Demand for Environmental Quality*. North-Holland, Amsterdam.

Solow, R.M. (1986). 'On the intergenerational allocation of natural resources', *Scandinavian Journal of Economics* **88**, 141–9.

Srinavasan, T.N. and Bhagwati, J.N. (1978). 'Shadow prices for project selection in the presence of distortions: effective rates of protection and domestic resource costs', *Journal of Political Economy* **86**, 96–116.

Starrett, D.A. (1988). *Foundations of Public Economics*. Cambridge University Press.

Stiglitz, J.E. (1986). *Economics of the Public Sector*. W.W. Norton, New York.

Stokey, N.L. and Lucas, R.E., Jr, with Prescott, E.C. (1987). *Recursive Methods in Economic Dynamics*. Harvard University Press, Cambridge, Mass.

Suen, W. (1990). 'Statistical models of consumer behavior with heterogeneous values and constraints', *Economic Inquiry* **28**, 79–98.

Tahvonen, O. (1991). 'On the dynamics of renewable resource harvesting and pollution control', *Environmental and Resource Economics* **1**, 97–117.

Tietenberg, T.H. (1992). *Environmental and Natural Resource Economics*, 3rd edition. Scott, Foresman and Company, Glenview, Ill.

Tinbergen, J. (1952). *On the Theory of Economic Policy*. North-Holland, Amsterdam.

Ulph, A. (1982). 'The role of ex ante and ex post decisions in the valuation of life', *Journal of Public Economics* **18**, 265–76.

Varian, H.R. (1992). *Microeconomic Analysis*, 3rd edition. W.W. Norton, New York.

Viscusi, W.K., Magat, W.A. and Huber, J. (1991). 'Pricing environmental health risks: survey assessments of risk–risk and risk–dollar trade-offs for chronic bronchitis', *Journal of Environmental Economics and Management* **21**, 32–51.

Viscusi, W.K. and Zeckhauser, R.J. (1976). 'Environmental policy choice under uncertainty', *Journal of Environmental Economics and Management* **3**, 97–112.

Weisbrod, B.A. (1964). 'Collective-consumption services of individual-consumption goods', *Quarterly Journal of Economics* **78**, 471–7.

Weitzman, M.L. (1974). 'Prices vs. quantities', *Review of Economic Studies* **41**, 477–91.

(1976). 'On the welfare significance of national product in a dynamic economy', *Quarterly Journal of Economics* **90**, 156–62.

Willig, R.D. (1978). 'Incremental consumer's surplus and hedonic price adjustment', *Journal of Economic Theory* **17**, 227–53.

Yunker, J.A. (1989). 'Some empirical evidence on the social welfare maximization hypothesis', *Public Finance* **44**, 110–33.

Index